Studying and Researching with Social Media

Education at SAGE

SAGE is a leading international publisher of journals, books, and electronic media for academic, educational, and professional markets.

Our education publishing includes:

- accessible and comprehensive texts for aspiring education professionals and practitioners looking to further their careers through continuing professional development

- inspirational advice and guidance for the classroom

- authoritative state of the art reference from the leading authors in the field

Find out more at: **www.sagepub.co.uk/education**

SAGE Study Skills

Studying and Researching with Social Media

Megan Poore

Los Angeles | London | New Delhi
Singapore | Washington DC

Los Angeles | London | New Delhi
Singapore | Washington DC

SAGE Publications Ltd
1 Oliver's Yard
55 City Road
London EC1Y 1SP

SAGE Publications Inc.
2455 Teller Road
Thousand Oaks, California 91320

SAGE Publications India Pvt Ltd
B 1/I 1 Mohan Cooperative Industrial Area
Mathura Road
New Delhi 110 044

SAGE Publications Asia-Pacific Pte Ltd
3 Church Street
#10-04 Samsung Hub
Singapore 049483

Editor: Marianne Lagrange
Editorial assistant: Rachael Plant
Production editor: Thea Watson
Copyeditor: Chris Bitten
Proofreader: Rose James
Indexer: Anne Solamito
Marketing manager: Catherine Slinn
Cover design: Shaun Mercier
Typeset by: C&M Digitals (P) Ltd, Chennai, India
Printed in India at Replika Press Pvt Ltd

© Megan Poore 2014

First published 2014

Library of Congress Control Number: 2013951478

British Library Cataloguing in Publication data

A catalogue record for this book is available from
the British Library

ISBN 978-1-4462-6971-8
ISBN 978-1-4462-6972-5 (pbk)

To Matthew

Contents

About the Author

Megan Poore is the PhD Academic and Research Skills Advisor at the Crawford School of Public Policy at the Australian National University. For over ten years she has worked as an academic, researcher, academic skills advisor, and an educational designer, giving her a unique understanding of the issues that confront both staff and students in the integration of social media into their every day study and research practices. Megan has won several awards – both nationally and internationally – for her SkillSoup podcasting project and is particularly known for her best practice approaches to risk management in the area of social media. Megan is the author of *Using Social Media in the Classroom: A Best Practice Guide* and co-author with Gail Craswell of *Writing for Academic Success* (Second Edition), both also published by SAGE. Megan holds a PhD in Social Anthropology from the Australian National University.

List of Figures and Tables

FIGURES

TABLES

Preface

This book is intended to help you harness some of the many social media tools and services in your study and research practices. It is both practical as well as conceptual: practical, in that it provides a general guide to the social media tools and services that can be used to support and enhance both study and research; and conceptual in that it gives insights into the social, academic, and quasi-legal contexts that we all must engage with when using social media either for formal assessment or for our own self-directed learning and professional development.

Social media are being increasingly used in teaching and learning activities, leading students to wonder what their lecturers are looking for in a blog post or how that might be different from writing an essay (or a wikipage or a Facebook comment ...). Similarly, researchers are progressively turning to social media to help them communicate their work to both specialist and lay audiences, and wondering if Twitter really can be used to build their online profile. *Studying and Researching with Social Media* helps you explore these and many similar issues. As such, this book is a little different from most study and research skills textbooks, which have typically focused on the more 'traditional' elements of the academic enterprise, such as essay and report writing, time management, handling information, giving seminars, doing exams, finding research articles, using library databases, getting published, and drawing up research proposals and literature reviews. It is also different from books that focus solely on the technical and procedural elements of social media, such as how to create a blog post, how to set up a wiki, how to record a podcast, how to edit a video, how to manage file formats, and how to embed widgets. Rather, this book combines the two approaches to give you a far more nuanced understanding of the modern academic environment. To this end, it does not give you step-by-step 'how-to' guides – you can find them readily enough if you conduct a simple Google search. The book instead takes a holistic approach and gives you both 'big picture' stuff as well as the nitty-gritty detail on how social media apply to the university context.

For students, you will learn how to maximise your grades when creating an audio-visual presentation, what your lecturer is looking for when they ask you to work collaboratively on a wiki, and how to be a good community member on a class-based social network. For researchers, the book will help you figure out what kind of online portfolio you should have according to your research and career goals, how to best use social media to find research materials, and how to communicate your research products to the audiences you want to target. For everyone, there is advice on how to use social media to improve academic productivity, how to build digital literacy, and how to handle ourselves (and others) online. Finally, there is a large focus throughout the book on keeping safe online. Although the final chapter is specifically dedicated to the legalities and practicalities of the online environment, in fact the entire book is about issues relating to privacy, risk, copyright, intellectual property, content distribution, Terms of Service, data collection, online security, and cybersafety. My main aim has been to equip you with the information you need to be able to safely and knowledgeably navigate the web.

There is, by necessity, a focus in some sections on writing and/or genre. Most people think that because they know how to write a report or journal article they therefore know how to write a blog post. Not so. Social media are challenging and expanding our understandings of what constitutes various academic 'genres' – the sooner you understand this point, and the sooner you learn to produce materials according to genre, the more effective your engagement with social media for study and research will be.

Using social media in your study and research will give you a richer, more dynamic, and, I believe, more rounded experience of the scholarly enterprise and all that it constitutes in the modern Academy.

I

Getting Started: The Essentials

Part I provides the basis for using social media for study and research. The first chapter takes a 'big picture' view by taking a look at a theory of teaching and learning in order to situate social media in both the educative and research context before describing the benefits – and peculiarities – of using social media in scholarly environments. Chapter 2 focuses far more on the everyday practicalities of social media, in particular looking at functional commonalities that apply across various tools and services before discussing social media communication expectations and practices.

1

Why use Social Media in your Studies and Research?

OVERVIEW

This chapter charts the rise of social media since the early 2000s and outlines why social media are important to twenty-first-century life and learning. It provides a brief overview of the educational theory that is relevant to social media and education as a way of helping you understand why lecturers might be using social media in teaching and learning. The chapter also describes the benefits of using social media for research, paying particular attention to the value of communicating with peers, keeping up with the latest research, improving efficiency and productivity, promoting your academic career, and disseminating your work. Issues around competency and 'digital natives' are also explored, as is the role of the VLE (Virtual Learning Environment) in the modern higher education context.

The focus of the chapter is on how social media can support effective learning and research, but it also aims to put less 'tech-savvy' readers at ease by explaining that, to use social media tech and tools, you don't need to have any special knowledge (for example, how to write html) and you don't need access to specialised hardware (for example, servers). Instead, it shows that using social media is easy and that anyone can teach themselves to use online digital technologies effectively to support their study and research.

WHAT IS 'SOCIAL MEDIA'?

Social media are simply those digital technologies that allow users to easily create and share material with others via the internet. The internet hasn't always been used in this way. In the early days, people needed access to special knowledge (such as how to write html code) and special equipment (such as servers) in order to make the internet 'work', meaning that web-based communication via the internet was largely uni-directional. By 2005, however, internet technology had developed to such a point that it became possible for ordinary people to have their own websites or, perhaps more accurately, their own web 'presences'. These days, we use sites and services such as blogs, wikis, Facebook, Skype, Twitter, and many others to publish our own material on the internet without giving a second thought to what makes it all happen.

What is the difference between the web and the internet?

The distinction is fine but important. Basically, the internet provides the underlying architecture or structure that supports the digital transfer of information. On top of this architecture sits the web, which is simply a platform used to deliver content via the structure of the internet. Taking it a step further, we can see that the apps that you have on your smartphone aren't websites but they still use the internet to transfer and present data.

The role of social media in twenty-first-century communication

The growth of social media in recent years is having quite profound impacts on how information and knowledge are created and distributed in modern culture. Whereas traditional broadcast media have been characterised by the 'one-to-many' control of information flows (through books, magazines, newspapers, television, etc.), social media are characterised by 'many-to-many' information sharing. Social media, then, are networked media and they allow for the instant and simultaneous sharing of material on the internet.

Clarifying terms

There are many different terms that get thrown around when people talk about social media. There are often used interchangeably, but we can, in fact, distinguish between them:

- *IT (Information Technology)*. Describes the 'inner' workings of digital technologies – that is, things that relate to Computer Science, coding, programming, software development, hardware development, scripting, etc.
- *ICT (Information and Communication(s) Technology/-ies)*. Refers to technologies that facilitate the social elements of digital life and to anything that funnels the flow of communications between *people*. The key term, here, is 'communication'.

- *Social media.* Signifies digital technologies that allow users to easily create and share material with others via the internet.
- *Web 2.0.* Describes the 'shift' or 'evolution' in internet technologies that occurred around 2005 when a 'second generation' of websites and services became available, allowing people to easily publish their own material on the web. Web 2.0 is thus closely associated with the growth of social media and is sometimes also called the 'read-write' web: that is, we don't just have to read it, we can also 'write' it.

Why does any of this matter to you as student and/or researcher? Well, quite simply, social media are providing us with new platforms for communication and, inasmuch as communication is one of the chief activities of both study and research, social media have the potential not just to provide new *tools* for communication but also to *change the nature* of communicative practices themselves. We are seeing this already in the diversity of writing 'genres' that are developing through people's use of internet-based services such as Facebook and Twitter.

As you move through this book, you will learn more about what constitutes appropriate 'genre' and communication practice on various social media platforms, but for the moment we can say that communication via social media is all about

- Participation
- Collaboration
- Interactivity
- Community building
- Sharing
- Networking
- Creativity
- Distribution
- Flexibility
- Customisation.

These qualities are exactly those that make social media so useful in education and research.

SOCIAL MEDIA IN STUDY AND RESEARCH

Social media are having large impacts on the way we conduct our scholarly enterprise. In particular, social media are not only helping us apply better pedagogies to our teaching and learning activities, but they are also proving beneficial at all stages of the research cycle. We will see how this works in more detail as we go through the chapters of this book; for now, though, we'll take a more conceptual look at how social media are influencing the study and research process.

Social media and a theory of education and learning

It may seem strange to include a section on educational theory in a study and research skills textbook, but having a basic knowledge of the kinds of teaching, learning, and scholarship that are best supported by social media will help you to make the most of social media in your academic endeavours.

Although there are various theories about how people learn – and how they learn best – the one that has most currency in social media environments is called 'social constructivism'. Social constructivism holds that learning is a collaborative, participatory process in which the creation of knowledge and meaning occurs through social interaction. In other words, we learn best in interaction with or when working with others. Based on this notion, it should be easy to see how social media, which so readily support collaboration and interactivity, can be harnessed to benefit not just the ways in which we learn (study), but also the ways in which we build on, interrogate, and share what we already know (research). Thus, both study and research benefit from activities that involve collaboration, participation, interaction, dissemination, sharing, connecting, networking, building, and creating – activities that can be easily achieved through the use of social media.

All of this is in contrast to approaches to scholarship that focus on the monolithic, individual learner or researcher, that is, someone who operates in isolation from others and who is either the 'receiver' (learner) or 'transmitter' (researcher) of knowledge. Whilst there can be some value in such approaches, they are nevertheless quite static and tend to limit the opportunities that both students and researchers have for constructing and sharing our knowledge of the world and our place in it.

Why lecturers use social media in teaching and learning

Social media tools are nimble, flexible, easy to use and often very powerful, allowing students to easily create their own content, websites, and learning spaces. In theory, this should lead to the types of socially constructivist learning approaches (mentioned above) that are student- and class-focused, rather than teacher-driven. John Dewey recognised the importance of such approaches a century ago when he stated that there should be 'more opportunity for conjoint activities in which those instructed take part, so that they may acquire a social sense of their own powers and of the materials and appliances used' (2004 [1916]: 39, emphasis removed). We can now readily create such opportunities for students because social media platforms can be used to put education at the centre – not the teacher – and thus allow students to take part more actively and creatively in their own education.

Not all lecturers, of course, use social media as part of their everyday teaching and assessment practice – in fact, most probably *don't*. The use of social media in university teaching and learning is still in its early days, leading many to be cynical or sceptical, others evangelistic, and perhaps most simply uninformed or indifferent. Nevertheless, as a student, you may increasingly find yourself taking courses in which the use of social media forms part of your assessment or part of the 'delivery' platform for basic course content. To this end, lecturers use social media for three main reasons:

1. *Education.* Lecturers who use social media in their teaching typically want you to share, communicate, collaborate, participate, interact, network, connect, build community, be creative, and distribute your work/findings/discoveries in a socially constructivist learning environment (see above). Tools such as blogs, wikis, social networks, and others are excellent for such activities. Lecturers might also want you to develop some of the technical and communication skills that will be of use to you when you leave university and enter the workforce (in fact, these skills might form part of your university's 'graduate outcomes') and using social media can help with that.
2. *Assessment.* Many lecturers are finding social media tools more and more useful and appropriate when it comes to assessing student work. Lecturers are still discovering their way a bit in this area, but those who are working within the social constructivist models of teaching and learning described above are developing forms of assessment that combine both formative ('as you go') and summative ('at the end') assignments. It's important to remember that lecturers working in this way are often those who have an interest in educational theory to begin with, which means that they are basing their teaching on informed pedagogy and not just on 'what has come before' or 'what has always been done'. This is important for improving student learning, but if you feel that you're not sure what it is that you have to do in order to complete your assessment, then don't be afraid to ask your lecturer for clarification.
3. *Administration.* Inasmuch as social media are geared towards the distribution of content, they provide excellent platforms for the delivery of course materials, meaning that they can be used to take the place of a traditional VLE (Virtual Learning Environment – see below). Your lecturer may prefer to employ just one system or service, such as a blog, to host everything course-related, or they may work with a 'hub and spokes' model in which case a variety of social media tools and services (for example, Twitter, Flickr, and newsfeeds) are fed into a central platform, such as a wiki.

Precisely how specific social media tools are used for these purposes is explored in the chapters that follow.

Benefits of using social media for your research

So far, we've looked at how social media can be used to support the educational activities of lecturers. But to the extent that education is a communicative practice, then so too is research. There is no point in conducting research if we can't disseminate it and build communities of scholars who share and critique ideas. Procter et al. (2010: 4040) define scholarly communications as:

conducting research, developing ideas and informal communications;

preparing, shaping and communicating what will become formal research outputs;

the dissemination of formal products;

managing personal careers and research teams and research programmes; and

communicating scholarly ideas to broader communities.

Social media support all these scholarly activities.

Conducting research, developing ideas, and informal communications

Social media can most obviously be used in social science disciplines that conduct research amongst *people*, that is, social media can be used – with ethics clearance, naturally – to gather data on human behaviour, thoughts, social interactions, etc. But social media can also be used as platforms for *search*. Twitter, blogs, and social bookmarking sites can all be checked for the latest articles, discoveries, and ideas in your field – you don't only have to rely on the databases in your library catalogue (or Google Scholar) to find scholarly material. You can use social media to work on joint-writing projects, to keep in touch with fieldworkers and research participants, and even to develop and share ideas via online mindmaps. See Chapter 8 for more detail.

Preparing, shaping, and communicating what will become formal research outputs

Research is often messy and keeping track of it, even messier. Social media allow you to host research material online (publicly or privately) and to access it from anywhere. You can keep notes, save and tag bookmarks and favourites, and manage references all using social media. Blogging allows you to present ideas and get feedback, whilst subscriptions (see 'RSS' in Chapter 2) feed the latest research and report updates directly to your online location. Social media can thus help you gain control over information channels at the same time as using those channels for getting pre-publication responses to your work. Again, see Chapter 8 for more information.

The dissemination of formal products

Most formal scholarly work is still disseminated in traditional formats such as those found in peer-reviewed journal articles and books. Nevertheless, many publishing houses are advertising and promoting the latest research publications via social media. Further, you can publicise your own articles and books using social media. Of course, you need to be careful that you don't upload entire works without your publisher's permission, but most publishers are more than happy for you to use social media to promote your own material, both pre- and post-publication.

Managing personal careers, research teams, and research programs

Perhaps one of the most powerful uses of social media for researchers is for the promotion of your own academic career. This may sound somewhat selfish and self-serving, but the reality of academe in the twenty-first century is that it is a competitive business: you are competing for grants, jobs, publication, funding, position, students. What's more, you are expected to have a set of career goals and to periodically apply for – and receive – promotion. Establishing and maintaining an online profile, and building credibility, reputation, and awareness, can greatly increase your chances of finding and retaining a position in the modern university system. In addition to this, however, social media can be very effectively mobilised to manage research teams and programs: you can keep in touch, share data, debate ideas, and collaborate on grants using various forms of social media. Chapter 7 looks at building your online profile in more detail.

Communicating scholarly ideas to broader communities

Finally, social media are being used to communicate what we do beyond the traditional bounds of the academy. No longer is research – in any of its forms or stages – obtainable only by those with special access to journals, people, institutions, and the like. Rather, with so much now available on the internet in so many different ways, links to the broader community can be fostered and our research disseminated to a much wider audience. This allows us not only to share discoveries and get feedback, but also to initiate 'citizen science' projects, develop outreach services, and to engage more publicly with industry, government, and policy makers and implementers.

Social media have become such an integral part of the ways in which we communicate that, simply by default, they are also becoming integral to the ways in which we conduct our study and research.

SOCIAL MEDIA IN THE UNIVERSITY ENVIRONMENT

Certain peculiarities of the university environment mean that the use of social media in higher education is not always straightforward. Firstly, there are social and demographic factors that impact on the assumptions we make about people's use of social media. And then there is the role that the Virtual Learning Environment (VLE) plays in delivering, controlling, and distributing electronic content. You need to understand this environment if you are to successfully use social media to support your study and research practices.

The 'digital natives' debate: Assumptions around your use of social media

The term 'digital native' was first coined by Marc Prensky in 2001 to describe those people who have grown up in digital environments and whose brains, as a result, exhibit certain physical characteristics that are different from those of 'digital immigrants', that is, those who have *not* grown up in digital environments (Prensky, 2001a, b). Prensky's paper sparked much debate – debate that continues today – about whether or not young people are, indeed, 'digital natives' or whether Prensky's claims are overstated. In some ways, Prensky has been both misinterpreted and misrepresented (Poore, 2012: 164), because he wasn't arguing that people born after a certain date suddenly demonstrated a spontaneous evolutionary shift in the structure of the human brain. Rather, he was saying that some people, as a result of growing up in digital environments, 'think and process information fundamentally differently from their predecessors' (Prensky, 2001a: 1, emphasis removed).

All of this is important because these debates and discourses aren't just theoretical or academic – they can actually lead to certain assumptions about what people 'know' about learning with social media. To this end, how others *think* about how certain groups use social media may directly impact *you* when you use social media in your studies and research. The remainder of this section applies largely to students, but you may also find that similar issues arise in the research environment.

Assumptions around competence

You probably use only a few websites and social media services on a daily basis: Facebook, YouTube, Google, Twitter, and Wikipedia are clearly the chief contenders. This is generally fine, but the problem is that we normally use only one or two main functions on each service and ignore the rest. For example, most people will watch YouTube clips, fewer will actually upload them, and fewer still will make their own videos for sharing. Similarly, we'll visit Wikipedia to get some quick information about a subject, but not many of us will actually edit an entry and add our own knowledge to the topic. By the same token, we tend to be quite familiar with one or two digital devices and are accustomed to how they work and how they are set up. As a result, we become competent in the use of a few things but can feel quite lost when asked to apply ourselves to something different. (In fact, services such as Facebook don't do you any favours in terms of teaching you how to add hyperlinks, embed videos using embed code, or complete similar actions because all these things are done automatically for you.) In the study context, you might be asked to create a blog, contribute to a wiki, produce your own podcast, or tag and share your bookmarks – things that you may have never done before.

It helps, here, to think about where you sit in the 'conscious-competence' learning cycle (Figure 1.1) as regards your skilled (or otherwise) use of social media in particular and digital technologies in general. The cycle works like this:

- *Unconscious incompetence.* You have no awareness of a certain area of expertise or set of skills – in other words, 'you don't know what you don't know'. You may never have heard of social bookmarking (see Chapter 7), for example, so it doesn't impact you.
- *Conscious incompetence.* You become aware of an area or skill leading you to 'know what you don't know'. For example, your lecturer might ask you to use social bookmarking for an assignment and suddenly you realise that there is a whole digital domain about which you know nothing. This is what I describe to students as the 'freak-out' stage because it can be quite stressful wondering how on earth you will manage what is being asked of you.
- *Conscious competence.* You start to gain skill or expertise in an area and you can perform at a reliable level. Continuing our example, you have set up a social bookmarking account and you can save bookmarks and tag them up (see Chapter 2 for information on tags) if you think about what you are doing.
- *Unconscious competence.* You can now perform the skill or operate in the area of expertise without thinking about it: it has become 'second nature'.

Thinking about competence is important for two main reasons. Firstly, your lecturer, perhaps working off certain ideas about 'digital natives' described above, might assume that you have full competence in any and all areas of

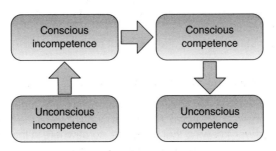

FIGURE 1.1 The 'conscious competence' learning cycle

digital media use. The result can be believing that you can easily transfer skills learnt from Facebook to the new medium and underestimating the support you really need to succeed in class. This is assuming 'conscious competence' on your part, when you might be at the 'conscious incompetence' stage and feeling quite anxious. Secondly, you, yourself, might overestimate your competence because you have gained confidence in using your regular sites, services, and devices on a daily basis. Further, you might often feel frustrated with others' 'slowness' when sitting next to them on a computer or looking over their shoulder as you try to help them make sense of their mobile phone. Be careful not to mistake your *confidence* in particular online and digital environments with *competence* in all such environments. In my experience, students who are, for example, quite used to working within Facebook can have initial difficulties when asked to find an embed code to display a video on a blog they've created on their own. Both you and your lecturer need to bear these things in mind.

Activity   Social media competency quiz

Complete the following quiz to see where you sit on the 'conscious competence' learning cycle in relation to social media.

1 Computers

  a) Can be broken ☐
  b) Are a means to an end ☐
  c) Are 'old skool'. I use my phone for everything ☐

2 I learn by

  a) Guessing and hoping ☐
  b) Reading or taking a class ☐
  c) Doing ☐

3 When I come across a new application or online tool, I

  a) Dread having to learn something completely new ☐
  b) Think about other tools I know and try to figure out how the current one might fit a pattern ☐
  c) Get in there and play around and see what happens knowing that I can't break it ☐

4 When I can't figure out how to do something in a social media environment, I

  a) Sit there thinking either 'I'm so dumb' or 'Computers are stupid' ☐
  b) Try the help function and, when that doesn't work, I email the helpdesk ☐
  c) Google an answer, knowing that someone, somewhere in the world has solved this problem before and has posted their answer in a discussion forum or similar ☐

5   When a dialogue box pops up in the middle of doing something, I

a) Click and hope, not really knowing what the options mean ☐
b) Read it very, very carefully and then decide which option I want to click on, knowing that I've definitely made the right choice ☐
c) Read it quickly, guess which option is most likely and then click, knowing that I've probably made the right choice but it doesn't matter because there's little chance I'll make the wrong one, anyway ☐

6   Problem solving

a) Is too hard. I'm not sure how to do it on the internet ☐
b) Is a good way of working through issues, but I don't have the time ☐
c) Is how I make things work ☐

7   Social media is

a) Intimidating ☐
b) Important for work, study and research ☐
c) Just there – I use it but tend not to think about it ☐

8   The pace of change

a) Makes me wonder how I will ever keep up ☐
b) Is to be expected in today's world. I'll manage ☐
c) I don't actually notice any 'pace of change' ☐

9   When it comes to integrating social media into my work, uni and personal lives, I

a) Must know it all before I can start ☐
b) Should learn stuff now, while I have some spare time ☐
c) Will learn it when I need to and be comfortable with that ☐

If you answered mainly 'a', then see the section on 'Attitude' in Chapter 2 for a discussion on how to adjust your perspective on social media – and how to deal with perfectionism and feeling overwhelmed – to help you move into the conscious competence stage. If you answered mainly 'b', then each chapter of this book will be helpful in giving you a greater understanding of how social media work in the university environment. If you answered mainly 'c', then the chances are that most of what is covered in this book will simply be 'revision' for you; however, take a look at the chapters in the final part of the text, as there might still be some skilling up you need to do as regards the more legal or ethical elements of using social media.

Assumptions around communication preferences

Some lecturers will assume that because you might regularly communicate with family and friends via mobile phone, text, Facebook, or chat, you will be quite comfortable with using these and similar technologies for study. Further, they may take for granted that you would prefer and/or can do without face-to-face contact with your lecturer and that you are quite happy to undertake your entire course online. In fact, the research shows quite the opposite in both cases, and has done so for some time (EDUCAUSE, 2012; JISC, 2007, 2008). Students want separate academic and private or social lives and prefer to use different communication formats for different audiences (EDUCAUSE, 2012: 25). Generally, text, Facebook, chat, and IM are preferred for friends and email for lecturers. Some lecturers may lose sight of this and assume that you are comfortable with – and have a 'natural' inclination for – interacting via what you see as more 'private' forms of communication. Similarly, in a recent study in the US 87 per cent of students said that face-to-face interaction with their teachers was very or extremely important (EDUCAUSE 2012: 26). Being aware of some of the assumptions that might exist around your communication preference can help you manage your course, and your own and your lecturer's expectations, when it comes to social media assignments.

Assumptions around using social media for learning

A final assumption that might arise out of digital native debates and discourses is the notion that you are 'OK with it'; that using social media is highly motivating for you because you use it in your social and everyday life and because you may have 'grown up' with it. You, on the other hand, might just feel confused and overwhelmed by what you are being asked to do and you can't see how using social media in your studies actually relates to or enhances your learning.

Although there may be a disconnect here, don't give up. Lecturers who use social media for student learning are normally highly skilled in its use at a functional level, but also understand and appreciate the benefits for education at a theoretical and practical level (see above). That doesn't mean, however, that all lecturers are equal when it comes to describing *how* to use social media for learning. In fact, studies show (EDUCAUSE, 2012; JISC, 2007, 2008) that students want more information on how to learn *with* social media and not on how to make things work in a technical sense (EDUCAUSE, 2012: 29).

If you aren't sure – or if your lecturer hasn't been entirely clear – about why and how their intended use of social media in your course will support your learning, then gently ask them

- Why are we using this tool over another, for example, a traditional lab report or essay?
- How will this help me learn what you want me to learn?
- How am I being assessed and under what criteria? Writing? Sharing? Critical engagement? Communication? Quality of group work? (See the individual chapters on blogs and wikis for examples of success criteria and marking rubrics.)
- What technical competencies can you or the university help me acquire? Will you or a central training department run workshops or am I expected to form a study group, perhaps?

Other questions, of course, will arise according to your specific context. Needless to say, don't be aggressive, defensive, or negative in your questioning (no matter how exasperated or panicked you might feel). If you ask respectfully – and only ask those questions either that you couldn't find your own answer to or that you really, really were unclear about – then your lecturer could well appreciate the opportunity to clarify what they are looking for in your assignments.

Always bear in mind that your lecturer has almost certainly chosen to do things this way for very good reasons; it's just that sometimes they might not communicate those reasons as neatly or as explicitly as students need them to. Remember that both you *and* your lecturer may still be feeling your way in the area of using social media in the classroom. How your lecturer gets skilled up in this is a matter for them and their professional development program. For your part, though, you need to start figuring out how to use these tools for *learning*, not just for social communication. And that is what this book hopes to guide you in.

The role of the Virtual Learning Environment (VLE) in higher education

Until recently, almost all online teaching and learning was conducted via teacher-controlled, centralised Virtual Learning Environments (VLEs, also known as Learning Management Systems or LMSs). It is worth spending just a little time, here, on understanding the relationship between VLEs and your lecturer's use of social media, as it will help explain why your lecturer has chosen to use an externally hosted social media service as opposed to your university-supplied VLE. As such, this section is of most use to students, but teaching academics might also find some of the principles explored to be of interest.

Virtual Learning Environments (such as WebCT, Moodle, Blackboard, Sakai, and others) are designed to provide stable, online class environments for both teachers and students. These systems excel in streamlining administrative and didactic tasks and are important for the management of course materials and information. However, VLEs tend to lack a degree of flexibility, usability, and functionality when it comes to helping develop rich, deep, and engaging learning experiences for students. In other words, VLEs are primarily *management* systems, not pedagogic ones, and they are often used to support didactic or transmission educative practices that push content at students (Fitzgerald and Steele, 2008: 27; Ullrich et al., 2008: 705). In this sense, they are sometimes used more or less as an 'advanced photocopier' that replicates old teaching practices based on mass communication, on processes of industrialisation, and on economies of scale (Attwell, 2007: 2–4).

Because centralised VLEs are designed to do several things all at once, they also have a tendency to provide 'watered down' versions of only a few social media tools and applications. For example, some VLEs have wiki or blog functions attached to them, but those functions are often poor imitations of 'real' wikis and blogs available on the web. Moreover, as already mentioned, traditional, centralised VLEs are teacher-controlled and often make it difficult for students to upload or produce their own content. In other words, VLEs often do not easily allow for the type of student engagement and creativity that many social media platforms encourage and that lecturers want from you. All of this can have a restrictive effect on students' creative and active participation in learning and presents dilemmas for both university administrators and lecturers alike:

> ... the rise of [social media] applications has challenged the role of institutional LMSs which tend to be closed applications specific to an institution or jurisdiction, and challenge[s] the policies of organisations and systems as teachers test, trial and experiment with collaborative tools that are only available outside their learning organisation. (SICTAS, 2009: 77)

Today, then, some lecturers, rather than be restricted by what the class VLE offers in terms of functionality, are starting to explore powerful, flexible, externally provided social media tools that support a better pedagogy. Stephen Downes encourages this approach in saying that we need to 'move away from large, centralized applications and instead make use of a network of connected applications' (2008: 1). On a related note, Fitzgerald and Steele point out that '[t]here is no one tool that provides a social software solution to support learning and teaching, nor is it appropriate to use the one technique for all disciples or even throughout the teaching of a particular discipline' (Fitzgerald and Steele, 2008: 31).

At this point, I need to make it clear that I am not advocating an overthrow of university-supplied virtual learning environments. Many lecturers find the tools supplied in a university VLE adequate for their administrative and teaching requirements; indeed, traditional VLEs can provide an acceptable baseline for the distribution of information about a course (which, arguably, all courses should have) in the VLE. Furthermore, a VLE links into the university's student database, which aids administration of courses. However, many lecturers, aware of what constitutes good teaching practice, want to use the best tool for the job – whether that tool is inside or outside the VLE. On this point I agree with Fitzgerald and Steele who state that 'institutional ICT systems like the corporate learning management system must be developed in ways that can work with web services that sit outside the academy' (Fitzgerald and Steele, 2008: 31).

Clearly, this book does not focus on how to use VLEs for study, but bear in mind that much of what is covered here can be easily applied to your institution's Virtual Learning Environment. For example, if your lecturer is using your VLE to set a blog or a wiki task, then much of the advice provided in this book will pertain to that situation.

SUMMARY

- Social media are those digital technologies that allow users to easily create and share material with others via the internet.
- Social media are all about participation, collaboration, interactivity, community building, sharing, networking, creativity, distribution, flexibility, and customisation.
- Social constructivism is a theory of learning that holds that learning is a collaborative, participatory process in which the creation of knowledge and meaning occurs through social interaction: we learn best in interaction or when working with others. Social media can thus support good teaching and learning.
- Lecturers use social media for educational (pedagogical), assessment, and administrative purposes.
- Social media can be used to conduct research, develop ideas, prepare and get feedback on early draft materials, build your online profile, and communicate your work.
- Debates around 'digital natives' may impact on you because some people will make assumptions around your competence with social media, your communication preferences, and how you use social media for learning.
- Understanding the conscious-competence learning cycle will help you identify your skill levels as regards your use of social media and digital technologies.
- Virtual Learning Environments (VLEs) provide largely didactic environments for the management of course materials and information, but they lack a degree of flexibility, usability, and functionality when it comes to helping develop rich, deep, and engaging learning experiences for students.

FURTHER READING

Dabbagh, N. and Kitsantas, A. (2012) 'Personal learning environments, social media, and self-regulated learning: A natural formula for connecting formal and informal learning', *The Internet and Higher Education*, 15 (1): 3–8.

Gruzd, A., Wellman, B. and Takhteyev, Y. (2011) 'Imagining Twitter as an imagined community', *American Behavioral Scientist*, 55 (10): 1294–318.

Hoffman, E.S. (2009) 'Social media and learning environments: Shifting perspectives on the locus of control', *In Education*, 15 (2). Available at: http://ineducation.ca/index.php/ineducation/article/view/54/532. Accessed 13 September 2013.

Kukulska-Hulme, A. (2012) 'How should the higher education workforce adapt to advancements in technology for teaching and learning?', *The Internet and Higher Education*, 19: 247–54.

McNeill, T. (2012) '"Don't affect the share price": Social media policy in higher education as reputation management', *Research in Learning Technology*, 20, Supplement: ALT-C 2012 Conference Proceedings: 152–62.

Procter, R., Williams, R., Stewart, J., Poschen, M., Snee, H., Voss, A. and Asgari-Targhi, M. (2010) 'Adoption and use of Web 2.0 in scholarly communications', *Philosophical Transactions of the Royal Society A*, 368: 4039–56.

Ullrich, C., Borau, K., Luo, H., Tan, X., Shen, L. and Shen, R. (2008) *Why Web 2.0 is Good for Learning and for Research: Principles and Prototypes*. Paper presented at International World Wide Web Conference, WWW 2008, 21–25 April, Beijing, China. Available at: wwwconference.org/www2008/papers/pdf/p705-ullrichA.pdf. Accessed 11 September 2013.

2

Social Media Basics

OVERVIEW

Chapter 2 prepares the ground for your social media explorations by examining the functions and features that are common to most online, social media environments. Firstly, the 'backbone' of social media, RSS, is explained before we move on to the basics of links, embed code, tags, and widgets. Guidance on setting up an account is given (for example, tips on choosing a username), as is advice on how to 'beef up' your password(s) and how to create backups in a variety of ways. The chapter also discusses matters relating to the 'socialness' of social media (for example, audience issues, online 'cultures', tone, privacy, sharing information) and includes a comprehensive discussion on how to communicate – and communicate appropriately – with lecturers using social media. Finally, the chapter discusses the need for a positive attitude or mindset – perhaps the most important pre-condition for successful study and research in the social media environment – and in particular, the need to believe and *know* that using social media is easy and that anyone can do it but that it is essential to be your own helpdesk.

FUNCTIONAL COMMONALITIES OF SOCIAL MEDIA

There are many characteristics and functions that are common to social media sites, services, tools, and applications across the internet. This section explores some of the most common. If you make an effort to understand the basics, then you will find yourself swiftly developing the 'transferable skills' you need to help navigate social media environments quickly and easily.

RSS: The foundation of internet content distribution and aggregation

RSS is short for either 'Really Simple Syndication' or 'Rich Site Summary' (there is no consensus on exactly what it stands for). More important than the abbreviation and what it signifies, though, is what RSS *does*. RSS provides the underlying 'architecture' for the distribution of content via the internet: it aggregates and 'feeds' content from one source to another, allowing you to follow people on Twitter or Facebook, to subscribe to YouTube channels, to link accounts, and to generally share material between sites and services. This is a big step on from the early days of the internet, when users had to visit each website independently to check to see if updates had been made to the site. RSS neatly circumvents this 'hit-and-miss' procedure by delivering updates directly to *you* on the site or service you are currently using.

Some sites and services display a small, square, orange icon somewhere on the screen along with some text that says 'RSS' or 'Subscribe' or 'Feed,' which indicates that you can subscribe to that page's content using a 'feed reader'. The advantage of using a feed reader over Facebook or Twitter (which pretty much act as their own feed readers for their own content) is that you can aggregate content from a much wider variety of sites and services than just a few, popular social networks. With a feed reader, you can subscribe to – and thus get the latest updates from – blogs, news services, publishing houses, government and non-government organisations, research councils, funding bodies, etc. Feed reading apps are very popular for smartphones and tablet devices as they neatly assemble content from multiple sources into the one spot (search for 'Feed reader' in your app store). This means that you don't have to continually open and close or switch between several different apps in order to view material across applications – all of which can greatly advantage your study and research practices.

Feeds usually operate quietly in the background and are only useful if you check them regularly, so try to make it a habit to check your feeds once a day for the latest information on topics that are relevant to your study and research.

Further uses for RSS in study and research are covered in Chapter 8.

Hyperlink etiquette

No doubt you already know what a hyperlink is (that is, a referral to a document, image, or any other object on the web) and how to click on one, but it's important that you know how to correctly embed a hyperlink in your blog, wiki, or other site if you are going to use social media as part of a study or research presence.

Some services, such as Facebook, automatically detect and insert hyperlinks whenever you post one. This is OK up to a point, but it should be noted that, as at time of writing, Facebook does not actually follow good etiquette (see the bullet points below) when it inserts hyperlinks automatically on your behalf. This is not a problem if you are using the internet solely for personal purposes; however, if you need to communicate at a more professional level, then Facebook-like 'sidestepping' (which you, as a user, cannot yourself side-step) is not helpful because it means that you don't have to bother learning how to use hyperlinks correctly. What is important, here, is that you know how hyperlinks work, and that you understand both the automatic and manual processes involved in inserting them.

Here is some basic hyperlink etiquette that you should follow on any site or service that allows you to insert your own links:

1. Insert the link *behind* the display text using meaningful, descriptive prose that reads like a sentence. CORRECT: 'Visit the *Studying and Researching with Social Media* website for more information'. INCORRECT: 'Read more http://sagepub.co.uk/studyingandresearching'.
2. Avoid consecutive one-word links such as 'here here here'.
3. For accessibility reasons, do not create links that open in new windows or tabs.

Some services, such as Twitter, automatically shorten any links you add. This is acceptable, because communication via these services is characterised by brevity and limits to the number of characters you can use in any one message. Where you have control over adding your own links, however, you should always follow the etiquette outlined above.

Tips for creating an account

In the course of your web explorations it is likely that you have created at least one internet-based account, whether it is for a social media service, for online banking, or for shopping. When you sign up for an account, you are basically creating your own folder on the provider's servers and you access that folder through the unique combination of username and/or email address and password. Here is the minimum amount of information you should be required to give away (in a technical sense) to any social media service:

- *Username.* You need to choose a unique username because no two users of the same service can have the same name (that is, no two folders hosted by a service can have the same designation).
- *Password.* Choose a strong password, and use a different password for every site or service you sign up for (see below). You can change your password in your personal account settings or administration area.
- *Email address.* You may have more than one email address, so make sure you create your account using an address that you access regularly. Further, you may be required to confirm your account request via email before you can start using a service, so you need to be able to access your email inbox at the time of sign up.

Too frequently we create accounts without much thought but you should give some consideration to the following:

- *Choose your username carefully.* Some services allow you to change your username but many don't.
- *Choose a username that is unique and that you won't forget.* Aim to create for yourself a standard username that you can take advantage of across the internet without having to pick a different name for each site you want to join.
- *Consider choosing a username based on your real name.* Your lecturer and/or professional audience will appreciate knowing exactly who it is that they are talking to. A username based on your real name is also easier to remember. If lecturers make a suggestion about what would be a good username for the course – and you are OK with that (see Chapter 12) – then follow their instructions.
- *Avoid usernames based on your student (or staff) number.* Some lecturers may require this, but, mostly, usernames based on student numbers make it difficult for both your teacher and your classmates to identify you.
- *Don't choose a frivolous username.* 'PinkladyNo3' and 'DirtBikeDemon' are OK to use with friends on a personal level, but do not reflect well in a study or research environment.

Passwords

Most of us have one, not-very-secure password that we use all over the internet. This obviously isn't good practice for security reasons as it leaves you open to identity theft, account hacking, and more. To maximise your safety on the internet, you need a secure password and a *different password for every account you create*. This might sound like a lot of hassle, but you can get around it by using a formula to create a master password that then becomes the base for developing a different password for every site or service you sign up for (see the activity below).

Avoid writing down your password(s) in a notebook (the book can easily be lost or stolen) and, of course, never give out your password to anyone – not even to friends. Finally, don't forget to log out of any open account on a shared computer and then to log off the computer itself; this is especially important if you use a computer at work or on campus.

 Activity   Create a secure password

If you are like most people, then you probably need to improve your password security. Do it now by completing the following steps:

1   Choose a word that you will remember, for example, 'pilaf'.
2   Reverse it: 'falip'.

---

3 Add some numbers that you will remember, for example, the year you started high school (avoid using the year of your birth – you have no doubt provided that information to various services on the internet already, which will compromise the security of your password): falip02.
4 Add some symbols: *falip$02%.
5 Add some more numbers, perhaps the year you started kindergarten: *falip$02%94. This is your master password. You base all your other passwords on it, so be sure to remember it.
6 Finally, add service-specific letters for each service you use – perhaps the first and last two letters of the service's name in upper and lower case respectively. So, for Facebook, your password would be FA*falip$02%94ok and for Google it would be GO*falip$02%94le.

You now have a secure, unique password that you should have little difficulty remembering and applying to each account you use.

Tags and tag clouds

Tags, also known as 'labels', are the keywords that are applied to the many different objects (photos, images, videos, audios, blog posts, wiki entries, etc.) on the web. The main purpose of tags is to help users classify their own materials and to navigate others' – without them, the content on many websites (such as blogs, YouTube, Twitter, and Flickr) would be virtually impossible to find.

Tags are often displayed in a 'tag cloud' (see Figure 3.1, next chapter), which is a visual representation of the tags that have been applied to the objects on a site. You'll notice that in a tag cloud words appear larger or smaller depending on how many objects have been given a specific tag. In other words, the larger the tag appears in a tag cloud, the more frequently it has been used.

Tags and categories: What's the difference?

Some social media sites and services allow you to create 'categories' as well as tags. Both are used to classify content, but the 'spirit' behind each is different: whereas content is given many tags, it is usually assigned to only one category. Categories act as a 'Table of Contents' and are thus generally more 'formal' and 'fixed' than are tags. So, a blog post in Anthropology about how Pakistani kinship networks form a basis for group loyalty might be given the tags 'kinship', 'family', 'villages', 'patronage', 'izzat', 'culture', 'clan', and 'biradiri' but be assigned to the general category of 'kinship'.

You can give an object any tag or tags you choose. For example, a picture of a polar bear might be given tags ranging from 'polar bear', 'bears', 'Arctic', 'carnivores', 'climate change', 'paws', 'ice', and even 'cute' or 'angry' depending on who is doing the tagging and to what purpose. In terms of your studies and research, it's obviously important to use tags that are sensible, descriptive, relevant, and meaningful. In some assessment tasks, you may, in fact, even be judged partly on how effectively or otherwise you have used tags in your work. There is no limit to the number of tags that can be added to an object, but, as a rule of thumb, you should aim for three to six, just so that you've got a balance between too little and too much information. In any case, avoid frivolous tags or tags that simply don't assist users in finding content on your site. Tags are important to get right.

Widgets and embed code

A widget (sometimes referred to as a 'gadget') is a small tool or application that you add to your website or page to show content that is actually being hosted elsewhere. You can use widgets to display videos, calendars, tag clouds, documents, maps, RSS, slideshows, graphs, and any amount of similar items on your site – the material still 'lives' on the original site, it's just that it's also displaying on your own.

Widgets work on what is called 'embed code', which is a small piece of web code (html or similar) that describes 1) where the original object (video, calendar, or whatever) can be found on the web, and 2) what it should look like when it is added to your site. Some sites and services allow you to drag-and-drop 'prefabricated' widgets into your site, which is great, but it doesn't actually teach you anything about how widgets work 'behind the scenes'. So, if, for example, you want to add a YouTube video to your website but there is no 'prefabricated' widget to do it for you, you will need to know to do it yourself from scratch:

1. Decide where, on your own site, you want to add the YouTube video (or other object).
2. Go to YouTube (or other host site) and find the video you want to embed in your site or on your page.
3. Find the video's embed code by searching the page for words such as 'embed' or 'share' or similar. The embed code will look something like this: <iframe width="560" height="315" src="http://www.youtube.com/embed/jL3nQt2kkPo" frameborder="0" allowfullscreen></iframe>.
4. Copy the embed code from the host site.
5. Go back to your own site and paste in the embed code in the place that says 'add widget', 'add embed code', 'add video', or similar.
6. Don't forget to hit 'save'.
7. Now, refresh your page to make sure that you have embedded the video (or other object) correctly on your site. You should now be able to click 'play' on the video on your site and watch it.

The example provided above shows you how to embed a YouTube video on your site but the same steps apply for any material you want to embed. The first time you successfully embed an object from scratch in your own site you'll feel a sense of accomplishment, which can be motivating especially if you are a little tentative about the whole social media enterprise. On top of this, embedding useful, rich media objects in your site can really impress your lecturer and show them that you are embarking on this 'learning with social media thing' in good faith.

Backups

If you are a student, then creating backups of your work should be integrated into your everyday study habits. In the 'old days,' students were meant to keep copies of any written or similar work that they submitted, just in case things got lost in the office or suffered some other unnameable, administrative fate. Although the format of assignments may have changed (that is, you now most likely submit your work electronically, not physically), you are still supposed to keep a copy of your work as a backup.

The implications of this should be clear: if you are asked to create your own blog (or wiki or podcast or whatever) for a course assignment, then it is *you* who has to make sure it is backed up. On-the-ball lecturers, as part of their risk management of social media use in the classroom, will repeatedly remind you to take backups of your work and will not accept 'the dog ate my homework'-type (in the world of social media these translate as 'the server went down' or 'I inexplicably lost all my online work') excuses. If your computer blew up (or whatever), they will simply ask, 'Where is your backup?' If you cannot provide one, then you may well fail the assignment.

So, the consequences of *not* backing up your work can be significant.

For researchers, backing up your precious data and written documents should already be a habit and you should already have systems in place for backing material up online. However, you need to know how to make *proper* backups: to lose years' worth of work because you kept things on a shabby old flashdrive that crashed can be heartbreaking, not least of all because you could have done more to keep your work safe. And as we all know, nothing is ever as good when you have to write it a second time.

Perhaps the most important thing to note is that backing up your work is different from simply making a copy of it. When you make a copy, you are simply saving a single, local version of your work to one digital location; a proper backup instead entails making a full file copy of your site or object and then placing it in *two* different digital locations. You might decide to keep one copy on your local hard drive and another somewhere on the internet (say, in an online dropbox or file-hosting service – see Chapter 9) or a flashdrive (but flashdrives have a tendency to crash, so be careful – instead transfer your files to your desktop and work on them there before saving them back to your flashdrive at the end of the day) or even a CD- or DVD-ROM. A simple, although not entirely elegant, solution is to email a copy of your backup file to your web-based email.

> You are responsible for backing up any site or digital object you create, manage, or administer.

 Activity Take a backup of a social media site

Many social media services provide a backup option that allows you to export a backup file to your local desktop or similar location; this can normally be done through your site settings or administration area. Some services, however, do not provide such a function, so you need to find your own solution. In this case, try one of the following:

1 Use your internet browser to take an html copy of each webpage containing your work. To do this, go to File > Save As (or similar) and save a copy of the page to a local disc and keep it safe. You can view your saved file simply by clicking on it: this will open it in your browser software, even if you are not connected to the internet. Note, though, that you would have to do this for *each and every page* you want to take a copy of.
2 Find a tool that will take an entire copy of your site. Search 'HTTrack' for PC and 'SiteSucker' for Mac and follow the instructions to save an html version of your work.

It's best to practise and to know how to do this *now*, before you have to do it 'for real' with an assignment or major research project.

Word and your social media use

Many people prefer to use Microsoft Word to formulate their work before pasting it into their blog, wiki, or whichever other social media service is being used for written work. This is a mistake for two reasons:

1. Word forces you into producing work that reflects a particular cognitive style of writing – usually one that is found in essays, journal articles, reports, and similarly formal pieces of writing, and that is inappropriate for communication via social media. It is by far better that you write directly into your social media interface (whilst saving often) so that your writing achieves the correct style and tone in the social media context. Specific advice on how to write for different forms of social media is given in the relevant chapters.

2. Copying and pasting from one software environment to another (for example, from Word to PowerPoint or from Word to a blog) usually leads to formatting problems. This can be frustrating, especially when you have written a long blog post or wikipage that now needs a complete re-format.

Finally, some people think – not unreasonably – that constructing their work in Word provides them with a form of 'backup' when writing lengthy or complex material. This is true to some extent, so if this is your rationale for using Word, then bear in mind (for the reasons outlined above) that it is best to write firstly into your social media site or service and *then* to copy and paste into Word or a text editor every now and then until you are ready to publish your final piece of work.

COMMUNICATION EXPECTATIONS AND SOCIAL MEDIA

Not all communication via social media is equal. Sometimes you need to very carefully attend to formal social and writing conventions that surround human interactions; at other times, a more casual approach will be acceptable. Being alert to, and practising, good communication etiquette via social media will help you navigate the sometimes tricky cultural landscapes that characterise social media. This section provides general advice on social media writing conventions but also places a special emphasis on how students can better understand their lecturers when it comes to communicating via social media in the teaching and learning context.

Writing conventions and style

Just as you adapt your communication style to suit various types of face-to-face interactions, so, too, must you adapt your style when using social media, regardless of whether you are using it for study or research. We all know that we act and speak differently in different social situations; for example, the language and tone you adopt in front of a selection committee at a job interview is different from the language and tone you adopt in front of your friends at a social gathering.

Make sure you understand the writing conventions around the type of social media you are dealing with. For example, expectations around grammar, levels of formality and informality, and the use of idiom and abbreviations all vary across different platforms. The chapters in Part II discuss these issues in greater detail, but, for now, some general observations can be made:

- *Blogs.* Standard English is expected (on academic and professional, as well as most other, blogs), meaning that you should pay attention to correct grammar, spelling, and punctuation. 'Textspeak' is not acceptable, although a more personal – even 'chatty' – style of writing can be very effective.

- *Wikis.* Again, Standard English is required. Wiki writing is generally more formal than is blog writing, but it should not be jargonistic or overly bookish.
- *Twitter.* Accuracy and brevity are key to writing effectively for Twitter. Full, expansive prose is not necessary but text-style shorthands (such as 'c u l8tr') are generally not acceptable.
- *Social networks.* Lapses in spelling and grammar are well-tolerated, but they should not interfere too much with understanding. Too much sloppiness, even on a fairly informal, relaxed social network, can frustrate your audience.

If you have used social media regularly for any length of time, you will probably have found yourself 'in trouble' at some point over something that was either misread, misinterpreted, or misunderstood by others, or plain ill-judged on your own part (see Chapter 11 for further discussion). For this reason alone, you need to understand communication practices as they apply to various social media formats.

Understanding your lecturer's other responsibilities

If you are a student then it is important that you understand that your lecturer is not just a teacher: in most cases, academics have a number of other things to deal with as part of their job. This means that they are not spending all their time on social media activities relating to your course. Understanding the multiple dimensions that make up academic life will help you to 'manage upwards' when it comes to making requests of or seeking assistance from your lecturer. Typical academic responsibilities include:

- *Teaching/lecturing.* Designing, developing, organising, delivering, evaluating, and reworking courses; assessing student work; providing feedback; supervising graduate research students.
- *Research.* Developing research proposals; applying for grants and other funding; collecting and analysing data; writing up results.
- *Publishing.* Conducting literature reviews; writing up research; targeting journals and submitting articles; making corrections based on peer review and re-submitting.
- *Community service.* Attending and participating in meetings and seminars; chairing committees; contributing to discussions about the direction a department or faculty might be moving in; mentoring new and junior staff; providing feedback to colleagues.
- *Administration.* Booking teaching venues; photocopying and/or adding materials to websites; typing up and distributing notes from meetings; entering grades into databases; handling student complaints and requests for extensions; looking into plagiarism cases; marking late work. In most universities lecturers must do these things themselves – there is not a 'secretary' or research assistant to do it for them.

Knowing a little bit about these other tasks will allow you to figure out where you 'fit in' with your lecturer's daily duties.

Communicating with your lecturer

No-one ever really tells you how to communicate with your lecturer, so spend a little time getting to know your lecturer's preferred communication style and how you should best approach them when you need to ask a question or get help. If you want a quick and adequate response to your queries, you need to communicate both clearly and well. The advice below is based on common sense, good practice, and courtesy. Use all three and you should have few difficulties in establishing a good relationship with your lecturer.

- *Know your lecturer's preferred communication channel(s).* Is your lecturer happy to respond to emails? Do they prefer to talk to students face-to-face or over the phone? Can you direct message them? Or are they fond of using a discussion forum for student communications? Use what suits them best.
- *Ask others first.* Got a question? Try to find the answer yourself first *before* you contact your lecturer. Check your course guide and/or website for anything obvious you may have missed, or put your question to the course discussion forum – often other students in the forum either have similar questions or can answer your question for you. Lecturers particularly like this kind of problem-solving because it means that the student community is contributing to and building its own repository of information relating to the course and how it is run; this is much better than having ten individual students email the lecturer with the same question.
- *Manage your expectations around email.* Most lecturers will respond to student emails, but how they manage those emails will vary. Some lecturers will respond immediately, others may take several days to get back to you, and some will not respond outside of regular work hours.
- *Get used to checking your student email.* Any formal announcements from your lecturer will be made via your student email so check it on a daily basis. There will be no excuse for not knowing about a change to the course if you have been notified about it via student email.
- *Email only one teacher at a time with your question.* Don't send separate messages on the same topic to separate recipients. If you have a question or want to make a point, then email one recipient and CC the others. This avoids having three different people tying up resources by working in isolation on a problem that could be solved by one.
- *Don't expect an immediate response to your solicitations.* Regardless of communication format, it is unreasonable to expect that your lecturer will respond immediately to your message.
- *Use mobile phone contact judiciously.* Some lecturers may give out their mobile phone number and prefer to use that over an office number. This is fine, but just remember that

29

a mobile is *mobile* and so might your lecturer be: they may be in a meeting or driving to a fieldwork site or dropping the kids off at daycare. Don't expect your lecturer to be in a position to talk immediately you call them on their mobile; in fact, they may allow your call to go through to voicemail while they sort out their other business and then get back to you later.

- *Think three times before texting your lecturer.* Generally speaking, you should avoid texting your lecturer, unless they have explicitly told you it is OK to do so or unless it is a dire emergency. Text messaging is quite possibly the last frontier when it comes to contacting your lecturer via electronic means, especially for undergraduate or coursework students.

Emailing your lecturer (or colleagues)

In many ways, emailing your lecturer should be a 'last resort': if you can find the answer elsewhere, then try to do so (see above). Of course, if you have privacy or confidentiality concerns about posting something in a public forum, then it is entirely appropriate – indeed, *only* appropriate – that you email your lecturer directly. (Although this section focuses on student–lecturer email communication, many of the points made also apply to colleague–colleague email communication.)

With these things in mind, know that your lecturer will likely have a certain set of expectations around what constitutes appropriate communication standards when it comes to email. In the first instance, it should be noted that contacting your lecturer via email is not the same as talking informally to friends and family via Facebook, chat, text, or messaging. Rather, an email to your lecturer requires a more 'traditional' approach – it doesn't have to be overly formal, but there are certain matters of style and tone that you should attend to. It is really, really important that you take some time when crafting any email message you want to send to your lecturer, so take care to construct a proper email. Remember, when you are emailing them you are normally emailing with a request, so be sure to put your lecturer in the right frame of mind from the beginning. Here are some tips:

- *Include a standard salutation.* You should always begin your message with 'Dear So-and-so' ('Hello' can be acceptable when you know your lecturer a little better). Always include your lecturer's name and *never* just write 'Hi' or 'Hey'. Lecturers can be put off by emails that lack an appropriate salutation, with some seeing it as a mark of disrespect. You want your lecturer to be well-disposed to your message from the outset, especially if you are seeking an extension or making a similarly tricky request.
- *Include an appropriate complementary closing.* Finish your message with 'Kind Regards', 'With many thanks', 'Thanks for your time', or similar. Avoid informalities such as 'Cheers' and 'See ya', although they are a marginal improvement on no complementary closing at all.

- *Don't forget to include your full name and student number.* You may not be the only 'Sarah' in the class, so 'Sarah Smith, u3869274' helps your lecturer identify you and avoid the frustration of having to email you back with a time-wasting 'Which "Sarah" are you?'
- *Be professional and courteous.* This may seem obvious, but it can be easy to lose sight of especially if you are emailing your lecturer with an issue or a frustration that you are experiencing with the course. Keeping things civil and polite whilst acknowledging that maybe you 'missed something' is a good tactic. Remember, emails, like all digital communications, can be archived and retrieved (not to mention forwarded!), so don't send anything that might portray you in a poor light if problems arise further down the track.
- *Use correct grammar.* You don't have to write a formal essay to your lecturer when communicating via email, but you should make an effort to write proper English. If your lecturer has to parse your email they may not be kindly disposed to your request or comment.
- *Use correct punctuation.* Punctuation is there to aid the reader in understanding your message, and lack of things such as full stops and correct capitalisation only add to the labour of reading a text. Remember, your lecturer is a busy person – make their life easier (and, by implication, your own) by getting things 'fairly' right. Of course, small errors in both grammar and punctuation are acceptable – this is email, after all – but too many errors will make a message difficult to read. Further, what is acceptable in text messaging in terms of acronyms ('brb', 'lol', 'ttyl') and contractions ('thx', 'plz', 'r', 'u') Is not acceptable in email. But perhaps the worst offender in this category is the use of a lower case 'i' for the first-person personal pronoun 'I': avoid this entirely.

Remember: email is king in the work world. Although a large degree of informal digital communication between people who know each other occurs via forms other than email (such as Facebook, chat, IM, etc.), email is still the primary form of communication in places of business – and that includes universities. You must be able to communicate effectively via email if you are to establish a good digital relationship with your lecturers and/or colleagues.

Attitude

So far in this chapter we have covered some of the more technical and social requirements for successful social media use in higher education. Although having good skills in both these areas is an excellent start, they will count for little if you don't also have the right attitude. By this, I mean that how you *choose to view* social media will determine your success or otherwise when it comes to using social media for study and research. If you are a keen social media user to start with, you might have to temper your enthusiasm somewhat; if you are sceptical you might have to open up a little to the educational possibilities that are generated by the application of social media in universities. In either case, you may well need to learn from scratch exactly *how* social media are being used for educational and research purposes – which might be completely new to you. Again, some of the focus here is on the student experience of social media, but similar issues – especially those around perfectionism – occur for lecturers and researchers, too.

Feeling confused by the task requirements

It is not uncommon for students to feel confused by what their lecturer is asking them to do as regards using social media to complete course assignments. Quite likely this is all new to you, irrespective of how much or how little you use social media in your personal life.

Informed lecturers will provide you with what's called 'scaffolding' – that is, the supports you need to achieve the learning outcomes for the class. It is called scaffolding because the various bits and pieces (for example, resources on what makes a good blog post, links on how to embed a video, guidance on how to structure your wiki, discussions on how to use the media in critical thinking) are provided at appropriate points in your learning and gradually removed: once you have learnt one thing, you are then able to move on successfully to the next part of the task. Other lecturers, however, may be working more on 'instinct' and may neglect to give you the scaffolding you need. In such cases, there is nothing wrong with constructively suggesting that a link to how to create a tag cloud might be useful for the class.

If you're confused or unclear about what is required of you for an assessment task, then *ask*.

Remember, the use of social media in university classrooms is still in its infancy, so in many cases both lecturers and students are learning together. Rather than see this as a deficit on the part of either lecturers or university education in general, take the opportunity to contribute profitably to *how* your lecturer teaches their course: make suggestions, test things out with and for them, and be instrumental in your own success in using social media in your learning.

Attitude towards your lecturer

This is a delicate subject, but one that nevertheless needs to addressed if we are to be honest about how both some students and some lecturers approach the use of social media for pedagogical purposes.

As mentioned above, the use of social media for educational purposes in universities is a relatively new thing, and both students and lecturers are still finding their way in the new digital environment. This can lead to a situation where some lecturers are trialing new things that don't always work smoothly and that students find frustrating. This can especially be the case if lecturers are working more on 'gut instinct' (which might be correct in terms of what they are trying to teach you, but which may lack a proper educative structure) than on a fully informed pedagogy. This is not to say that lecturers are 'hopeless' or 'bad teachers' or 'ill-informed'; rather, it points to the fact that most university lecturers do not gain formal training in teaching and learning either as a field of studies or as a practice.

In many ways, this makes it all the more laudable when lecturers want to explore methods that *improve student learning* and that don't involve the simple replication of methods, tools, and techniques that have been around, literally, for several hundred years, or the possible reproduction of assignments they may have been setting for the past dozen. Further, and this is something that many students don't realise, lecturers who *are* trying to improve student learning through the use of new methods sometimes work in environments where their colleagues don't 'get' what it is that they are trying to do and who also aren't afraid to voice their opinions that the only way to teach students is to get them to write essays. Unsupportive work environments can be stressful for lecturers who are simply trying to do better by their students.

However, such praiseworthy efforts do not in themselves justify an 'anything goes' approach – especially when marks are involved – and lecturers need to understand that student concerns over how social media are being used in a course are often genuine and not just examples of 'carping' or whingeing about a difficult task that students simply don't want to do.

If you find yourself in a situation where you are frustrated by the lack of clarity or coherence around a set task, I suggest you look carefully at how to handle things. If you are feeling confused, the chances are that your lecturer knows that there is something wrong with how they have gone about setting up the task and how they have communicated their requirements. It's important to be open in such circumstances and to avoid defensiveness – on both sides – for defensiveness only leads to the shutting down of communication channels that really need to be open if a problem is to be resolved (see Chapter 11). So, rather than getting defensive, angry, or irritated, the best attitude to adopt in this situation is one where you 'cut your lecturer some slack'. Offer them solutions ('we need a handout' or 'give us some links to relevant resources'), not problems. Your lecturer should welcome supportive, encouraging comments, especially if they help the course to run more smoothly, thus decreasing everyone's stress levels.

Perfectionism and feeling overwhelmed

Higher education often exists within high-stakes, competitive environments in which people are measured against their grades, publications, and/or research output, rather than effort or degree of improvement. Under such conditions, those who produce the most 'flawless' work – and, by implication, those with perfectionist tendencies – often believe they have the advantage over others when it comes to succeeding in the Academy. This is usually not the case. Experienced academics know that being a perfectionist is not actually helpful when it comes to producing good work that engages the scholarly community to take up key issues and debates around a topic.

In fact, the top academics are usually those who can put ideas together quickly and who can communicate them well enough so that peers can review them and take them further: an unpublished, 'almost perfect' paper sitting on your computer cannot compete with a 'pretty good' paper already submitted to a journal and on its way to publication. In other words, 'near enough is often good enough' and there is no point waiting until something is perfect before you send it on its way. This approach, however, can often be a little threatening to those of us with a proclivity for perfectionism and may, indeed, be a problem if you

- Feel you have to read 'everything' before you can start on or hand in an essay.
- Are embarrassed by that grammatical error that slipped into your paper.
- Won't get a colleague's feedback on some text because it's 'not finished yet' and everything needs to be 'just right'.

Perfectionism can be a big trap in social media environments. So, work on yourself and your attitude and try to embrace the following advice, if only to help you manage the stress of working within unfamiliar territory.

Perfectionism is not your friend in social media environments.

- *You don't have to know or do it all.* It's impossible, anyway. There is so much information online that you can't conceivably know or read everything that is out there. Choose the one or two things that best suit you and the task, and stick with them. Don't keep looking for the 'perfect' way of doing things – you'll never find it, not least because online environments are being updated all the time.
- *Relax your standards around certain forms of writing.* Different social media environments require different 'genres' of writing (which are explored throughout this book), all with different standards of grammatical expression, punctuation, etc. If you feel challenged by producing anything other than faultless formal or Standard English for everything you write – regardless of genre – then you will simply not be able to take part effectively and efficiently in many online conversations.
- *Accept ambiguity.* Many things that get posted via social media are unfinished. This can be quite confronting for perfectionists because you are being asked to publish 'incomplete', 'deficient' work online for all the world to read. Moreover, you might have

to do it in a digital environment that you aren't quite sure how to control in a technical sense, meaning that you might accidentally hit 'submit' or 'publish' before you are ready, or that you just cannot get that video centred on your wikipage and you don't like the way it looks. Using social media means that you might have to accept a level of ambiguity or imperfection in your life that you are not happy with and not used to.

- *Give up some control and be flexible.* You will not be able to control everything that goes on in social media environments, whether it's the way a heading is formatted or the way other people 'behave' or write. A level of acceptance and flexibility as regards how these environments work will greatly assist in keeping your stress levels down.

What matters is that your ideas and research are getting out there – not that the image you inserted in your blog post is two pixels too wide. That said, do take care with your design process, but be sure to know when you are being a perfectionist and when the amount of time you are spending on fixing the size of an image, for example, is disproportionate to the value of communicating your work in good time.

Don't get overwhelmed. Temper your standards for yourself and others, know that you can't control or know everything, and aim for 'pretty good' as opposed to 'perfect' and you will have a good chance of doing well with using social media for study and research.

Problem-solving

If you have any experience at all with social media you will have noticed that there is rarely a helpline available to deal with your questions or problems (unless you pay for it, of course). Further, there is almost never an instruction manual provided, as the service you are using is being updated all the time, meaning that such manuals quickly go out of date. In fact, an instruction manual should be unnecessary in a well-designed social media environment, as all the instructions should be there on the screen already: from 'post' to 'add link' to 'insert video'. Additional help, of course, can often be found in discussion forums and FAQs accompanying the site or service. But not everything can be solved via the site or service itself. Therefore, the best skills you can develop in digital environments are those of problem-solving and troubleshooting when things go wrong. So, help yourself by trying these strategies when you just can't figure out how to do something, where to find something, or how to make something work:

- *Read the FAQs.* Most social media sites and services provide a page or pages of 'frequently asked questions', written in plain English, to help you figure out how to use the service. The focus of FAQs is on things such as 'How do I add a blog post?' and 'What are tags?', that is, the functionality of the service itself.

- *Search the discussion forum.* A discussion forum is the place to find answers to problems that you have encountered in using the site or service; for example, you may want to know how to display an RSS feed on the site of your wiki, or you are having trouble getting a podcast widget to play your audio. If there is a good-sized community of users of the service, then the chances are that someone can respond to your forum post and help solve your problem.
- *Google it.* There is a very good possibility that you are not the only one with this particular problem or trying to do this particular thing. Type your problem into a search engine and see what you come up with. Solutions can often be found on blogs or on other forums that exist outside of the service you are having problems with.
- *Watch a video tutorial.* People are always posting tutorials on all kinds of topics on YouTube. Get used to using video-sharing sites as a way of learning how to do things with social media.
- *If you can imagine doing it, you probably can.* Even if a site or service doesn't 'natively' allow you to upload a folder full of pictures all at once to your wiki, the chances are that you can make it happen with a bit of tweaking. Google what you want to do and see if anyone else has managed to do the same thing. You'll be surprised at how much extra you can do on a site if you really want to.

It's all about you

The final thing to remember about your attitude to and in social media environments is that it's 'all about you'. How you choose to react to and use social media depends on *you*. So, take some pressure off yourself and bear these things in mind:

- *You can't break it.* Social media services do not allow you to access and mess with the underlying code that runs the tools you are using. This means that you can't break anything (not unless you are hacking into a service, in which case you are likely involved in some form of criminal act). So, jump in and explore and play without thinking that you are going to 'hit the wrong button' or 'make a mistake' – but always make sure you hit 'save'.
- *Start small and build.* Don't try to learn everything all at once. Start with one or two things, gain some confidence, and then work your way into some of the more advanced functions of the social media service you are using. 'Quick wins' are always motivating.
- *It's not the software, the computer, the service, your lecturer, your students, or the assignment: it's YOU!* By focusing on your own 'user incompetence' or 'user error' (as opposed to the other things just listed) you can magically reduce your anxiety and stress levels in social media environments. When something 'doesn't work', look for the error *you* made: perhaps you signed in with the wrong email address, perhaps you provided the wrong image link, perhaps you clicked on 'yes' when you should have clicked on 'no'. Alternatively, maybe you didn't ask your lecturer to clarify what they wanted as regards part of the assignment, or conceivably you 'zoned out' when they were describing the level of English they were expecting on your wiki. Maybe the information is out there, but you haven't looked hard enough for it. In any case, you can't break it, whatever it is, and the chances are that you can always salvage things.

SUMMARY

- RSS provides the underlying 'architecture' for the distribution of content via the internet: it aggregates and 'feeds' content from one source to another.
- It is important that you follow hyperlink etiquette when adding links to your blog, wiki, or other site.
- The minimum amount of information you need when setting up an account on a social media service is a username, password, and email address.
- Having a secure password is important: really, really important. You should have a 'baseline' password that you use to create a different password for every account you create.
- Tags are keywords that are applied to different objects on the internet. They help us navigate the huge amount of web content that is out there.
- A widget is a small tool or application that you add to your website or page to show content that is being hosted elsewhere. You can use widgets to display videos, calendars, tag clouds, documents, maps, RSS, slideshows, graphs, and any amount of similar items on your site.
- Taking backups is vital. You must back up any site or digital object you create, manage, or administer.
- You need to understand the writing conventions and style expectations that govern various types of social media.
- Make sure you know how to communicate effectively with your lecturer and with others when using social media. Pay special attention to email communications.
- You may need to cultivate a good attitude towards the use of social media in your course. Know how to problem-solve, and keep a check on perfectionism.

FURTHER READING

Nichol, D., Hunter, J., Yaseen, J. and Prescott-Clements, L. (2012) 'A simple guide to enhancing learning through Web 2.0 technologies', *European Journal of Higher Education*, 2 (4): 436–46.

O'Reilly, T. (2005) *What is Web 2.0? Design Patterns and Business Models for the Next Generation of Software*. Available at: http://oreilly.com/web2/archive/what-is-web-20.html. Accessed 11 September 2013.

Settle, Q., Telg, R., Baker, L.M., Irani, T., Rhoades, E. and Rutherford, T. (2012) 'Social media in education: The relationship between past use and current perceptions', *Journal of Agricultural Education*, 53 (3): 137–53.

Shen, D., Cho, M., Tsai, C. and Marra, R. (2013) 'Unpacking online learning experiences: Online learning self-efficacy and learning satisfaction', *The Internet and Higher Education*, 19: 10–17.

Xu, C., Ma, B., Chen, X. and Ma, F. (2013) 'Social tagging in the scholarly world', *Journal of the American Society for Information Science and Technology*, 64 (10): 2045–57.

II

Core Social Media Formats

The second part of *Studying and Researching with Social Media* describes four formats that could be said to make up the 'core' of social media: blogs (Chapter 3), wikis (Chapter 4), social networks (Chapter 5), and audio-visual presentations (Chapter 6). This part focuses on how each is used in higher education and discusses not only technical features but also how to successfully engage with each format as well as any special considerations you might have to account for when using the tool or service in study or research.

3

Blogs

OVERVIEW

This chapter begins by describing how blogs work and how to set one up. The core blog characteristics of comments, posts/entries, and reverse chronological ordering are detailed, and the importance of tagging is highlighted so that you understand how material is navigated on blogs. We discuss how blogs are used by lecturers to solicit critique and reflection – as well as the evaluation of ideas or positions – from students. Two main models of blogging you might encounter are presented: the 'whole of class' blog, and the 'teacher only' blog. The chapter also points out special blogging considerations including how to write a blog post, how to write a blog comment, the need for appropriate style and tone, and the difference between a blog and a discussion forum. Advice is also provided on how blogs are assessed and we look at some of the special considerations for blogging, such as choosing a blog address, posting appropriate material, and why blogging is different from Facebook. For how to use a blog to build your online profile, see Chapter 7.

WHAT IS A BLOG?

A blog is a website that allows you to make regular entries (called 'posts') on a topic or range of topics. Some blogs are pretty much personal journals (indeed, this is how blogging started, with people recording 'web logs' of happenings in their daily lives), whilst others might have a more professional focus. Blogs are most commonly written by individuals, but there are also blogs written by groups of people who share a common interest. Posts (or entries), comments, tags, and reverse chronological ordering are all typical of blogs.

Posts

A post is simply something that you write or put on your blog. Posts are the core part of your blog, and may include commentary, opinion, descriptions of events, reflections, links to other sites and materials, embedded videos, images, polls or slideshows, etc. Posts normally include the date the post was created, several tags (see below, and Chapter 2), and are automatically archived.

Comments

Comments are responses that readers of your blog make to your post. Readers normally reply to the initial post and generally not to each other's comments (unlike in a discussion forum – see below – where members respond to the discussion as a whole), although the more powerful blogging services do allow for such 'nested' comments.

Tags and categories

Tags are keywords that are added to each post by the blogger as a way of classifying content so that the post can be retrieved later on. Most importantly, however, tags help your readers to find material on your blog, which is essential given the dynamic, continually changing nature of most blog content. Tags are nimble and flexible and can be quite informal or personal. For example, if I were to post a picture or a story about a beagle puppy, I might tag it with 'beagle', 'puppy', 'dog', 'pets', and 'vaccination'. My 8-year-old nephew, on the other hand, might tag the same object as 'puppy', 'fun', 'Fido', and 'cute'.

Tags are often displayed in a 'tag cloud', that is, as a group of words, some bigger, some smaller (the larger the appearance of the word, the more often it has been added as a tag to posts on the blog). Readers use the tag cloud to navigate your blog. So, using the example tag cloud in Figure 3.1, if readers want to read all the posts on 'digital literacy', then they simply click on the tag 'digital literacy' and the blog's content gets automatically

Being social **Blogs and blogging** Business Careers advising CIBER **Culture** Digital divide **Digital literacy** EdCom Editing **EduBusiness**

Educational leadership

Education politics Educause Format **Futures** Internet Learning environments **Learning online** Legal issues

Lifeline **LMSs** MCEETYA

Net Gen

Opinion PLEs

Podcasting

Podcasts Podcasts and podcasting **Podules**

Reports and studies Resources Scripts Social issues **Social networking**

Target Tech'n'Teach

Technology Tips

Trends University **Web 2.0** Web Two Wowsers

Wikis and wikiing

Young people

FIGURE 3.1 An example of a tag cloud

sifted to show only those posts that have been tagged up with 'digital literacy'. Posts that relate to learning online, podcasting, social networking, and wikis and wikiing won't be shown.

Categories, like tags, are ways of classifying your post and they help your readers find content on your site by serving as a table of contents for your blog. Unlike tags, however, posts normally only get assigned to one category and not all blogs use categories. See Chapter 2 for further discussion.

How blog content is organised

Blogs are dynamic and display the latest posts at the top of the page, that is, posts or entries are displayed in reverse chronological order. This can occasionally confuse first-time bloggers who somehow feel that their work should be displayed in chronological or 'narrative' order from first post to last. Again, the more powerful blogging services do allow you to display content in this way if you want to, but this should be discouraged as a blog is not a 'story' to be read from start to finish; rather, it is an unfinished work-in-progress that doesn't follow a traditional narrative structure of beginning, middle, and end.

Blogs versus discussion forums

As stated earlier, a blog is usually written by a single person who contributes an original blog post and then gets comments from people about the original post. With a discussion forum, however, anyone can make an initial contribution, and replies generally move the discussion forwards, rather than stick to the original post. Of course, in practice, there is often some cross-over in how these online tools are used.

VIDEO CLIP Blogs in Plain English

To get an overview of how blogs work, watch CommonCraft's 'Blogs in Plain English' video on YouTube (search 'Blogs in Plain English').

Choosing a blogging service

Perhaps the most well-known – and even most highly regarded – blogging service is provided by WordPress.com. WordPress is a powerful blogging tool with excellent functionality – that is, you can do lots with it, from writing simple posts to embedding rich media, to controlling exactly who can comment and under what conditions. Simpler services include Blogger (hosted by Google, so if you have a Google account then you already have access to Blogger), and Tumblr (a very popular, streamlined, rich-media-friendly service).

Depending on how your lecturer is using blogging in your course (see below for common blogging models), there may or may not be a blog already set up for you. If you have to contribute to a blog that is already being used, then make sure that you agree to the Terms of Service (see Chapter 12) before signing up. If you have the liberty to choose your own blogging service, then perhaps check out the three providers mentioned above (WordPress, Blogger, and Tumblr), and see which suits you best. My usual advice to students is to just use WordPress because it is relatively easy to operate, and, given that it allows you to do so much, you can 'grow into it' as you learn. However, many students prefer the simplicity of Tumblr (but be warned: both tag and comment functions aren't part of the default Tumblr settings, and adding them can be a little tricky). If you want to explore services outside these three, then you can conduct a comprehensive comparison at WeblogMatrix.org (search 'WeblogMatrix').

Essential widgets

Add these widgets (or 'gadgets') to your blog's 'appearance' or 'theme':

- Tag cloud
- Archive
- Search box
- Pages (if using static pages)
- Links

Using a blog and your blog's dashboard

If you are required to set up your own blog for your course, firstly check to see if your lecturer has provided any instructions about which service to use, what kind of username to pick (sometimes they will suggest something based on your student number, but see Chapter 2), and what email address you should associate with your account (often they will prefer that you use your university email). If you are happy with these instructions (or if you can simply do your own thing), then create and verify an account (see Chapter 2) after reading and agreeing to the Terms of Service (see Chapter 12).

Once that's done, you'll notice that there are two main parts to your blog. Firstly, there is the administration or 'dashboard' area where you build, write, and manage your blog. From the dashboard, you can write and publish posts, change the appearance or theme of your blog, add users, control comments, set your site to public or private, and do all of the things that generally make your blog work. Note that only you and any other approved authors on your blog can view the dashboard, and only then when you are logged in. The second part of your blog is your 'front page'; this is the bit that the 'rest of the world' can see, that is, the part on the web that is viewable by regular visitors to your site and the part where they make comments.

TIP Working between your dashboard and your blog's front page

Keep two tabs open in your browser (if you don't know about tabbed browsing, then google it to find out) – one for your dashboard and one for the public face of your blog (that is, the front page of your blog site itself). Switch between your dashboard and your site to make sure that the changes you *think* you have made in your dashboard are actually showing on your site. Don't forget to refresh the screen to be sure that you are viewing the latest saved version of your site.

Make sure that you know how to access your blog once you've logged out – in other words, know your blog URL (web address) and remember the username, password, and email address you used to sign up for your blog account.

Visit WeblogMatrix.org to compare blogging services.

BLOGGING IN HIGHER EDUCATION

Blogs are used in particular ways in higher education, both as learning tools and as tools for communicating research and ideas. Although the focus here is on the student experience of blogging, researchers will also benefit from the following sections, as blogs can be used in similar ways to support the research process (see Chapters 7 and 8 for more information about blogging for research). For students, though, if you have a sense both of how your lecturer will be using a blog in your course (that is, the blogging 'model' they are working from) and of the typical blogging tasks they might ask you to undertake, then you are on your way to meeting the requirements of your blogging assignment.

Blogging models

Lecturers have three main options when it comes to how they want to use blogs in their course. It's a good idea for you to identify the blogging model that your lecturer is working from so that you can think about what is expected of you when it comes to engagement with, and assessment of, blogging in your class. To this end, lecturers use blogs in three main ways:

1. *Administration blog.* Some lecturers prefer using an external blogging service over their institution-supplied VLE. This may be because they find a blog easier to use than a VLE, because they want your and their work to be more generally available on the web and not locked behind a university login, or because they simply favour the aesthetics of a blog. On this model, the lecturer uses the blog to post learning materials, readings, links, assignment information, announcements, etc. Thus, the blog favours transmission approaches to teaching and learning (see Chapter 1) where the lecturer is the sole blogger and provider of information – although students are often invited to ask questions about the course via the comment function of the blog.
2. *Whole-of-class blog (learning-focused).* There are two main versions of the 'whole-of-class blog'. The first is where the lecturer is the only blogger and students are either required or encouraged to make comments on the lecturer's posts. Posts are based on the course content that the lecturer wants you to engage with or demonstrate an understanding of. The second 'whole-of-class blog' is the kind where everyone in the class has author access to the blog and is required to both write posts and make comments. Again, the exact requirements of the task will vary, so check with your lecturer if you are unsure.
3. *Individual student blogs (learning-focused).* On this model, you set up your own blog and give the teacher your URL so they can access and read your work. For some students, this means that your main audience is your lecturer (who is assessing your work), but, in many instances, students are put into 'blogging groups' where four or five of you have to read and comment on each others' blog posts for marks. Sometimes, however,

this kind of blog is used purely as a way to get you to write regularly on class topics, and it's not necessary that others read or comment on your work. This can be extremely valuable in that it helps you improve your understanding of, and develop ideas about, key course themes.

Your lecturer's choice of blogging model is (or least should be) determined by their educational focus (see below), that is, what they want you to learn, understand, and/or do in order to successfully complete their course. If they choose a purely administrative blog, then their focus is chiefly on furnishing you with course materials. If, however, they chose a learning-focused blogging model, where you are being asked to either blog or comment or both, then their emphasis is on getting you to critique and reflect upon your own understandings of key course concepts. This kind of learning-focused blogging is usually characterised by the types of tasks that lecturers want you to carry out on a blog.

Typical blogging tasks set by lecturers

If your lecturer is using a learning-focused blogging model (see above), then you will probably be asked to undertake one or more of the following tasks:

- *Writing blog posts (either on your own, individual blog or on a whole-of-class class blog).* Lecturers usually specify word limits for blog posts (often sitting around the 300–500 word mark) and they frequently set a minimum *or* maximum number of entries you should make on a topic. For example, you may be asked to 'write a minimum of four blog posts of up to 500 words per entry'. Alternatively, you may be allowed to blog as much as you want, but be asked to submit your 'best five' (or whatever number) blog entries for grading.
- *Making comments.* You may be asked not to blog at all, but, rather, to simply comment on the posts that your lecturer writes on the class blog. It could be that you are required to comment on every post your lecturer writes, or just on a set number; your comments may be assessed for marks, or you may be given a fixed, passing grade simply for making a minimum number of replies; you might get to choose the posts on which you comment; or you might be asked to comment on a particular week's or theme's topics only. Regardless, you need to be sure about the task requirements, so seek any clarifications you need from your lecturer.
- *Being part of a blogging group.* You may be put in 'blogging groups' or 'blogging circles' where you are required to both write posts of your own as well as comment on others' work. Often these groups are quite small – four or five students at the most – because your lecturer knows that you don't have time to read and comment on every student blog in the course.
- *Creating a private blog.* On rare occasions your lecturer will ask you to set up a private blog that is only shared between you and them. This is particularly the case if you are

being asked to blog some quite personal reflections on a class topic and/or if you are dealing with sensitive subject matter. Such assignments are not set lightly by lecturers. However, you yourself must be comfortable with what is being asked and you must bear in mind that nothing that gets posted on the internet is ever completely private (see Chapter 12). If you are being asked to do something that doesn't sit right with you, then don't do it; instead, approach your lecturer and respectfully outline your concerns and suggest some solutions (see Chapter 2).

Being sure about task requirements is key to successfully blogging for your course. Normally your lecturer will give quite specific instructions about how you should go about your blogging task, so make sure you follow those instructions and that you stay within the limits of the set assignment; just as there are limits set for more traditional assignments, so, too, must there be limits for blogging assignments.

WHY LECTURERS WANT YOU TO BLOG

If you know *why* your lecturer is asking you to blog, then you can enhance your learning – and your grades. Take some time to think about what your lecturer is trying to achieve, both for themselves and for you, and you will have a better sense of what blogging at university is all about. (Again, if you are using blogs for research purposes, being clear about your purpose – or the research team's purpose – in using a blog will help you blog more effectively. See Chapters 7 and 8 for further discussion.)

Educational and intellectual purposes

Blogging is becoming popular amongst university lecturers because it encourages critique and reflection, making it particularly well-suited to constructivist pedagogies (see Chapter 1) in which you build your understanding of a topic bit by bit, either on your own or with other students. This form of blogging is arguably favoured in the humanities and social sciences, but that does not mean that students in the hard sciences (for example, biology, chemistry, and physics) are never asked to blog. For example, an English literature lecturer might want you to write a series of blog posts on how a poet uses metaphor to express meaning; a sociology lecturer might want you to blog your ongoing observations about the gendered nature of workplaces and to describe how those observations are or are not reflected in the literature; and a chemistry lecturer might ask you to use your blog to record your experiments and observations over a period of time.

In any case, blogging is not a 'one-off' thing: it is usually done over a semester or longer to allow lecturers to track the development of your thinking as you make frequent, generally short, posts on a topic or topics. The advantage of this (both educationally speaking and for your lecturer) is that your early ideas about a topic are exposed, allowing you to get feedback from others; this should be used to inform your later posts as your understanding matures. Blogging is therefore quite different from the fait accompli that is essay-writing, where you present a (hopefully) coherent, logical, well-reasoned, and critically argued piece of work all in one go.

Where blogging *is* similar to essay-writing, however, is in the evaluation of ideas: lecturers want to see how well you can assess different scholarly opinions on a topic, and, in some cases, they want to see if you can contribute meaningfully to current debates in an area. Thus, blogging is not simply about describing the literature or summarising, over a number of posts, the different positions on the subject; rather, it is about genuine intellectual engagement with central course concepts. Bear this in mind and your blog posts and comments should achieve good grades.

Practical purposes

Lecturers also use blogging for more practical reasons. In many instances, they are looking for how well you write, especially in terms of focus, coherence, style, tone, grammar, and even punctuation (see below). Although most lecturers don't want your blog posts to resemble formal mini-essays on a topic, neither do they want to read incoherent, rambling, irrelevant, poorly worded text; instead, they want to know that you can put together a focused, informed, thoughtful, well-expressed post in 300 words or less (or whatever word limit is specified).

Moreover, lecturers will also often be looking for the kinds of information you can source, present, and disseminate. Relevance and value are key here: ideally, you want to share material (for example, links, videos, images) that your lecturer and others would not only find 'interesting', or that would make them hit the 'Like' button, but that they themselves would want to forward to or post on their own site.

Finally, lecturers use blogs to give feedback through the 'comments' function. Although they may not comment on each and every post, they may still comment on a few posts, or ask other students to comment on your posts. Lecturers may choose to do this because it bypasses the need to download your assignment from the VLE, open it up, write comments in track changes or in a new document, and then upload your assignment again. Being able to comment directly on your blog is a convenience as well as a well-informed teaching strategy.

SUCCESSFUL ENGAGEMENT WITH BLOGGING

Once you have gained an understanding of the blogging model your lecturer (or research team) is working from, the task you have been set, and the intellectual and practical purposes behind the use of blogging in your context, you will be in a position to really maximise your use of this form of social media in terms of your learning, your grades, and/or the distribution of your research.

The information provided in this section is, by necessity, very general. I strongly urge you to talk to your lecturer or research team leader/blog owner if you are unsure about what they are expecting. For example, I suggest below that blog posts are typically under 500 words in length; however, your lecturer might expect you to write something either much longer or much shorter. If you aren't sure, then ask – you must have a complete understanding of what it is that your lecturer or research team wants you to do in terms of blogging for them.

Writing

Writing a blog post is an art in itself and requires an understanding of genre just as much as writing an essay does, for there are certain techniques and characters of style, tone, form, etc., that come together to make a blog post a blog post and not an essay or a report or a novel or a tweet. Some basic advice for writing a blog post is as follows:

- *Write simply and clearly using Standard English.* Blog language is less formal than essay language; however, you must still use correct spelling, punctuation, and grammar. Use simple, jargon-free Standard English, and make clear statements about your ideas, reflections, opinions, commentary, and such like. Using formal, 'academic' English is generally considered inappropriate, and should be reserved for essays, reports, journal articles, and the like. At the same time, though, 'textspeak', masses of abbreviations, and incorrectly used punctuation will not reflect well on your blog post.
- *It's OK to use 'I'.* There is often a good deal of confusion on the part of students, especially, about the use of the first-person personal pronoun, 'I', in their university studies. Some lecturers place a strict ban on the use of 'I' in the belief that when a student uses it they will fall into the trap of expressing a personal opinion (along the lines of, 'I think that the government is bad') as opposed to a scholarly one (for instance, 'I believe the poor fiscal performance of the government can be explained by three main factors ...'). In fact, it is quite common in the humanities and social sciences (less so in the hard sciences) to see 'I' used when an author positions themselves in relation to other authors and ongoing debates, and/or when a writer wishes to be very clear about an argument they are developing, for example, 'In this paper, I contend that democratic governments must

quickly address major fiscal imbalances if further monetary crises are to be avoided'. With this preamble, it should become clear that the use of the term 'I' is totally appropriate in blogging, itself a less formal kind of communication than the academic essay or report. One thing that you must not do, however, is to incorrectly punctuate 'I': little 'i's can indicate sloppiness or haste in your work.

- *Keep it short.* Blog entries are usually under 500 words (but check your task requirements, as above) and some can be just a couple of lines. Your lecturer will penalise you if you ramble, and other readers won't read a comment on your post if it looks too long. Of course, occasionally you may want or need to write a longer post – but, as a rule, keep it short.
- *Stick to one point per post.* This can be tricky, especially if you are used to writing lengthy essays, articles, or reports in which you are at liberty to explore and present complex ideas and findings over a number of pages. However, blogging is a different genre of writing and requires you to concentrate on only one or two aspects of a problem or issue at a time. If you feel you need to make several points, then think about splitting your blog entry into a number of different posts.
- *Keep it focused.* Related to the previous point, blogging is an exercise in focused writing. If your writing is disjointed and incoherent, and if readers can't follow your train of thought, then they won't read your work.
- *Break up your text.* Write short paragraphs, even to the point of breaking an otherwise unified and coherent paragraph up into several bits. If you are writing a longer post, then break it up by inserting sub-headings – but if you are adding sub-headings, then you might need to consider whether or not your post is getting too big and unwieldy and should instead be spread across several different posts. The bottom line is, perhaps, that your post should be easy to scan.
- *Edit your post (and comments) before you publish.* Edit for style, tone, grammar, spelling, and focus. If your blogging service has the facility, then do a 'post preview' before you hit 'submit'. Poorly structured and worded text will not enamour you to your reader – who might just happen to be your lecturer.

Posts and comments

In general, your posts and comments should be focused, relevant, on-topic, raise insightful questions, share useful links and other media, challenge readers to think more deeply on a topic, and provide accurate information. Here are some tips for writing good blog posts and for making helpful blog comments:

- *Choose a catchy title for your post.* The idea of a blog post is to get people (not just your lecturer) to read it, so make your post title interesting. You should also give an indication of your topic, argument, and/or opinion in the title.
- *Link to other things.* Linking to related content or embedding videos or images in your blog posts will demonstrate to your lecturer the types of intellectual or reflective connections you are making on a topic. Make sure that whatever you share is relevant, though.

- *Appropriate use of lists is OK.* Providing a bulleted list in a blog post will help your readers digest your material quickly and will give a simple structure to what you're trying to get across. But be sure to know when lists are appropriate and when you should be using intact prose to express yourself. Your lecturer may well penalise you for using only, or too many, lists. Remember: part of what they are wanting to see is that you can write coherent, grammatically correct English.
- *Express your opinion.* Yes, your lecturer really wants to see this! But be certain that you are expressing a *scholarly* opinion and not a personal one. Any opinion in posts or comments needs to be based on considered, critical, scholarly reflection, and should be constructed in reference to relevant, peer-reviewed (that is, academic) literature. So, don't shy away from writing what you 'think', but make sure there is some intellectual musing going on.
- *Put some of yourself into it.* Blogs provide a less formal type of assessment or exercise than do essays or reports, so you are allowed to put a bit of your personality into your posts and comments. Humour is acceptable, as is a bit of emotion or passion, but be sensible in your writing, and be aware of things that might offend or put your readers offside, even if you don't mean for them to (see below).

Presentation

- *Think carefully about categories and tags.* Categories and tags help readers navigate your blog, so choose carefully. Use tags that clearly describe your content: do not use tags that are too 'way out' or indecipherable, and make sure your categories are general enough to capture the main areas of content in your blog.
- *Attend to the appearance of your blog.* A good-looking blog shows that you care about your reader's experience when they visit your site. Use an uncluttered theme that makes for easy screen viewing. Also be consistent in the small things, such as font styles, font size, use of captions on images, etc. Bear in mind that some lecturers will specifically dedicate marks to the 'aesthetics' of your blog; this can include everything from ease of navigability, effective use of tags, relevant use of rich media (videos, images, audio, etc.), overall appearance, even accessibility in terms of 'friendliness' to people with vision, hearing, or other impairments.

 Activity   Analyse some blogs and blog posts

Step 1 – Find some blogs. Track down half-a-dozen or so blogs – it doesn't matter if they are academic blogs, business blogs, personal blogs, community blogs; in fact, looking at a range of blogs is probably a good thing for this exercise. You may already know of, or regularly read, a few blogs, but if not then you can find blogs using Google's blog search (go to Google.com, type in your search term, and click on 'blogs' at the top of the page – Google will search only blog content for your search term).

Step 2 – Analyse some blogs. Once you have found your blogs, do a quick analysis of the different posts:

Writing

- How long are the posts? If short, are they too short? If long, too long? Has the author attempted to break up lengthier posts? If so, how?
- What style of writing is used? What is most/least effective?
- Are the posts focused? Is the purpose of the post (or, indeed, the entire blog) clear? Or do they ramble?
- How has the author handled paragraphing?
- Have the posts been proofread?

Posts and comments

- Do the posts present a balanced view? Do they need to?
- How much 'opinion' is too much opinion?
- What topics are people writing about? How are they approaching those topics?
- What kinds of posts keep your attention?
- What kinds of posts seem to get the most comments? The most 'hits' or 'likes'?
- How has the blog author dealt with comments? Does the author respond or not?

Presentation

- Does the blogger use rich media? If so, is it effective? Or just distracting? Has it been embedded properly?
- Are there useful links added to the posts?
- How easily can you find your way around the blog? How has the author used categories and tags?
- Are any of the bulleted lists helpful?

Step 3 – Reflect on your findings. This is where you synthesise what you have learnt from Step 2 so that your approach to blog writing is as informed and structured as any other kind of writing.

- What surprises you about blog writing?
- What will be the biggest difficulty you will have in writing blog posts?
- What will you try to emulate? Avoid?
- How is blog writing different from essay writing? Report writing? Other writing?

How blogs are assessed: What lecturers are looking for

As discussed earlier, blogs are excellent tools for eliciting critique of and reflection on a topic. As such, lecturers will use blogs to assess both how deeply you are thinking about the issues you are covering in class and how your ideas and understandings about key course themes have developed over time. But this is not all that lecturers are looking for. Just as with essay- or report-writing and similar, they are also looking for focus and coherence in your writing, critical engagement with the literature, your understanding of content, and your ability to stay within the parameters they have set for the task.

Table 3.1 provides an example of how you might be marked for a blogging task. This example is based on an 'assessment rubric', that is, a criterion-based tool used by some lecturers to guide them in their appraisal of your work. Read the rubric carefully to see how lecturers might judge where your work 'sits' in terms of quality and what they are looking for. Even if your lecturer doesn't use such an explicit tool, they are nevertheless likely to be measuring your work along these lines.

TABLE 3.1   Example of blogging assessment rubric used by lecturers to guide their evaluation of your work

Criterion	Unsatisfactory	Satisfactory	Good	Very good	Excellent
Understanding of issues	Little evidence of knowledge or understanding of issues relating to the topic being researched. Extensive confusion about the topic.	General or vague comments on issues with little evidence of close understanding of the topic being researched. Some confusion about the topic.	General comments on issues, backed up with some reference to specific aspects of the topic being researched. No significant confusion about the topic.	Commentary on specific aspects of the issues with evidence of close understanding (e.g., examples and cases) of the topic being researched. Clear comprehension of the topic.	Evidence of careful, broad, and deep understanding of the detail of the issues relating to the topic being researched. Inconsistencies and differing positions or approaches are noted and accounted for.
Critical engagement with issues	Does not identify key issues related to the topic being researched. Champions personal views rather than those backed up research.	Identifies key issues but provides limited critique of the topic being researched. Tendency towards description or personal reflection rather than analysis. Little reference to the research.	Demonstrates an adequate level of critique on the topic being researched with some analysis of opinions related to the topic being researched. Some reference is made to research reports or studies.	Responds to issues raised by the topic being researched, presents arguments and opinions on the topic based on research reports and studies.	Demonstrates broad and deep analytical engagement with the topics being researched. Presents arguments and opinions based on the research and demonstrates an ability to relate the material to different contexts.

Criterion	Unsatisfactory	Satisfactory	Good	Very good	Excellent
Development of thinking	Critique, opinion, or general ideas do not move past the initial understanding of the topic. Issues are not explored.	Critique, opinion, or general ideas begin to move past the initial understanding of the topic but show no significant evolution over time.	Critique, opinion, or general ideas mature past the initial understanding of the topic. Some degree of intellectual evolution as it relates to the topic under study.	Critique, opinion, or general ideas mature and grow well beyond initial understandings. Noticeable intellectual evolution and expansion as it relates to the topic under study.	The current end point of the thinking provides for extension and movement into a higher intellectual engagement with the topic under study. Links to related areas are made explicit in terms of future research.
Navigability of blog	Almost impossible to access and navigate blog content. No use of tags or other organising devices. Titles poorly used or meaningless.	Difficult to access blog content. Limited use of tags or other organising devices. Titles poorly used or almost meaningless. Links and media (e.g., videos) are poorly embedded.	Blog content can be accessed via tags or other organising devices. Titles used well. Links and media (e.g., videos) are adequately embedded.	Easy access to blog content. Good use of tags or other organising devices. Links and media (e.g., videos) are adequately and accurately embedded and show a good understanding of web authoring etiquette.	Excellent access to blog content of all descriptions. Extended, relevant, and sensible use of tags or other organising devices. Links and media (e.g., videos) are intelligently and accurately embedded and show an excellent understanding of web authoring etiquette.
Scholarly communication style	Refers to fewer than four reputable sources. It is difficult to understand the critique.	Some mistakes in spelling and/ or grammar; lack of clarity in the writing. Sometimes difficult to understand the critique. Refers to at least four reputable sources.	Adequate spelling and grammar. Critique understandable. Refers to at least four reputable sources.	Clear presentation of points of view, concisely expressed. Refers to at least four reputable sources.	Clear, concise, articulate, enjoyable to read. Refers to at least four reputable sources.

SPECIAL CONSIDERATIONS FOR BLOGGING

Blogging brings with it a set of special considerations that are almost unique to this form of social media. Make sure you account for the items discussed below in any blogging project you might undertake.

Setting up your own blog

You may be asked by your lecturer to set up your own blog as part of the task they've set you. Rather than see this as an irksome chore, instead embrace the opportunity to create something that is uniquely your own – besides, when else do you get to set up your own website for a university assignment?

First, however, you need to be comfortable with what your lecturer is asking of you, because, although lecturers may suggest that you use a particular blogging service (for example, WordPress or Blogger), they should not 'require' this of you. I say this because most universities have rules against forcing students to sign up for externally hosted web services in order to complete an assignment. See Chapter 12 for more information, but, in short, the reason for this is that you cannot be compelled to sign up to a Terms of Service if you don't agree with those Terms. That said, prudent lecturers will have conducted a risk analysis of their intended use of blogging in their course and will have chosen a blogging service whose Terms of Service are likely to be acceptable to you, that is, the Terms do not require you to give up your copyright or to give away a sub-licensable licence to your intellectual property, amongst other things (see Chapter 12). If you already have a blog, then you might reasonably ask your lecturer if you can use that blog for your assignment, even if your own blog isn't hosted by a service recommended for use in your course.

So, assuming that you are happy with what you are being asked to do, create an account with a blogging service and take some time to 'get to know' your blog. Explore your dashboard area (see above), change the theme or appearance of your blog, make (and delete) some test posts, add videos, links and images, and practise adding tags. Spending an hour or two just playing around on your blog and becoming familiar with how it works will build your confidence in using this form of social media for your study. Once you have some 'technical know-how', and once you feel comfortable with the functionality of your blog, you can start to focus on where most of your marks come from – and that is from your thinking.

Choosing a blog address

If you have the chance to set up your own blog, then consider carefully the address or URL you give your blog. Some students choose an address based in some way on the course title or number, for example, 'afshanIDEC3056. wordpress.com'. This is fine if you are sure that you only want to use your blog for that particular course, but if you are thinking ahead to perhaps using your blog as the basis for your eportfolio (see Chapter 7), then you should choose something a little more 'sustainable', that is, something that you can use into the future. So, if it's available, then a URL based on your name would be smart, for example, 'afshanjabeen.wordpress.com'. See Chapter 7 for more on building your eportfolio and Chapter 12 for more on considerations relating to using your real name on the web.

Extending your blogging outside the classroom

You can, of course, just do the bare minimum that is required of you in your blogging tasks and (theoretically speaking, at least) get a pass. Hopefully, though, you want to achieve more than this.

Take the opportunity of starting your own blog to explore the blogging medium: What is its value as a communication platform? How can you use blogging to get across your ideas and (informed) opinions? How can you link into others' blogs as a way of delving more deeply into a topic? What do people write about on blogs? What resources do they share? What characterises the blogging genre in terms of writing and communication? In addition to this, you should really be thinking about how your blog can be used as the basis for your eportfolio: blogs make excellent instruments for both hosting and distributing content relating to you and your work (see Chapter 7).

Appropriate material

Knowing what is appropriate to post on your blog requires good judgement. It should go without saying that you should not post material that could be seen as racist, sexist, xenophobic, unduly critical or disparaging of others, derogatory, abusive, pornographic, offensive, threatening, or similarly hostile or antipathetic (in fact, when you sign up for a Terms of Service with a reputable service provider you are agreeing not to post such material, anyway; see Chapter 12). However, sometimes it can be difficult to know when you have overstepped a boundary. For example, you may be asked to use your blog as a journal for recording your experiences on an internship or practicum. What if you observe what you consider to be a 'dodgy' incident and then you blog about it? Is this a breach of privacy if those involved are identifiable? On the other hand, what if you *don't* refer to any names or places but still those involved find your blog and can identify themselves in what you've written? Although you may not have breached any privacy laws, or, indeed, done anything 'wrong', you may still find yourself in a difficult situation where another party feels tremendously aggrieved about what you have written. Alternatively, you may be asked to blog about discussions you've had in face-to-face tutorials. Will you make explicit mention of points raised by particular students and then criticise those points? A general rule-of-thumb, here, is to be sure that you are critiquing ideas and practices and not criticising people. The distinction can be delicate, however, and in some cases there is simply nothing you can do to account for others' reactions.

A public or private blog?

If you feel genuinely uncomfortable about having a blogging presence on the web, then discuss the matter with your lecturer. In particular, you should provide them with a well-thought out argument or reason as to why you don't want to blog. For example, being cyberstalked for the past two years should be sufficient grounds for your not wanting to have an extended online digital footprint. If the lecturer agrees that your concerns are genuine, and not just a means of getting out of having to write a blog, then they should find some other way for you to submit work for assessment, a way that enables you to still meet the success criteria and/or learning outcomes for the assignment. For example, they (or you) may suggest that you still write up entries in 'blog style', but that you submit them in hardcopy or via your courses' VLE (see Chapter 1). Just remember, though, your lecturer probably has a right to ask if you are on Facebook, or if you have a Yahoo account, or if you have a Hotmail address and to question why you are willing to have a profile on those sites but not on a blogging service. You need to be prepared to counter such questions. Finally, remember that some blogging services, such as WordPress, allow you to make your blog private but not searchable by search engines. This means that whoever has the direct link or direct URL can access your blog, but Google and Yahoo and other search engines won't be able to find it.

> People often confuse the term 'blog' with the term 'post'. So, you'll hear people say, 'I wrote a blog today'. Actually, what they mean is, 'I wrote a *post* on my blog today' – the term 'blog' applies to the whole site, not to the individual pieces of writing that appear on it.

Blogging is not Facebook

One thing certain to impact negatively on your marks for blogging is to treat blogging as if it is the same as Facebook. It is not. In the first instance, Facebook wall comments are not the same as blog comments: wall comments are largely social and often fun in nature, whilst blog comments are topic-focused and need to be professional. Secondly, status updates are not the same as blog posts: status updates are usually posted quickly, with little thought, when you want to share something, whereas blog posts need to include some element of deliberation. Remember: Facebook is personal and social; blogging for university should be professional and academic.

Some blogs are not 'real' blogs

Some platforms, such as your VLE or a group-based social network such as Ning (see Chapter 5) provide 'blogs' as part of the functions included in their service. Although these functions allow you to write blog-style posts, they are not 'real' blogs in the sense that they do not operate as a stand-alone, personal site that you have administrative control over. Nevertheless, your lecturer may ask you to use the 'blog' function on VLEs and similar sites; if this is the case, then make sure that, as per the above, you know what is expected of you as regards the requirements of the task.

SUMMARY

- A blog is a website that allows you to make regular posts on a topic or range of topics and to get feedback from readers in the form of comments.
- Blogs display content in reverse chronological order, use tags and categories to organise content, and can be made either public or private.
- Typical blogging tasks set by lecturers include writing blog posts, making comments, being part of a blogging group, and creating a private blog.
- Blogs are used by lecturers because blogging elicits critique and reflection, can be used to track how students build understanding of a topic over time, and requires students to write concisely.
- Blog posts should be well-written, short, focused, and expressive of your scholarly opinion.
- Special considerations for blogging include choosing a suitable blog address, knowing what kinds of material are appropriate to post on your blog, and whether or not your blog should be made public or private.

FURTHER READING

Kirkup, G. (2010) 'Academic blogging, academic practice and academic identity', *London Review of Education*, 8 (1): 75–84.

Powell, D.A., Jacob, C.J. and Chapman, B.J. (2012) 'Using blogs and new media in academic practice: Potential roles in research, teaching, learning, and extension', *Innovative Higher Education*, 37 (4): 271–82.

Shema, H., Bar-Ilan, J. and Thelwall, M. (2012) 'Research blogs and the discussion of scholarly information', *PLoS ONE*, 7 (5). Available at: http://www.plosone.org/article/info%3Adoi%2F10.1371%2Fjournal.pone.0035869. Accessed 12 September 2013.

Top, E. (2012) 'Blogging as a social medium in undergraduate courses: Sense of community best predictor of perceived learning', *The Internet and Higher Education*, 15 (1): 24–8.

Weller, M. (2012) 'The virtues of blogging as scholarly activity', *Chronicle of Higher Education*. Available at: http://chronicle.com/article/The-Virtues-of-Blogging-as/131666/. Accessed 12 September 2012.

4

Wikis

OVERVIEW

A wiki is a website that anyone can edit, depending on how you set it up and depending on your privacy settings. This chapter describes different levels of user access for wikis and the core functions of editing, 'history', and discussions. We look at how lecturers use wikis to elicit collaboration, knowledge construction, and knowledge sharing from students and describe the various wiki models you might come across. The chapter also advises on how to deal with the common wiki problem of not wanting to edit others' work and provides advice on how you can develop and structure content, contribute effectively to a wiki, and improve navigability. We also shed light on how your lecturer or wiki owner (and other members) can track your wiki contributions, on how to deal with version control, and how to set up your own wiki. The chapter also quickly looks at the issue of Wikipedia and how lecturers view its use by students. Advice is also provided on how wikis are assessed.

WHAT IS A WIKI?

A wiki is a website that allows people with access to easily edit, add to, and delete webpages and/or their contents. Wikis are very similar in appearance to ordinary websites that have 'static' information on them; the difference is that you cannot edit regular websites but you *can* edit a wiki. Wikis are thus typically created by groups of people as they seek to build and share knowledge on a topic or topics (unlike blogs, which are normally – but not always – written by individuals). In this way, wikis are about the ongoing process of knowledge construction around a particular topic and contributors collaborate on a wiki to build a webspace that constantly changes, according to what the community knows at any given point. Therefore, a wiki is by its nature a 'work in progress' and the knowledge that it contains is always 'unfinished'.

Wikipedia is probably the best-known example of a wiki. Wikipedia is a website that anyone can contribute to by creating and editing articles on any topic. It is important to understand that Wikipedia is just an example of a wiki – not all wikis are Wikipedia, however.

Pages and editing

Wikis have pages (similar to webpages) that make up the core of a wiki; these pages are editable by those who have editing access to the wiki (you normally need an account with a wiki service and to be a member of a wiki before you can edit it). Some wikis are fully editable by anyone and some wikis, or even individual wikipages, are 'locked off' so that only certain people can access them. It will depend on how the wiki you are using has been set up.

To edit a wikipage, all you need to do is sign in and click on the 'Edit' button. This then turns the wikipage into something resembling a Word document, that is, a toolbar appears across the top of the page allowing you to format text, change headings, add bullet points and tables, and insert images, videos, widgets, and links (see Chapter 2). This is called 'WYSIWYG' editing, or, 'What You See Is What You Get' (most wiki services also allow you to edit the special wiki code or 'wikitext' if you want to be a bit more advanced about things).

Once you have added your content or made your changes, you then click 'Save' to secure your work. At this point, there is usually the option to add a comment to what you have just added to the wiki; this is important if your wiki is being edited by a lot of people and you need to explain to them why you made the changes you did.

Discussion forum

Each wikipage usually comes with a discussion forum attached to it, although sometimes the wiki is set up so that the forum is site-wide rather than page-specific. The purpose behind the discussion forum is technically to allow contributors to discuss the reasons behind any changes they've made to the page; however, many lecturers use the discussion forum more generally to facilitate conversation amongst students about key course themes (see below).

History revision and restore functions

One of the most important characteristics of a wiki is its 'history revision' function. This distinguishing feature allows wiki users to compare the different saved versions of a wikipage and to revert a saved wikipage to a previous version. The history function also allows wiki editors to track which users have made which changes, making it indispensable to lecturers who want to find out how much work you have done on a class wiki and what type and quality of work it has been. Related to this is the 'restore' function, which allows wiki users to return a page to any previously saved version. This is invaluable if you decide that an earlier version of the page was 'better', if you have become the victim of 'wiki vandals' or if an 'edit war' breaks out (see below).

Privacy settings and user access

Wikis can be public or private, editable by anyone, or editable only by members. Exactly how your class wiki works will depend on how your lecturer has set it up. If you're not sure about the settings on your particular course wiki, then ask.

WIKIS IN HIGHER EDUCATION

Wikis are used for both study and research purposes, but this section focuses primarily on wiki use in the classroom. That said, much of what is discussed here applies in the research context, so don't be tempted to skip over this section if you are a researcher – instead, take the information here and apply it to your own situation. If you are a student, however, then you need to know that there are some typical educational models that lecturers work within when they ask you to complete an assignment by using a wiki. Having a general 'feel' for how your lecturer (or research team, if you are a researcher) is using the wiki, and appreciating the rationale that lies behind such use, will help you understand what's required of the particular wiki task you have been set.

Wiki models

First, you should know that your lecturer is probably using one of three main models when it comes to setting a wiki assignment for their course. Familiarise yourself with each of these models so that you can start to identify what your lecturer wants from you in terms of your use of the wiki medium.

VIDEO CLIP   Wikis in Plain English

To get an overview of how blogs work, watch CommonCraft's 'Wikis in Plain English' video on YouTube (search 'Wikis in Plain English').

1. *Administration wiki.* Just as some lecturers prefer to use a blog in place of their institution-supplied VLE (see Chapter 3), so, too, will others prefer to use an externally hosted wiki service. Wikis are excellent for building resource repositories and FAQs, meaning that the lecturer can easily post course materials such as readings, assignment information, notes, rich media, links, references lists, etc. Lecturers also frequently use the wiki's discussion forum to post announcements, get feedback, and to start course-related topics, allowing them to combine the administrative features of a wiki with more learning-focused ones, as described below.

2. *Single class wiki (learning-focused).* This is, perhaps, the most common form of learning-focused wiki. On this model, everyone in the class contributes to building wikipages on a single wiki around course topics – sometimes in groups, sometimes individually (see below). The main point is that by the end of the course your class will have built, developed, and refined an information source (hopefully a fairly high-level one, given that it is being created by university students or researchers) that can be accessed by others and not just by those enrolled in your course. Arguably, this type of learning focus takes the best advantage of the wiki format in educational terms, that is, it uses the wiki as the basis for a socially constructivist approach to teaching and learning (see Chapter 1), where students co-construct knowledge on a topic in a group setting.

3. *Multiple class wikis (learning-focused).* On this model, students are split into groups, each with responsibility for building their own wiki. Each wiki is then linked to via a central portal, usually the main class wiki, in a kind of 'hub-and-spokes' framework. The educational purpose is the same as the single class wiki, above, that is, you are expected to build knowledge on a topic in a group setting.

4. *Individual student wiki (learning-focused).* A less common form of the learning-focused wiki is the one where individual students are asked to set up their own wiki as part of a learning portfolio, eportfolio, or similar. As regards a learning portfolio, students create pages and post information around key course themes, slowly building their portfolio until the submission deadline. An eportfolio is slightly different in that it might include components related to your 'learning' (that is, elements of what you did in class), but it may also include things such as a resumé or CV, examples of your work from other courses or elsewhere, contact information, etc. (see Chapter 7). In both cases, it could be asserted that a blog actually provides a more appropriate format for both kinds of portfolio (see Chapter 7 for a discussion on using wikis and blogs as eportfolios); so, if you already have your own blog, or would prefer to use a blog for such a task, you might want to approach your lecturer to see if they would allow you to use a blog as the basis of your portfolio.

Your lecturer's approach to how wikis are used in their course will be based on their intended learning outcomes for you, the student; that is, they will consider their educational objectives and match them up with how they employ the wiki for their course. So, if they want simply to 'push' information and materials at you, then they will use an administration-type wiki; if they want you to construct and demonstrate your own understandings of key course concepts in conjunction with classmates, then they will use a class wiki that is learning-focused. Note, however, that because wikis are flexible in how they can be structured as a whole, both the administration wiki and the class wiki models can be combined; this means that pages or areas can be set up that host fairly static information (for example, course outlines, readings, assessment information) whilst other pages – and, indeed, the discussion forum – can be dedicated to class participation and learning.

Typical wiki tasks set by lecturers

Learning-focused wikis (see above) are generally used when lecturers want you to undertake one or more of the following tasks – again, research teams often use wikis in a similar fashion:

- *Contributing to pages.* The main feature of a wiki is its pages. Wikipages are, as mentioned earlier, just like regular webpages except that people can easily edit them and add their own content (think of Wikipedia). How the pages are organised and structured will depend on how your lecturer has designed the wiki task. In some cases, your lecturer will expect the class to structure the wiki itself, that is, from scratch; this means that students decide as a whole how best to organise the wikipages. In other cases, however, your lecturer will already have created a 'shell' or a set of pages that provides a basic structure for your wiki. This structure is, of course, usually based around key course themes, and provides an example of the single class wiki described above. Your job is to take the basic shell and add to it – but how this happens will vary. Some lecturers will want everyone just to build the wiki in a fairly ad hoc manner, with people deciding when and where they want to contribute; other lecturers will put you into small groups and ask you to contribute to one section, theme, or area only. Small group tasks such as this may be undertaken either on a single class wiki or on multiple class wikis (see above). Sometimes, lecturers will set a word limit on pages. You need to know if this applies to your situation.
- *Contributing to and using the discussion forum.* Your class wiki's discussion forum can be used in one or both of two ways. First, if your lecturer is using a wiki purely for administration purposes then you will likely be expected to post any administrative queries (such as those relating to readings, assignments, lecture times, etc.) in the forum, as opposed to emailing your lecturer directly. Second, you may be asked to contribute to the forum as part of the assignment you have been set, which will mean that you are expected to participate in online discussions around course themes and content – that is, the intellectual content of what you are meant to be studying.

- *Being part of a wiki group.* Some lecturers use the wiki medium as a way of getting students to do group work; after all, wikis are perfect for this purpose. Your group will be expected to build a page or set of pages around key course themes and then have your contributions assessed – either as a group, individually (remember, your lecturer can track your individual activity on the wiki by using the history function), or both. If you're not sure about how group work is being assessed, ask your lecturer (and see below for more advice).
- *Editing others' work.* The whole point of a wiki is that its content gets built up over time as the wiki community adds to and refines its understanding of a topic. If your lecturer is using a learning-focused wiki model then it is *highly likely that you will be expected to edit other students' work.* Some students find this idea uncomfortable for a number of reasons, as outlined below, but, for now, know that there is a very high probability that your lecturer will require you to undertake wiki tasks that may require the alteration of others' contributions.

Wiki tasks can sometimes be quite complicated, mostly because they involve group work *and* the structuring of pages and content. As with any assessment activity, lecturers should give explicit directions about what you need to do to successfully complete any wiki task they set, but if you are unsure then ask.

WHY LECTURERS WANT YOU TO USE A WIKI

Lecturers don't want you to use a wiki just for the sake of it: they usually have some well-thought-out educational purpose behind what they want you to do and why they want you to do it. Having an understanding of what your lecturer wants you to achieve, educationally speaking, will help you target your efforts and maximise your learning. As per the above, much of what is stated here also applies to your research endeavours.

Educational and intellectual purposes

Wikis are about knowledge construction, presentation, and dissemination and this is why lecturers favour them when wanting you to demonstrate your comprehension of a topic. They are almost the perfect tool for lecturers working within socially constructivist pedagogies (see Chapter 1) because wikis encourage you to collaborate with others to create knowledge together. So, unlike blogs, which are principally about ongoing, individual, critical questioning and reflection (see Chapter 3), wikis are more likely to be judged on whether or not you've understood a topic and how well you've communicated that understanding. The bottom line, then, is that lecturers want you to explore a topic in depth and to present what you know in a clear, structured format.

With that said, lecturers are not just interested in the final product, because, although the wiki may look static at any stage, actually it is a dynamic store of information that is continually being reviewed, amended, and (hopefully) improved. Recall that each and every wikipage comes with a 'history' or 'revision' function that allows users to see who has done what and when on the wiki. By using this function, lecturers can spot how both individual students and student groups have built, developed, refined, and mediated their subject knowledge. In a practical sense, then, lecturers want to see that you have been able to source, analyse, synthesise, and evaluate appropriate materials for inclusion in the wiki. This all requires high-level cognitive engagement with key course themes on your part, which you can demonstrate not only on the wikipages you are contributing to yourself, but also via the site's discussion forum (see below).

Finally, lecturers use wikis for investigative group projects that often span whole semesters: if you are given a wiki assignment, it is likely to be part of an ongoing, integrated assessment regime in which each assessment item builds on the last. So, you may have a first assessment item that relates chiefly to the setting up and structuring of your wiki content, a second item that focuses on how well your wikigroup is working together to build understanding, and a third that evaluates the content and presentation of the material you've contributed to the wiki.

Practical purposes

Lecturers use wikis not only for the more erudite and instructional reasons outlined above, but also because they want to see how well you source, handle, organise, present, acknowledge, and disseminate content. This includes everything from checking your writing (especially for structure, coherence, focus, clarity, and readability) to evaluating the validity, trustworthiness, impact, and usefulness of the resources you've chosen to present. And, as with most assignments, lecturers are also measuring how well you can stay within set parameters such as word, page, and content limits. All of this comes in addition to gauging how well you have understood the subject matter.

But perhaps one of the most valuable reasons that lecturers use wikis is because they can easily track contributions to the wiki, student by student. This allows them to determine the type and quality of the content you have added as an individual as well as to see what kind of 'team player' you are. The discussion forum also provides a convenient way of measuring student interaction and dealings with each other, and many lecturers will make the effort to see how you are communicating with other students on the forum.

Finally, the co-operative elements of wikis should also not be overlooked. Many universities list 'graduate outcomes' that include ability to work collaboratively in teams and they may well use a wiki task to ensure that they are meeting their obligations to involve you in group work at some level. So, show your lecturer that you can play well with others in an online environment and you'll be well on your way to achieving success in your wiki endeavours.

 Activity   Create your own wiki

The purpose of this activity is to get you thinking about some of the issues you might encounter when using a wiki in class. The main idea is that, in setting up your own wiki, you will see things from the point of view of the site administrator (that is, your lecturer). If you can do this, then you will be able to work effectively, as well as being able to identify any potential problems that might occur with how the wiki is being used in your context. So,

1   Get an account with a wiki service (search, 'Free wikis') and create a wiki (follow the instructions).
2   Go to your wiki, click the 'Edit' button, and add some content to the homepage – maybe add some text, include a list of bullet points, add an image or video, create a table, etc. Just play around – you can always delete things later.
3   Add some new pages to your wiki and make sure that they are added to the navigation menu; this might happen automatically, or you might have to do this manually – just try things out and see how they work.
4   Get to know how pages work: explore the 'history' or 'restore' functions, figure out how to rename, lock, or delete pages.
5   Now, it's time to investigate your 'admin' sections. Check out the wiki's settings or management areas. In particular, see how the wiki handles memberships, privacy and permissions, notifications, and discussions. What levels of access are there? How much can the administrator(s) control? What problems can you see with the different kinds of settings that can be applied to your wiki?

Knowing how wikis work from an administrator's point of view puts you in a better position to appreciate how your lecturer is using the wiki in your class. But not only that, it gives you an understanding of what can and cannot be done with the wiki, and such an understanding is invaluable in helping you handle any problems you might encounter along the way.

SUCCESSFUL ENGAGEMENT WITH WIKIS

When you understand the basics of wikis – what they are, how lecturers or research teams use them to support class or research activities, and what they hope to achieve intellectually – you can begin to focus on some of the more nuanced aspects of contributing to a wiki. For students, note that, as with traditional assignments, such as reports and essays, subtlety is appreciated by lecturers, so being an astute wiki user should improve both your grades and your learning experience.

Contributing to a wiki

Make yourself 'visible' on the wiki. By this, I mean make sure that you frequently contribute high-quality material and that you are an active – but respectful – editor of wiki content. The key here is *quality*: you need to make substantive, relevant, meaningful additions to the wiki that demonstrate to your lecturer or research team leader your high-level intellectual engagement with key themes and with the work of your peers.

Use the discussion forum

Don't neglect the wiki's discussion forum: it can provide a very powerful means of communicating with your lecturer, research team, and/or classmates. Use the forum to ask questions, make comments and observations, explain reasons for changing content (you can also use the 'comment' function at the point when you save the page to do this), or to answer others' queries before your lecturer does; it is true to say that positive, helpful, and active forum contributors get noticed by lecturers! Naturally, make sure that your posts and responses are constructive, relevant, encouraging, and supportive and *never* post anything that could be seen as negative, aggressive, or sarcastic – that kind of thing only generates contempt amongst the community and can severely diminish your standing with your lecturer or study or research colleagues.

Changing other people's content

One of the keys to successful engagement with wikis is to change other people's content. This can seem 'wrong' at first, because you know that someone else has industriously developed and posted material that they think is worthy of distribution or because you don't want to 'offend' anyone by altering all their hard work. Regardless, you need to overcome such reactions and simply get on with it. Remember, your task on the wiki is to construct and disseminate knowledge in a community-based online environment: for students, your lecturer wants to see that you can do this in a mature, intelligent, and also considerate, fashion. In fact, your marks may depend on it.

Group work

Related to the above point, you need to prove to your lecturer (or team leader) that you are a good 'team player' – that you understand that wikis are about collaborative effort and that you are confident in, and capable of, working successfully in a group environment. Many students (and, indeed, academics), however, are unfavourably disposed towards group work, sometimes because of bad experiences (where, in the past, you have had to carry 'free-loaders') and sometimes because the purpose and/or assessment method is unclear to you (if this is the case, then see below). Further, group work does not come easily to some, not least because you have moved further and further away from such work ever since you finished primary school. However, bear in mind as a student that your lecturer has chosen to use a wiki as an assessment item for sound, educational reasons, that is, because they feel that a wiki is the best way for you to achieve the learning outcomes they have set for you. So, acknowledge the validity of the group work approach and show your lecturer that you can co-operate with others in the building of a truly excellent online resource.

Writing conventions

In general, you should aim to present your page content in Standard English. This means that you use grammar, vocabulary, punctuation, and spelling that are accepted and that can be understood by most Anglophone speakers of English. You should also abide by conventions for the structuring of text, namely, your paragraphs should be unified and coherent, your points should develop logically, and you must include citations and references for all work that is not your own. Headings are quite acceptable, as is the odd bulleted-list (where necessary – be careful not to overdo bullet points). Idioms and informal constructions should be avoided, as should jargon, overly formal scholarly writing, and the word 'I' (which is acceptable in blog writing, but not on wikis, see previous chapter). Of course, it's quite OK to relax your writing style when you are posting in the wiki forum – once again, be aware of the appropriate use of language as it applies across genres (see Chapter 2). In sum, wikis are about the communication and dissemination of knowledge (not only its construction) and thus the style and tone of language should aid these activities.

Presentation

It is crucial that you clearly structure and present your wiki content if you are to achieve good grades for your wiki assignment or if you are to communicate your research effectively. There are two main things to address here: navigability and appearance. In terms of navigability, your pages must be logically ordered and they must relate to each other sequentially. Think about your wiki readers: how will they make their way around your site? Do you need to structure things alphabetically, or should pages be arranged in such a way that they reflect the development of key course themes? It's always a good idea to ask someone outside of your wiki group or circle to see how easily they find it to navigate your wiki and to give you feedback. As regards appearance, the general rules of any good web authoring apply: keep the page clean, uncluttered, and consistent in all things, including font sizes, heading levels, image sizes, colours, object positioning, and so forth. Your readers (one of whom, at least, is your lecturer!) should not feel frustrated by unattractive, disorderly, and disordered pages; instead, they must be free to evaluate your content without distraction.

How wikis are assessed: What lecturers are looking for

Because wikis are about knowledge construction, lecturers most frequently use them to assess your understanding of a topic at the completion of a course. However, it is rare that 100 per cent of your grade will be allocated to the final wiki product. Rather, a wiki assignment is more likely to be broken up according to 'milestones' (Milestone 1 might measure your progress to date; Milestone 2, the final product) and, in many cases, grades will also be given for both individual and group work.

Bearing this in mind, then, you could be assessed on all or any of the following as regards wikis: the content or subject matter itself (measured via the final product), the development of your understanding of the subject matter over time, your individual contribution, your contribution to the group, structure and organisation, navigability, presentation and writing, development of thinking (which can be determined using the 'history' or 'restore/compare' functions), etc. The bottom line is that you need be very clear – very clear indeed – about how your contribution to the wiki is being assessed. This means you need to know about any weightings that are being attributed to any assessment criteria your lecturer has developed, you need to know about word limits (if there are any), and you especially need to know how any group work is being assessed. If you aren't clear about any of these things, then consult your lecturer.

See Table 4.1 for an example of an 'assessment rubric' based on how you might be marked for a wiki assignment. Lecturers may use such a tool to help them determine the quality of your work as it applies to various 'success criteria'.

TABLE 4.1   Example of wiki assessment rubric used by lecturers to guide their evaluation of your work

Criterion	Beginning	Emergent	Proficient	Advanced
Quality of group work	Little evidence that group members have worked together. The work has been divided up amongst group members. No discussions about wiki contents. No encouragement of other members.	Only one or two wiki members have notably contributed to the wiki's development. Wiki contributors have tended to focus on only one type of task (for example, proofreading, adding images, or finding links). Few discussions about wiki contents. Little encouragement of other members.	All members have contributed to the wiki's development. Wiki contributors have engaged in a variety of tasks. There are discussions relating to the development of the wiki's contents. Members encourage each other.	All members have made significant, broad and deep contributions to the wiki's development. Contributors have engaged in a variety of tasks. Discussions relating to the development of the wiki's contents are focused and insightful. Members encourage each other and offer help and suggestions to others.
Content	Content on the wiki is irrelevant or inadequate. It does not focus on key themes and is trivial or superficial.	Content is broadly relevant to the topic and the key themes but does not consistently meet the learning curriculum for the task.	Content is relevant and focused. The wiki demonstrates a clear appreciation of the topic and the key themes. Meets curriculum objectives.	Content is relevant, focused, and demonstrates a perceptive understanding of the topic and key themes. Exceeds curriculum objectives for the task.
Structure and organisation	The wiki has no discernible structure. The wiki is disorganised with extraneous content appearing on pages. No sense of how the pages connect or how topics or themes are linked. No logic to the wiki.	The wiki has a loose but often confusing structure. Some content is organised on the correct pages, but other content is peripheral to the page's focus. Pages and topics are vaguely connected. Little logic to the wiki.	Clear structure to the wiki in which content is well organised and presented. Connections between themes and topic are coherently made.	Wiki content is clearly and logically organised. Structure is logical and coherent. Key themes are kept discrete but connections between them are made explicit.

SPECIAL CONSIDERATIONS FOR WIKIS

Wikis bring with them their own, distinctive issues, most of which relate to group work and collaboration and the fact that neither is often done particularly well in many higher education contexts.

Correcting errors

Because wikis are about the community of users, anyone can fix errors at any stage. Of course, anyone can also *produce* errors at any stage, so that is why building a wiki needs to be a collaborative exercise – so that false or inaccurate information can be rectified quickly. Do not feel embarrassed about correcting others' errors (but, at the same time, do not take an unhealthy delight in doing so!).

Disagreements over wiki content ('edit wars')

'Edit wars', in which contributors simply edit each other's content back and forth, are not helpful to the creation of a successful wiki. If disagreements about content occur, then editing of a wikispace should cease and a discussion about the problem should take place in the wikispace's discussion forum. Using the forum will allow collaborators to make arguments for and against the edits they've made, and (hopefully) to reach a consensus about what goes into the wiki.

'Farming out' the work

Wiki users – and especially students – are sometimes overly reluctant to edit or correct others' work, which can lead to the 'farming out' of different segments of the wiki work. For example, a small group of three that is working on a page or set of pages might decide to apportion the work so that one person is responsible for finding information, another for structuring it and 'knocking it into shape', and the third for editing it and making it look nice. Farming out the work in this way is a mistake. In the first and perhaps most important instance, you are compromising your learning: your lecturer has set this kind of task based on sound educational reasoning, that is, so that you build your knowledge of a topic in a socially constructivist learning environment (see Chapter 1). Secondly, you are likely to end up with a disordered, poorly structured, incoherent mess of unlinked ideas and content and this will be reflected in your final grade. Just as importantly, though, you are also missing the chance of working collaboratively with others and all the opportunities that that brings in terms of practising compromise, showing leadership, displaying humility, and learning from others. Finally, you may be damaging your grades because the chances are that you are being marked on your 'ability to work in a group' or similar; recall that your lecturer can tell who has done what on a wiki, so they know if you've been adding substantive content or if you've just been correcting punctuation errors.

Tracking your wiki contributions

Your individual wiki contributions can be tracked by pulling up a page's revision history. The revision history will tell others (for example, your lecturer) who has made what changes to the wiki, so they can see whether you have made significant, content-based contributions to the site, or whether you have simply corrected others' grammar and punctuation. In the context of assessment, the former (that is making substantive additions based on key course themes) will earn you higher grades than the latter. Don't make lots of little, ineffective edits (such as edits that simply change commas or formatting) as a means of pushing your username to the top of the revisions list – lecturers or wiki admins who use social media in the classroom are usually fairly tech-savvy and are on to this kind of tactic.

Developing and structuring content

Clear, logical structure is key to a good wiki: if your readers can't find their way around, they will quickly become frustrated and will leave your site. It is a smart idea to sit down and map out the organisation and design of your wikipages before you even begin to add and build on your content. You and your groupmates (if you are working in groups) may wish to get early feedback from your lecturer about your intended structure.

Dealing with 'freeloaders'

One of the things students complain most about in any group work situation is 'freeloaders', that is, those people who take advantage of the work of other students and who don't contribute to the group's activity but who still end up with a good grade. In many ways, spotting freeloaders is easier in a wiki environment, because your lecturer, as we know, can track individuals' contributions through the wiki's history function. This means that your lecturer can quite easily assign an individual grade for each student as well as a group grade for the wiki task. This is all well and good, but there remains the issue of the freeloader getting a good mark for group work that they haven't actually contributed to. This is a tough one in anyone's book and there are no easy solutions.

Perhaps the best thing you can do is to look over the task carefully before it gets underway, and do this in the first week of lectures. Many universities, as a matter of policy, allow students to raise issues about assessment in the first week of a course, meaning that you can make suggestions, at this time, about possible changes as to how coursework is evaluated. If no individual grades are being given out, then you might want to gently suggest that, because lecturers can track individual contributions to the wiki, then both individual *and* group grades should be given. If both group and individual grades *are* being given, then check the weighting of those grades; you might find an 80 per cent group and 20 per cent individual grade partitioning unfair or unreasonable and you could respectfully suggest that an adjustment be made.

Finally, if you cannot address the issue directly with the student(s) concerned, then you might simply have to trust that your lecturer is checking to see who is doing 'real' work on the wiki, and who is freeloading. Often lecturers just hope that students will work together nicely with everyone making equal contributions so that grades can given out fairly. In reality, however, many students know that this sometimes does not occur.

Reluctance to change others' content

It is essential to understand that a wiki is not really about you and your work as an individual: rather, it is a collaborative space where contributors put aside an individual viewpoint to create a resource that best reflects the state of knowledge within the wiki community. Changes to others' content shouldn't, then, be based on personality factors, but instead on what is best for the wiki. If you are going to make major changes to someone else's content, then it is good etiquette either to explain the change in a comment at the point when you save the page or to start up a thread in the discussion forum about why you've made major alterations.

Concurrent editing and conflicting edits

Very occasionally, two or more people will be editing a wikipage at the same time from different access points (computer, tablet devices, mobiles, and such like). This is known as 'concurrent editing'. When it comes to time to save, conflicts can occur between the different versions of the page that have been edited. Don't be too concerned about this, however. In the first instance, if no conflicts have occurred then the wiki system you are using will simply merge the edits. If there are conflicting edits, though, the system normally displays an onscreen message letting you know that concurrent editing is occurring and will give you a number of options for dealing with the issue – for example, you can elect to overwrite others' edits or to remove the conflict before saving. Concurrent editing is simply a side-effect of good wiki use.

Successful wikis

Truly successful wikis are built on more than just technical and academic foundations – there is a decisive human element, too, as discovered by Jonathan Davies in the excellent work he conducted for his Masters thesis some years ago:

- *Wikis must have a common goal* (Davies, 2004: 64). If your wiki group is uncertain about the purpose of the wiki, then unfocused and/or low-level contributions are the result.
- *Trust is everything* (Davies, 2004). This is about effective teamwork and team members feeling that everyone is contributing equally, behaving appropriately, and that any differences of opinion can be sorted out in a supportive atmosphere.
- *Wikiing must be valuable on a personal level* (Davies, 2004: 66). Despite the sizeable element of group work that occurs on wikis, wikis still need to provide individual contributors with a sense of satisfaction that comes from the combined effort.
- *Encouragement is essential.* Again, this is based on human values, not on technical ones. Contributors should motivate and inspire each other to produce an all-round excellent wiki.

Should you use Wikipedia?

This issue is not actually directly related to the topic of the current chapter, but I include it here because students always ask about it and researchers always use it, but tend to not admit it! It is probably fair to say that the consensus is that consulting Wikipedia is well and good for gaining a basic, background understanding of a topic, but that it should not be used to back up your arguments and should not be presented as an authoritative source. So, don't cite Wikipedia articles in your work (bearing in mind that lecturers and peer-reviewers are alert to the fact that some writers simply cite the references that the Wikipedia article itself cites!) and treat it as a peer-reviewed source. See Chapters 8 and 10 for further discussion on what constitutes authority in academe and how it relates to using social media for study and research.

SUMMARY

- A wiki is a website that anyone can edit, depending on how it is set up.
- Wiki contributors work together on pages that are continually updated as the wiki grows and that can be made either public or private.
- Wikis are characterised by pages, discussion forums, and history, revision, and restore functions.
- Typical wiki tasks set by lecturers include contributing to pages, contributing to the discussion forum, being part of a wiki group, and editing others' work.
- Wikis are used by lecturers because wikis support knowledge construction, presentation, and dissemination, and can be used to track your comprehension of a topic and how well you can work in a group.
- In contributing to a wiki, you should use the discussion forum, change other people's content, undertake group work, and write in Standard English.
- Special considerations for wikis include correcting others' errors on the wiki, edit wars, 'farming out' the work, developing and structuring content, concurrent editing, and dealing with 'freeloaders'.

FURTHER READING

Arazy, O., Yeo, L. and Nov, O. (2013) 'Stay on the Wikipedia task: When task-related disagreements slip into personal and procedural conflicts', *Journal of the American Society for Information Science and Technology*, 64 (8): 1634–48.

Arnold, N., Ducate, L. and Kost, C. (2012) 'Collaboration or cooperation? Analyzing group dynamics and revision processes in wikis', *CALICO Journal*, 29 (3): 431–48.

de Laat, P.B. (2012) 'Coercion or empowerment? Moderation of content in Wikipedia as "essentially contested" bureaucratic rules', *Ethics and Information Technology*, 14 (2): 123–35.

Kummer, C. (2013) *Factors Influencing Wiki Collaboration in Higher Education*, 29 January, Social Science Research Network. Available at: http://ssrn.com/abstract=2208522. Accessed 12 September 2013.

5

Social Networks

OVERVIEW

Although many of us are already familiar with personal social networks such as Facebook, fewer are familiar with group-based social networks – and especially with group-based social networks that are used in universities. The chapter begins by outlining the characteristics of such group-based social networks, including discussion forums, sub-groups, profiles, events, and announcements. Next, we examine two main social network models used in higher education and the many different kinds of tasks (and how they are assessed) that can be set by lecturers who use social networks as part of their teaching practice. An important point for both students and researchers is that *process*, rather than *product*, is one of the chief attributes of social networking, meaning that such sites can often be dynamic, messy places that encourage certain kinds of communication, knowledge sharing, media sharing, and feedback from the network's community. We also look at how to effectively contribute to a social network before discussing some of the issues around privacy, bullying, data collection, and security.

WHAT ARE SOCIAL NETWORKS?

Most forms of social media are 'social networks' at some level because they allow people to communicate freely over the network of the internet. In general usage, however, social networking describes the sites and services that provide people with platforms that enable them to connect and to build relations, and to share events, photos, videos, links, activities, news, and such like.

VIDEO CLIP   Social Networking in Plain English

To get an overview of how social networks work, watch CommonCraft's 'Social Networking in Plain English' video on YouTube (search 'Social Networking in Plain English').

Of course, the most famous (and largest) social network is Facebook. But Facebook is only 'a' social network: it is not 'the' social network. In fact, there are two main types of social networking service on the internet: the personal social network and the group-based social network. Personal social networks are usually provided free of charge and revolve around the individual; they include services such as Facebook, MySpace, Foursquare, Bebo, Orkut, and Hi5. Group-based social networks, on the other hand, typically hinge on topics of interest to a number of people. Group-based social networks include services such as Ning, Elgg, Groupsite, and SocialGO, and usually involve the payment of some kind of fee on the part of the person setting up the network on behalf of the group. Although sites such as Facebook do, indeed, support 'groups,' they are generally not appropriate in academic environments (see below under 'Special considerations' for more information on Facebook groups). It is thus the latter kind of social network that you most typically find used in higher education, not least because most students and researchers want and need to connect at a professional level rather than a personal one.

Search for comparison tables

Do a Google search for 'Social network comparison table' to find charts that survey the various functions and tools offered by different social networking services.

Just as the two kinds of social network have different purposes, they also have slightly different features (although many, of course, overlap). Personal social networks will more strongly feature activity streams such as 'news feeds' and things such as wall comments and status updates are important because they convey information about the individual. Group social networks, however, favour features that help the group as a whole to operate. As such, discussion forums, sub-groups, events, announcements, and profiles all become important. Because group-based social networks are the kind you are most likely to encounter in the university environment, we'll look at some of these components in turn.

Discussion forums

This is perhaps the most important element in a group-based social network. As a student, your lecturer will use the discussion forum to start topics relating to course subject matter as well as posting course updates or information, perhaps, on how to complete assignments. You can (indeed, 'should' if a discussion forum is provided for you anywhere – not just on a social network; see Chapter 2) also put your own questions for your lecturer into the forum. If you have a question about an assessment item, due date, list of readings, broken link, or similar, the chances are that someone else has the same question, so do everyone a favour and post your question in the forum. Researchers can use discussion forums to raise and refine research questions, to troubleshoot problems with research design or method, to get feedback on early ideas for a project or an article, to share insights with colleagues, or to network with colleagues at different institutions. Of course, not all academics feel comfortable with this type or amount of sharing, but it has to be said that the potential for seeking and providing advice amongst colleagues is tremendous in a group-based discussion forum that pivots around your particular research area.

Sub-groups

Group-based social networking services normally provide a way for group members to form into sub-groups, which can be either made visible to or kept private from each other. If your lecturer is using a social network as part of your assessment, the chances are that you will either have to assign yourself, or already be assigned to, a sub-group for the purposes of your study. The sub-groups may be based on key course themes or even be set up according to surname (to get you into manageable groups to discuss all course themes) – it will depend on what your lecturer thinks is best (of course, if you can see a better way of doing things, you can always make a gentle suggestion, but read the advice on communicating with your lecturer in Chapter 2 before proceeding). Sub-groups can also be particularly effective for larger research groups, and particularly for those that come together as part of a cross-institutional grant or project. In these instances, various sub-groups can be set up according to the different roles played by those collaborating on the project.

Announcements

Any well-functioning, group-based social network will have an active announcements board. In the study environment, this feature is essential to providing quick updates on assignments, lectures, and changes to various parts of the course. Your lecturer may not post this information elsewhere, so be sure to check the announcements regularly. For research groups, announcements will often include information relating to how to access certain parts of the network, about the progress (or otherwise) being made on various aspects of the project, about career opportunities, or about the actual running of the group. Make sure you subscribe to or receive email notifications of any announcements made to the group by adjusting your profile or account settings accordingly (but see Chapter 12 for more discussion).

Events

Group-based social networks thrive best when the members share and participate in community events, whether they be face-to-face or online. As such, conferences, meetings, get-togethers, professional development opportunities, seminars, lectures, etc., can all be posted to the group using the events calendar. You can also usually let people know whether or not you are attending an event, which can be most helpful for event organisers.

Profiles

As a student you may or may not want to add information to your profile on a coursework-based social networking group. You may feel uncomfortable about giving away personal information on a study site or you may decide that you couldn't be bothered building a profile on a site that's dedicated to only one semester's work. However, if you *do* want to add information, then, of course, make sure it is professional and not frivolous and do not give away any compromising personal information (see Chapter 12). In any case, you will need a basic profile and that should involve choosing a username that at least identifies you to the rest of the group (more information on this can be found in the section on 'Tips for creating an account' in Chapter 2).

For researchers, however, the situation is slightly different. If the social networking site you are joining is relatively large, active, and (or at least has the potential to be) well-known, then take some time to carefully construct your profile. This will be an investment of time that could pay good dividends very soon: the more you participate, the more you become known on the network; the more you become known, the more likely people are to check your profile, learn about your research interests and background and to get in touch with career opportunities. For further information about building your profile online, see Chapter 7.

Despite the fact that you may use a social networking service daily to keep in touch with friends and family, using a social network for either study or research purposes can be quite a different proposition. The following sections will help you focus the 'professional' aspects of social networking, allowing you to appropriately participate in social networking for academic purposes.

SOCIAL NETWORKS IN HIGHER EDUCATION

This section describes the various ways in which social networks are used by lecturers, but many of the general points (as opposed to the detail) also apply to researchers and research teams. As always, there is no one, single model that suits all lecturers or research teams – be sure to know how any social network is being employed in your situation.

Social network models

Although some lecturers will use social networking as part of their assessment regime, many others, in fact, do not. In these instances, the social network is used primarily as originally intended, that is, as a communication and networking platform. Thus, there are two main models when it comes to the ways in which social networking might be used in your course:

1. *Communication, networking, administration.* Using a social network in place of a university-supplied VLE (see Chapter 1) can be a good option for net-savvy lecturers: externally hosted social networks are often more intuitive to set up, build, and maintain than are sites on the VLE, and they tend to mimic certain online environments that students are familiar with (that is, Facebook). In particular, these networks typically give both lecturers *and* students more control over how their community works and develops as there are usually quite fine-grained and multiple communication, networking, and profile options available to members. Lecturers working from this model will use the social network to encourage *everyone* to post and share course-related information, links, videos, events, comments, blog entries, discussions. As a result, these kinds of environments can be hugely dynamic and stimulating when working well.

2. *Assessment.* Social networks are perfect for any number of educational activities including brainstorming, collaboration, knowledge and object sharing, opinion building, providing and receiving feedback, and the presentation and dissemination of information. Sometimes lecturers will attach grades to how – and how well – you use the class social network to take part in these activities. For example, you may have to work in sub-group or groups, develop your profile space, start and run discussions, or even take part in role plays. Some students find such activities difficult because they haven't encountered them in an educational setting before and can't see the point in them. This is where it's important to recall that academics are using social media in their teaching because such platforms allow students to be more active in their own learning, which, as we know, supports effective, socially constructivist approaches to education (see Chapter 1).

Sometimes your lecturer will combine both models so that the entire online learning environment for your course is an administration, communication, and learning space all at once. This means that these sites are often dynamic, messy places that reflect real-world learning as a *process* and not just as a *product*. Pedagogically speaking, this is much better for your learning than the didactic, transmission-style practices that you may be more accustomed to. It's important to keep this in mind if you are feeling a little anxious about the whole exercise (see the section on 'Attitude' in Chapter 2 if you think it will help).

Typical social network tasks set by lecturers

Regardless of whether or not you are given marks for the work you do on a course-based social network, your lecturer may expect you to undertake various tasks in various ways on the site:

- *Participating.* Lecturers don't set up course-based social networks without expecting students to participate in the course community, that is, they want you to share, collaborate, network, and give feedback to each other. You may be given marks for your level of participation; if so, be sure to know how, exactly, you are being measured (see below for a sample assessment rubric that addresses this issue).
- *Sharing useful links, videos, and similar objects.* Lecturers may specify the number of things they want you to share and they may also be looking to see how well, in a functional sense, you do that. For example, they may require that you share at least two videos and two links and that the videos need to be properly embedded in the site and the links need to follow proper hyperlink etiquette (see Chapter 2 for both).
- *Starting and contributing to discussions.* Unlike some discussion forums which are controlled solely by the lecturer, forums on social networks are almost always community-driven. This means that you may be expected to not only respond to discussions started by your lecturer but also to start threads of your own.
- *Being part of a sub-group.* You may be placed into a study sub-group or be expected to start your own and the group may be public or private – it will depend on how your lecturer has set things up and to what purpose. Further, you may be assessed according to how well you participate in the group, either or both in terms of engaging with the course's intellectual content or in terms of engaging with other students in the group.
- *Writing 'blog' posts.* The first thing that needs to be cleared up about 'blogs' on social networks is that they are not really 'blogs' in the truest sense of the term: your blog on a social network doesn't have its own web address and there is no dashboard (see Chapter 3). Having said that, your lecturer may not want you to create a full-blown personal blog that classmates can only access by leaving the course's social network. Rather, they may prefer instead that you write blog-type posts that show up in the network's activity stream and so the blog on a social network – as a simple space where you can put together a paragraph or two on a topic, tag it up, and then post it for comment – fits the bill perfectly.

- *Role playing.* I have known lecturers to use social networking services such as Ning for role-playing assignments. The lecturer first sets up a scenario that supports various viewpoints on an issue and students are put into sub-groups corresponding to those viewpoints. The sub-groups are then made private, allowing the members of each group to discuss their group's position on the issue 'behind the scenes' without the groups knowing exactly how each will argue their case. After a number of weeks, the lecturer then invites all sub-groups to engage with the scenario using the site's discussion forum or similar. Students may be marked individually, in groups, or both, according to how well they've engaged with the scenario.

The variety – and sometimes the complexity – of tasks that can be undertaken using social networks means that you need to be very clear about what is expected of you if you are asked to use this kind of media in your course. Remember, and as a main theme of this book, if you are in any way uncertain about why or how you should complete certain tasks, then ask.

WHY LECTURERS WANT YOU TO USE A SOCIAL NETWORK

The educational and practical purposes behind your lecturer's use of social networks in your course often intersect as social networks provide functional platforms that inherently support the collaborative side of good teaching and learning. Nevertheless, we *can* make some general observations – observations that you can also apply to your particular research context.

Educational and intellectual purposes

We saw in Chapter 1 that, if nothing else, education can be said to be a collaborative, participatory process in which knowledge and meaning are created through social interaction. As such, social networks, with all their potential for collaboration, sharing, interaction, participation, and networking, are almost the perfect tools for social learning – perfect, that is, if used well.

As alluded to earlier, *process* is perhaps more important in the social networking environment than is *product*. Wikis and blogs both easily support 'products' (that is, things such as wikipages, blog posts, and blog comments) but the exchanges on social networks tend to be more ephemeral in nature. Thus, your contribution to a course-based social network is likely to be measured in an ongoing fashion (maybe week-by-week as it would be in a tutorial group or a lab demonstration) as opposed to being measured according to one or two milestones that you meet along the way. In some instances, you may not even be awarded marks for your contribution; this especially applies if your lecturer is using the social network chiefly as a way to get you to share videos, links, and items of interest as the course unfolds. What is important, here, is to understand that, firstly, your lecturer is using the network to support a valid, constructivist pedagogy in which students create knowledge and meaning via social interaction (see Chapter 1), and, secondly, that not everything needs to be given marks to be of educational merit. This latter point can be easy to lose sight of when assessment (which is not the same as education) is accorded such a high value in mass education systems.

> Assessment is not the same as education. If your lecturer asks you to do something without being given marks for it, it may be because it is good for your learning.

That said, of course, you may well be given marks for your participation in your class's social network, particularly if you are assigned one of the more specific tasks (such as group work, role plays, or writing blog posts) described above. In such cases, you are also more likely to be given marks for the intellectual rigour of your contributions. You may feel on more familiar ground, here, as you might sense you have a 'clearer mission' to undertake, and one that links in better with your expectations of what constitutes legitimate educational activity at the university level.

Don't get too hung up on marks and grades, though. At the end of the day, regardless of whether or not you are given marks for your 'work' on a social network, you should embrace the opportunity to engage in the high-level, constructivist learning that social networks afford.

Practical purposes

As stated earlier in the chapter, lecturers sometimes use social networks – just as they might use blogs and wikis – as a replacement VLE; this is not just because it's more convenient for them, but also because students themselves may already be familiar with this kind of communications environment (that is, Facebook). This won't apply to all students, but certainly to a growing majority. Social networks are convenient, too, for both lecturers and students when it comes to providing feedback or interacting with each other via comments, wall posts, discussions, 'Like' buttons, etc. This can be an important consideration for lecturers who want to avoid the often-didactic or 'transmission-based' practices that undergird more traditional forms of university teaching (see Chapter 1).

Lecturers who use social networks also want to see you engage with a variety of media – videos, audios, 'mash-ups', slideshows, links, animations, not just with written text – and social networks provide both you and your lecturer with an easy method of sharing relevant, course-related material. In getting you to share such material, they can evaluate how well you are understanding the course (and, for the better, more diligent teachers, how well they are teaching it) at the same time as helping you build your digital literacy skills (see Chapter 10).

Lastly, your lecturer may be using a social network for building community, an activity which, in itself, supports the interactive, collaborative, participatory educational purposes outlined above. Community-based learning environments are not only pedagogically sound (although there are, of course, some students who simply prefer individual learning in any situation), but they can provide shy students who perhaps don't like to speak up in face-to-face groups with a safe space for contributing to the class as a whole. Lecturers want you to engage with others, play nicely together, and help each other – and social networks provide an ideal way of making that happen.

SUCCESSFUL ENGAGEMENT WITH SOCIAL NETWORKING

Social networks – perhaps more than most social media environments – can seem chaotic and disorganised, and not particularly well-suited to what some students regard as the necessarily 'structured' nature of university education. Although students (indeed, all of us) do need structure, the apparent lack of it in social networks does not automatically mean that social networking supplies a poor form of education or communication. In fact, social networks can arguably provide one of the most effective forms of education and/or communication because they are excellent for social learning and sharing, as stressed earlier in this chapter.

Don't confuse structure with thinking

Our university system teaches us that thinking can be found in the final products we present for assessment. But thinking itself is not a product and it is not often entirely structured – instead, it is mostly a jumbled, disordered, iterative process. Many lecturers use social media because social media can help expose your thinking about a topic *as that thinking occurs*. How we *present* our thinking and learning as a final product, however, should indeed be structured if others are to make sense of what it is that we are trying to convey as regards that thinking.

Accept chaos

The dialogical nature of the interactions on social networks is what makes this form of learning valuable in and of itself. That is to say, you can put forward an idea, thought, opinion, or impression and see what direction others take it in. This is quite different from 'individualistic' educational models where the main learning relationship is between you and your lecturer and where your ideas are normally fully formed (or as fully formed as they can be before the due date) before you present them for assessment. In social networking environments, your 'assessors' are often your classmates, in the sense that they are the ones to provide feedback, extend ideas, suggest further avenues for exploration – and all of this can happen in quite 'unstructured' ways. The trick is to not get too overwhelmed by the messiness of social networking as a learning mechanism and to not expect that your thinking needs to be fully formed on a topic before you post something on the network.

Be a good community member

This may sound rather nebulous and mysterious, but one of the things your lecturer will be looking for is how you participate in your course's social network. This primarily means how well you 'play' with others in encouraging them to contribute, in responding to their posts, and in how you demonstrate respect for their opinions. Lecturers are particularly impressed by 'class leaders', that is, those students who take the initiative to engage not only with course themes and topics but also with other students and who can negotiate positions effectively in terms of both course subject matter and different class 'personalities'.

Writing conventions

It may seem a banality to say that the benchmarks set for Standard English frequently do not apply in social networking environments; this can be irritating to some and emancipating to others. This is just another area in which social media are both challenging what we know about acceptable writing standards (see Chapter 2) and asking us to develop new genres of writing.

Things can be especially tricky for users of social networks in this area. If you are used to Facebook and similar sites – which are primarily about *personal* communication – you will be accustomed to quite relaxed and informal writing practices. The standard for communication on *group-based* social networks, however, is ever-so-slightly higher: while there will always be some leeway for lapses on social networks, you still need to adhere to *generally* correct spelling, grammar, and punctuation. This has more to do with making sure that your ideas are expressed in such a way that others can understand them and less to do with judgements being made about whether or not you have used the semi-colon correctly. In the absence of anything better, conventions of spelling, grammar, and punctuation have evolved to help us accurately communicate meaning to one another – don't neglect them entirely, especially if doing so will obscure your message.

Tone

Communication on social networks such as Facebook often works at the 'speed of thought': as soon as you think of something, you share it. This can be great in the university learning environment if you come across something that you think will be of interest or value to your classmates – you can quickly add it, get comments and feedback from others, and perhaps spark a new direction of thought on a topic. It's not so great, however, if you post a comment in a moment of pique or exasperation (see Chapter 11). Remember: this is not a *personal* social network but a group-based one, and the group has formed not because of any private or intimate connections between people but through the rather arbitrary fact that you all happen to be taking the same university course at the same time. This means that you should treat it like a work environment, not a personal space.

Contributing to discussions

If you are going to be given marks for anything on a social network, there is a high probability that it will be for your contribution to discussions. That notwithstanding, you can demonstrate good faith in the community by being active on the forum, taking the initiative to start discussions, and being sure to respond in a timely and supportive manner to others' posts and replies. Your social network will be something that you are expected to – or should – contribute to on a regular basis so you should visit it often and add items and comments that are useful to other students or users.

How social networks are assessed: What lecturers are looking for

We saw earlier that there can be a wide variety and high complexity of educational tasks undertaken in social networking environments, which would make it almost impossible for us to say exactly *what* lecturers might be looking for when they formally assess (for marks) your contribution to a social network – if they assess it at all! But we do know that social networking in higher education favours process over product and that, as a result, communication, knowledge sharing, media sharing, participation, and feedback are important in such online spaces.

As such, your lecturer will *generally* be looking to see what kinds of exchanges you are involved in, for example, information and object sharing, collaboration, networking, dissemination of opinion, providing feedback to classmates, starting discussions. They will also be looking to see how well you can synthesise large amounts of information and how you build your viewpoint over time – again, process is the focus, here. Your lecturer will also be assessing the intellectual content of your contributions, in which case the usual criteria of understanding the issues, showing analytical engagement with current research, and synthesising arguments or opinions will all apply. Finally, your lecturer is wanting to know how effectively you can build ties and engender positive relationships with other students.

RESEARCH FOCUS

As already stated, a good deal of what has been discussed above will also apply in the research context; however, there are some research-specific factors to take into account when using social networks to enhance your research activities.

Setting up your own research-based social network

More and more academics are seeing the value of using social media – and in particular, social networks – to connect with other researchers for the purposes of sharing ideas or raising the profile of a research area, or for managing entire projects with a project team. These kinds of social networks are, of course, typically group-based (as opposed to personal), meaning that they usually develop on services that best support group activities through features such as discussion forums; document sharing, storage, and access; calendaring and event publication; announcements; and the formation of sub-groups. In other words, if you are seeking to set up your own research-based social network, then a service *other* than Facebook will probably be more suited to your needs.

Terms of Service

As a researcher, you must understand the Terms of Service you sign up for when you create a group-based social network. For more information, see Chapter 12, but, for now, know in particular that you need to consider how a social networking service handles your copyright (Do you retain it? Do you even own copyright in materials you create?) and how it distributes your intellectual property (Are you granting the service a sub-licensable licence to your intellectual property? If so, there could be problems). These issues are covered in detail in Chapter 12. The main point is, as a researcher, you should never enter into a Terms of Service without fully understanding the implications of those Terms for the materials and ideas you produce.

Raising the profile of your network

Social networks can be invaluable for raising the profile either of a particular research area or of a particular research project, so consider carefully whether you want your network to be private or not. If your network is devoted to a particular field of research, then it should probably be publicly accessible. You should thus be sure to invite people to join your network, as invitations can alert people to both the existence and purpose of your network. If, however, your network is based around a specific project, and you intend to host certain kinds of data or similar on the network, then you should consider making it private and only accessible to members who you can approve. In both cases, you should also attend to various levels of membership: make sure that you have one or two other people who can accept responsibility for administration of the site, and that you both 'promote' and 'demote' people according to need.

SPECIAL CONSIDERATIONS FOR SOCIAL NETWORKING

Using social networks in the university environment can be a complicated business, not least because there are so many things to consider when trying to keep everyone safe online. It is crucial that you understand exactly how social networks function if you are to manage the risks associated with their use.

Private and public networks

Some lecturers or research team leaders will set up a private network, but others will want a public network and their reasons for this will vary. (Note that issues related to privacy per se are covered in Chapter 12.) For example, if the topic you are dealing with covers delicate matters that might elicit and/ or propose controversial ideas, your network administrator could want to make the class network private. In some classroom instances (and as sometimes happens), your lecturer may not want their teaching exposed to the world for critique, which could also lead them to close their network and make it visible to invited members only. Alternatively, your lecturer might decide that having a public network, open to and viewable by all-comers, is actually an educationally sound best-use of social networking for your particular course. For certain research teams, the decision to have a public or private network will be simple; for others, it will all depend (see above).

In any case, you need to know *exactly* how private or public your network is: Who can see the site? Who can join the site? Who can contribute to the site? If you aren't sure about anything to do with your social network's visibility, then ask: you may have some say in how all this works.

Data collection

Social networks – whether personal or group-based – provide the almost perfect environment for giving away information about yourself, simply by virtue of the fact that these networks are based on 'sharing'. Some information will be innocuous but other information may be compromising and it can be difficult to know what the dividing line is because social networks collect a *lot* of data about their users beyond their contact details; they can also 'mine' your profile for information that you have either knowingly or unknowingly given away about your likes, interests, personal opinions, sexuality, ethnicity, philosophical or religious views, political standpoints, relationship status – even your pets. Everything you share, view, post, play, click on, don't click on, link to, upload, publish, vote up, vote down, like, don't like, recommend, listen to, and download can all contribute to an online profile of you and your habits. This data may be sold on to third parties and, even if collected anonymously, can still be linked to any internet-connected device's Internet Protocol (IP) address meaning that, eventually, it could still be traced to *you*.

Finally, know that your information is regularly cached and archived, not only by the service you are currently using, but also by search engines such as Google. So, even if you delete something from public view this does not mean that it has gone forever; the chances are that people can still access it by viewing a 'cached' version of the page you removed the material from. This means that once you post something online it cannot be retrieved. For more detail, see Chapter 12.

Security

Not only might you be giving away information about your online habits, you might also be giving away information that compromises your own or others' personal security. For example, if you post a wall comment saying

90

that you are heading off to do the shopping, or that you are going to the movies on Saturday night with friends, you are also telling other people that you – or your friends – won't be at home at those times (this also applies to 'geotagging' through sites such as FourSquare and any location-based mobile phone apps).

Before you join any social network being used in your course it is essential that you read – and understand – the Terms of Service (see Chapter 12) and if you aren't sure about anything, ask your lecturer about it *before* you sign up. Further issues around security and data collection are explored in Chapter 12.

Cyberbullying and cyberaggression

Cyberbullying and cyberaggression are not restricted to school kids; nor are they restricted to social networks. In fact, any digital medium that supports communication between two or more parties can become a channel for bullying and aggression. Nevertheless, social networks, perhaps because of their purpose in sharing and connecting in real-time (as opposed to, say, wikis or blogs, whose purposes are more knowledge- and critique-based) seem to be particularly well-suited to the cyberbullying and cyberaggression phenomenon. Don't think that just because you are working with adults in a group-based environment that you are immune to being bullied online: staff can bully students, students can bully students, and students can even bully staff.

Universities have policies, guidelines, and codes of conduct around bullying and harassment that can help you if you are a victim of cyberbullying or aggression. But just as you have rights under such policies, you also have responsibilities – you need to observe them. Further, there are likely to be laws in your country that address hate speech, racism, misogyny, and vilification of any kind – you need to obey them. Sometimes, the apparently liberal, even laissez-faire, environment of the Academy can make us feel free to act in ways that we shouldn't be proud of. But don't *only* base your actions and responsibilities around what a policy or guideline or even a law says: if something is wrong, it's wrong – don't be bullied, don't *be* a bully, and don't stand by and watch. Cyberbullying and cyberaggression are covered in more detail in Chapter 11.

Uploading contacts or address books

It is quite common for people to upload database files full of addresses or lists of contacts to a social network, allowing you to easily add or invite your friends to a network you are using. This practice should be avoided. Firstly, the data you upload is not yours to share – it doesn't belong to you. Instead, it belongs to the person whose name, address, phone number, and email the data describe. You may be in breach of privacy legislation in your jurisdiction if you give away such details without a person's permission. Secondly, many social networking services use the data you upload to target you (and others) with marketing and advertising messages and/or to build a profile of your online habits and of people you know – you may be surprised by exactly how much data companies collect about you and how they use it. Chapter 12 addresses these issues more thoroughly, but, for now, understand that you should not, under any circumstances, give away information about other people without their permission.

Should I friend my lecturer on Facebook?

The simple answer to this is 'No'. Just as you prefer to keep your study, work, and personal lives separate, so, too, do your lecturers. Also, they might not like being put in the position of having to decline a friendship request from a student, which they 'should' do because to friend some students and not others could be perceived as playing favourites. That said, it is usually OK (it may even be expected) to become friends with a lecturer – or, indeed, anyone in the class – on a class-based social network, as opposed to Facebook.

Facebook groups

Sometimes your lecturer (or team leader, in the case of researchers) will set up a Facebook group for your class, usually as a way of allowing students to easily communicate about course-based matters. This makes sense, because many students are already on Facebook, it avoids the issues around having to sign for 'one more thing', and you don't have to become 'friends' in order to join the group. However, if you are not already a member of Facebook, and do not want to become a member, then you cannot be compelled to join. Similarly, you should not have to become a member of Facebook – or any social media site – in order to successfully complete an assignment (see Chapter 12). If you have genuine reservations about joining Facebook (or other social media service) for the purposes of your studies, then you should discuss them with your lecturer. As a researcher, you need to consider Facebook's Terms of Service very carefully: if Facebook (or any other service) asks for a sub-licensable licence to your content, then you are effectively giving away to third parties any intellectual property that may have resulted from your research activities.

SUMMARY

- Social networks allow people to connect and build relations, and to share events, photos, videos, links, activities, news, and such like.
- Higher education favours group-based social networks over personal social networks. Discussion forums, sub-groups, announcements, events, and profiles characterise the kinds of tools used by lecturers for course-based social networks.
- Lecturers use social networks for communication, networking and administration, and for assessment.
- Typical social networking tasks set by lecturers include sharing useful links, videos, and similar objects; starting and contributing to discussions; being part of a sub-group; and writing 'blog' posts.
- Social networks are used by lecturers because they encourage collaboration, sharing, interaction, participation, and networking, and are thus almost the perfect tools for social learning.
- Social networking in higher education favours process over product.
- To successfully engage with social networking in higher education you need to accept chaos, be a good community member, watch for tone in your communications, and contribute to discussions.
- Special considerations for social networking include whether the network is public or private, how much and what data are collected, and being alert to security, cyberbullying, and privacy concerns.

FURTHER READING

Cao, Q., Lu, Y., Dong, D., Tang, Z. and Li, Y. (2013) 'The roles of bridging and bonding in social media communities', *Journal of the American Society for Information Science and Technology*, 64 (8): 1671–81.

Curşeu, P.L., Janssen, S.E.A. and Raab, J. (2012) 'Connecting the dots: Social network structure, conflict, and group cognitive complexity', *Higher Education*, 63 (5): 621–9.

Meyer, K.A. (2012) 'The influence of online teaching on faculty productivity', *Innovative Higher Education*, 37 (1): 37–52.

Sanchez-Franco, M.J., Martín-Velicia, F.A., Leal-Rodriguez, A.L. and Oliva-Vera, I.M. (2012) *Acceptance and Use of Social Network Sites. An Analysis Among Undergraduate Students*. Proceedings of the 5th International Conference of Education, Research and Innovations, 19–21 November, Madrid, Spain. pp. 2340–3095.

Veletsianos, G. and Kimmons, R. (2013) 'Scholars and faculty members' lived experiences in online social networks', *The Internet and Higher Education*, 19: 43–50.

6

Audio-visual Presentations

OVERVIEW

This chapter begins by describing various audio-visual formats (AV) used by lecturers and researchers to support tasks such as creating a narrated slideshow, interviewing an expert, making a mini-documentary, and producing an ongoing video or audio series. We look at how AV presentations can be used to help you develop skills in constructing a coherent narrative on a topic, build your visual and auditory literacies, and improve your technical competency in recording, editing, and publishing video and audio. Next, we look at how to successfully engage with AV media through adopting suitable style and tone in your work, attending to visual and auditory 'grammar', and planning for content and structure. What lecturers are looking for in terms of assessment is covered, as are special considerations relating to the production of your AV presentation, such as the importance of getting started early, sticking to time limits, scripting and editing effectively, and handling perfectionism.

As with previous chapters, this chapter does not present step-by-step 'how to' guides; instead you are encouraged to seek out for yourself some of the excellent audio and video recording guides on the web for further information. And also as with previous chapters, although much of the focus might appear to be on the student experience, most of what is covered here can also be transferred to the research context.

WHAT ARE AUDIO-VISUAL (AV) PRESENTATIONS?

Although there are many forms of AV presentation, the three we focus on here are slideshows, videos, and podcasts as these are the most common formats used when you undertake some kind of AV task.

Slideshows

Most students and researchers will be familiar with the slideshow format as an essential part of lectures, seminars, demonstrations, and tutorials. Slideshow software such as PowerPoint (for PC) or Keynote (for Mac) is typically installed directly on your computer desktop or tablet device, but an increasing number of users are choosing to create, store, and share their slideshows 'in the cloud', that is, on the web via a service such as Google Drive's 'Presentation'. Other services such as Slideshare.net and Voicethread.com will convert an uploaded slideshow to a flash-type 'movie' that permits viewers to easily click through the presentation and even to download it – assuming you've given permission for people to do so. But you don't have to be restricted to the sequential arrangements intrinsic to more traditional presentation software: many lecturers and students are using sites such as Prezi.com to design a dynamic, less 'linear' visual environment for their oral presentations.

Other forms of visual media used in higher education

- Photosharing
- Videosharing
- Animation
- Comic strips
- Multimedia/mashups
- Virtual worlds

Slideshows displayed on an online service (Prezi, Slideshare, VoiceThread, etc.) can be made public or kept private and, of course, viewers can like, share, and comment on your work if you want them to. The online services also tend to generate an embed code for your slideshow, allowing you to easily display your presentation in your wiki, blog or other site. Finally, most slideshow software and services, whether online or loaded on to your computer, enable you to add a voice-over narration to your slideshow, either by way of adding an mp3 file to your presentation or by recording directly into the slideshow itself; Voicethread extends this with a function for annotating and even drawing on your slideshow in line with your commentary.

Audio

Audio presentations can be recorded via a number of devices equipped for the task: computer, laptop, smartphone, 'dumb' phone, hand-held digital voice recorder, tablet, or stand-alone digital recorder and mixer. Once you have a recording, you can edit it on your desktop using simple sound editing software such as Audacity (which is free, downloadable from Sourceforge.net, and suitable for both PC and Mac) or GarageBand (which normally comes free as part of the software already installed on a Mac). More powerful software such as Adobe Audition (PC and Mac) and Final Cut (Mac only, and also a video editor) is available, but it can be expensive. There are also free, online audio recorders and editors available – do a Google search for 'Free online audio editor' or similar and conduct a comparison. Audio presentations can be hosted on websites such as PodBean.com and PodcastDirectory.com; many are put into iTunes as part of an ongoing podcast series. As with most social media, listeners can like, share, and comment on your audio.

Video

Video recording is an almost banal affair these days, with even the most basic mobile phones being equipped with a video camera. Of course, you can also film material using a dedicated, high-definition video recorder, just about any digital camera, a webcam, or a camera built-in to your computer or laptop. But the trick is turning your recording into a 'movie', which involves a knowledge of editing and file formats (see below for both). You will probably have little control over the recording software you use, as it will already be loaded onto your recording device, but you will be able to find editing software that suits you: the most popular desktop software is probably Windows Movie Maker for PC, and iMovie for Mac. There are many more available both free for use on the web, for download to your desktop, or for purchase from a computer store – do a Google search and compare the features to see what suits you. Once you have recorded and edited your video, you can host it on one of the many videosharing sites on the web. YouTube is clearly the most ubiquitous videosharing site online, but Vimeo and Blip.tv are others (photosharing sites such as Flickr often also allow videos to be uploaded, but file size and running time are normally quite limited).

Equipment and file formats

You don't need expensive equipment to create effective AV presentations: most computers come pre-loaded with slideshow software and some also with video- and audio-editing software. If the software isn't pre-loaded, then you can usually download reasonably good software from the web, or you can use an online service to create your work 'in the cloud' (that is, directly online) without having to download anything at all to a desktop.

Creating a slideshow should be fairly straightforward (more so than creating an audio or video) and shouldn't require the purchase of any specialist equipment on your part. However, I recommend that, where possible, you always convert your slideshows to PDF file format, as PDF can be read by most computers and devices (regardless of operating system and regardless of the software version number being used to read the file) and is the best format for uploading to sites such as VoiceThread and Slideshare as it preserves your original font sizes, styles, and layouts. Video and audio editing, however, both require a certain amount of equipment and a basic knowledge of file formats in order to make things work properly.

Video and audio equipment

You will first need a recording device. This could be a computer, laptop, mobile phone, camera, tablet, digital voice recorder, or dedicated digital video or audio recording device. The chances are that you have a digital recording device within easy reach right now. The only thing to be mindful of is that you have enough recording capacity or disc space available for your recording, as both video and audio files tend to be quite large.

Separate microphones are optional for recording (most devices have a mic already built-in) and if you choose to buy microphones be aware that you get what you pay for. Cheap mics will do a passable job, but if you want things to sound super-professional then you could be paying quite a deal of money.

The same goes for headphones: again, they should be optional because your laptop, mobile phone, or other device will likely have a speaker (no matter how small) through which you can listen to your recording. That said, headphones can be useful when it comes to editing your work. You probably have a set of ear buds lying around that will serve well enough, but note that they won't assist you in listening for background noise that might need to be edited out. As with microphones, you get what you pay for when it comes to headphones. That said, you should only invest in a good set of headphones (either those that sit over the entire ear or on the ear) if you are serious about audio quality.

What is bandwidth and why is it important?

Bandwidth refers to the amount of data that can be sent across a network at any one time: the more bandwidth, the more data can be sent, and vice versa. Bandwidth is important to you in two main ways:

1 Sending large files takes up a lot of bandwidth. If there is not enough bandwidth, it will take longer to download or upload a file.
2 Playing or streaming embedded media (such as video or sound) on a site can be interrupted if there is a lot of 'traffic'.

Try to keep your file sizes in check to avoid irritating people who are trying to access them.

Video and audio file formats

This is where things can seemingly get a little technical; however, there are only two things you really need to know:

1. Size and quality matter. File formats that produce smaller files are preferred over larger ones, as long as quality is not too severely compromised. File size is important in terms of the amount of disc space used to save the file as well as the amount of bandwidth a file uses when it is played online.
2. Compatibility is essential. Your file must be playable in commonly used media players either online or on your desktop.

Mp3 is the most commonly used audio file format as .mp3 produces reasonable-quality sound in a relatively small file size. That said, there are many, many other audio file formats, including .wav, .flac, and .ogg. In fact, many dedicated digital audio-recording devices and softwares use the .wav file format, which produces higher-quality audio than .mp3 – but .wav usually needs to be converted to .mp3 if you want your audio to be playable on most mobile and digital devices.

Common video file formats include .avi, .mp4, .mpeg, .mov, .wmv, .swf, and .flv. These formats are all generally acceptable in terms of file size, although .mov often needs to be compressed before uploading to the net. These file formats can be played on at least Windows Media Player, Apple QuickTime, RealPlayer, Adobe Flash Player, and/or VLC (in fact, VLC is, perhaps, the most ecumenical of the lot). If you make a video in one format and a viewer objects that they can't watch it, then suggest that they try a different video player.

AV PRESENTATIONS IN HIGHER EDUCATION

Lecturers have been assessing various kinds of student presentation for a long time now; usually, such presentations have taken the form of a talk given in class either by individuals or by small groups. But digital media and computer software such as PowerPoint now give lecturers the option of having you complete oral work without your actually having to be in the room to present it. This short section focuses on presentations that are *not* given face-to-face and/or in class.

Typical AV tasks set by lecturers

Lecturers may ask you to produce an AV presentation either individually or in a group. Regardless, AV tasks are normally assigned very clear time limits, for example, you might be restricted to 8 minutes maximum for a narrated slideshow or mini-documentary or 3 minutes for each 'episode' of an ongoing audio or video series. Whatever you do, don't go over the time limit (see below).

- *Creating a narrated slideshow.* You should already be familiar with how to create a slideshow using software such as PowerPoint, but you may not have added a voice-over track before. Once you have created your narrated slideshow you may be asked to upload it to your class site or a site such as Slideshare so that other students can view and comment on it. This kind of task is most likely to be done by individual students, not by groups.
- *Interviewing an expert.* Recording an audio or video interview with a subject expert can be a terrific experience. In some instances you will be asked to find your own expert (in which case sites such as ExpertGuide.com.au are useful); in others, potential interviewees may already be lined up for you by your lecturer. Alternatively, you may be asked to 'buddy up' in pairs or work in small groups and to interview each other *as if* you were experts on a topic.
- *Making a mini-documentary.* Some lecturers will require you to put together a video or audio documentary or one-off 'radio' (audio) or 'television' (video) show. You may be given a format to follow or you may have to develop your own, in which case you could consider including interviews, narration, music and/or sound effects, tips, vox pops, reports, etc. Mini-documentaries can be produced by groups or individuals.
- *Producing an ongoing video or audio series.* This kind of task is, clearly, a semester- or even year-long proposition and requires you to use a variety of skills. Firstly, you will have to conceptualise your series, develop a format for it, script individual 'episodes', record material, edit it, and distribute or publish it. This can be done either individually or in groups.

Audio-visual assignments are often weighted fairly heavily in grade terms in recognition of the amount of time and effort that it normally takes to complete the task. And because of the time involved, you need to start early. To submit your presentation for assessment you may be asked to upload it to your VLE. Alternatively, you may be able to host it yourself on a site such as YouTube, Vimeo, or PodBean, meaning you can simply submit your URL.

WHY LECTURERS WANT YOU TO CREATE AV PRESENTATIONS

As already mentioned, audio-visual tasks are normally *big* tasks and, as such, they combine a number of skill sets, both intellectual and practical. On the whole, lecturers want you to create coherent narratives and build various kinds of literacy.

Educational and intellectual purposes

AV presentations are not only about the presentation and dissemination of information, but also about the important intellectual skills of analysis, synthesis, and evaluation and how you demonstrate those skills through visual and/or auditory means. This requires from the very outset that you make important decisions about how to handle a set topic; and that includes identifying key themes, figuring out how best to arrange them, selecting what material to use (and what should be left out), assembling it so that it makes sense, and then choosing an appropriate structure and format for the presentation of it all. Every choice you make in creating an AV presentation will help you develop the higher-order skills of selecting, explaining, interpreting, combining, integrating, assessing, explaining, reasoning, and judging – assuming, of course, that you are thinking about the task and not just throwing something together with little heed.

Lecturers also use AV presentations to help you develop skills in building a coherent narrative on a subject. Many students (even at the graduate level) struggle with putting together a logical, cogent 'story' in their work – a story that guides a reader, viewer, or listener clearly through a topic without requiring them to parse the work for missing or out-of-place bits and then reconstruct it in their own mind so that it makes sense. Being able to construct a coherent narrative is perhaps even more crucial for audio-visual texts than for written ones: with written texts, a reader can quite easily go back over a section, paragraph, or sentence and try to make sense of it again; this isn't so easy with audio and video, as listeners or viewers have to stop, 'rewind', and play again. And, in the case of a live broadcast, they miss this opportunity all together! Being conscious of such issues helps you to build audience awareness.

Finally, lecturers use AV presentations to encourage the development of multiple literacies. If you are using a voice-over or narration, you are, of course, expected to demonstrate traditional literacy in putting words together in an intelligible fashion. But more than this, your lecturer wants you to develop visual and auditory literacies – they want you to develop the ability to understand, interpret and present visual images and/or sound in such a way that they make sense and convey meaning (see below). At base, this is all about effective communication.

Practical purposes

Having to do audio-visual presentation tasks also forces you to develop more practical skills. The most obvious of these are the technical skills related to recording, editing, and publishing video and/or audio. Less obvious skills include project management skills, which include developing project goals, designing a project plan, conducting research, co-ordinating interviews and recordings, scheduling time for editing, and determining how to publish or distribute your final product.

AV presentations that require you to work in pairs or groups obviously need you to build your peer learning and collaboration skills as you test your social skills in negotiating with other group members to create a coherent, final product. Further, teamwork is often listed (in various forms) as a graduate attribute, so, in addition to using them to support effective education practice, lecturers also use group projects to fulfil university benchmarking requirements.

A final comment. Audio-visual presentations are not normally easy for lecturers to mark: they take a lot of time, concentration, and attention to detail, and cannot be 'skimmed' as an essay or other written piece can. In addition, lecturers often encounter difficulties when students submit files that cannot be opened, have an incorrect extension name, are in a non-standard format, take too long to download or stream, or just won't work. So, unlike some other forms of assessment based on using social media, you cannot assume that there are time-management benefits for lecturers in asking you to put together an AV presentation as part of the assessment for a course.

SUCCESSFUL ENGAGEMENT WITH AV PRESENTATIONS

Depending on your viewpoint, it can be exciting, daunting, or confusing to have to produce an AV presentation for class. In any case, you will be most successful if you can perform according to the following advice.

Style and tone

Style refers to the forms and techniques of communication that you choose to convey a message; tone means the 'mood' you adopt to convey that message. With written work, style and tone are usually proscribed by 'genre' conventions; that is, blog posts must sound like blog posts, essays must sound like essays, and reports must sound like reports. AV presentations, on the other hand, often give you greater flexibility when it comes to choosing the style and tone you will use to get your point across. So, for example, if you are adding a voice-over narration to your AV presentation, then an informal tone coupled with a conversational style could be appropriate. Or, if you are filming an interview, then a casual tone and a style involving a bit of banter might be acceptable.

Note, however, that a highly idiosyncratic style is usually hard to pull off when it comes to demonstrating academic engagement with key course themes. It is important, also, that your style and tone should be natural and not forced: if you feel uncomfortable with a more 'relaxed' design, then aim instead for a strategy involving a 'Standard English' approach. With all this said, it is still really important that you check with your lecturer to see what are the limits to the style and tone they will accept for AV assignments. In general, most lecturers want to see some 'personality' in your AV work – but not at the expense of serious, critical engagement with the scholarship on a topic.

Visual and auditory 'grammar'

Grammar comprises the systems and structures of language that help us communicate effectively. Mostly, we use the term 'grammar' to refer to the written word, but the notion of grammar can also be applied to auditory and visual forms of communication, in which both sound and vision have their own 'language' – a language that needs to be structured and presented in ways that make sense and that can be easily decoded by listeners and viewers. So, a highly developed visual grammar will communicate a message using everything from line, form, surface, size, colour, position, spacing, rotation, mirroring, inversion, movement, dimension, perspective, depth, juxtaposition, angle, focus, texture, background, foreground, scale, weight, and the many other elements that constitute visual design. A highly developed auditory grammar communicates using elements such as tempo, speed, pitch, tone, background, modulation, volume, silences, fill-ins, sound effects, music, rate of delivery, slow and fast fades, truncation, and echo.

This seems like a lot to get right, but as with any system of language simple, clear communication is key. Accordingly, overloading your assignment with sound effects, clashing colours, or poorly focused video will impede, rather than enhance, your work. Sounds and images (still or moving) need to be relevant, match the content, and be competently presented. This means that your auditory and visual material should demonstrate a degree of sophistication that reflects the fact that you are working at a university level. So, choose and present images and sounds judiciously.

 Activity   Build your visual literacy

Step 1 – Read The Visual Literacy White Paper *by Anne Bamford* (search for 'Visual Literacy White Paper Adobe Bamford'). Bamford distinguishes between 'visual syntax' and 'visual semantics'. Syntax refers to the form of an image and concerns elements such as perspective, light, and shadow juxtaposition, contrast, motion, and cropping (p. 3). Semantics, on the other hand, describes how images are comprehended, interpreted, and presented to create meaning in a particular (often sociocultural) context about history, society, identity, events, beliefs, and so forth (p. 4).

Step 2 – Find a dozen or more visual objects from a variety of sources. Include, perhaps, digital photographs, diagrams, posters, paintings, graphics, displays, illustrations, webpages, etc. Sort the objects into three groups: 1) a group for objects that you think 'work', 2) a group for objects that you think don't work, and 3) a group for objects that you are undecided about.

Step 3 – Analyse the first two groups. Start with the objects that work, then move on to those that don't. Consider the objects' syntax. How are the objects constructed in such a way as to them either effective or not? Use Bamford's syntax list (and google things you don't understand) to help you. Consider the objects' semantics. How do you understand or interpret the objects? What meanings can you elicit (or otherwise)? Again, use Bamford's list.

Step 4 – Analyse the final group. Given your analyses of groups 1 and 2, can you now make a decision regarding the objects that you're not sure about?

Step 5 – Apply what you've learnt. As you build your visual grammar, be sure to apply it to any visual presentations or materials you have to produce. The more you learn about how visual objects are composed, the better your visuals will appear.

Creativity and format

AV assignments give you the opportunity to show that you can do more than just write. In fact, the level of creativity allowed to you in producing an AV presentation can be quite high and you might very well have the leeway to record real or imaginary interviews, produce mini-documentaries, gather vox pops, add sound and visual effects, or assemble an animation. Before embarking on a creative response, however, check with your lecturer to be sure that you have the freedom to do something different or original with your presentation. Give them a sense of what you are thinking of doing and ask them 1) whether or not they think it will work, and 2) for any suggestions they might have in terms of content, format, or traps to avoid.

In the end, be careful, though: creative responses to assignments still need to demonstrate rigour in thinking. You will only receive good grades if you succeed in 'answering the question', in engaging intellectually with current debates and/or findings in the area, and in getting your point across.

One of the most delightful assignments I ever saw came from a student who had enlisted fellow classmates and friends to act out a pretend TV panel discussion between the major theorists and philosophers in her particular discipline. The 'panel members' (most of whom were not all contemporaries and indeed were long since dead!) made their points, argued with each other, and presented opposing opinions and the whole thing was mediated by the student who scripted herself as the facilitator. It was not only a wonderfully clever idea, but it was also well executed and intellectually rigorous.

Content and structure

Getting content and structure to come together to form a coherent whole is vital if you are to effectively communicate using any audio-visual medium. This is, of course, the same for a written piece of work, but, arguably, more is at stake with AV presentations because your audience doesn't have the benefit of being able to skim your work to get a sense of its overall quality before scrutinising it in more detail: once someone has hit 'play' they are pretty much committed. Thus, making the right choices at the planning stage is essential if you are to engross your audience.

- *Content.* In choosing your content ask yourself: What outcome do I want? What do I want to convince my audience of? What is the most effective evidence I can marshal to support my main points and how can I best present it? You may not be limited to 'the literature' in an AV presentation: images, sounds, video, animation, could all be acceptable. Your content for any AV presentation needs to be not only relevant but also engaging.
- *Structure.* Any form of academic communication, whether it be written, visual, or auditory, needs to be competently structured if your audience is to follow your argument. But ensuring that you have an adequate structure is perhaps even more important for an AV presentation than it is for an essay or report – if the structure of a written piece at any point breaks down, then the reader can always flick back and forth and try to establish how your argument hangs together; this isn't so easy with AV presentations. So, introduce your topic properly, allowing your audience to orient themselves to what is coming up in terms of argument, and subject matter, present your points logically, and end with a clear and concise summary and/or discussion of the implications of what you have presented.

Select your content wisely. No matter how slick or showy your presentation, it won't save poor content.

Engaging with and citing the literature

Students often ask how they should engage with the literature when building an AV presentation, and, especially, they ask how they should 'cite' their sources. If you are using a narration for either a slideshow or a video, then an easy way of doing both things is to simply integrate your sources into a natural speaking style. This should take the form of 'Smith, writing in *Modernity and Communication*, argued that not everyone liked using the telephone'. (Avoid saying 'Smith, two thousand and three, page one-hundred-and-sixty, argued that not everyone liked using the telephone'.) You can then provide a list of references either as your final slide or as part of your end credits. If you are creating a pure audio presentation, that is, one without any vision at all, you may want to submit a separate document containing your references list. In any case you need to find *sensible* ways of both demonstrating that you have an appreciation of the scholarship in the area as well as referring to that scholarship. If you aren't sure, then tell your lecturer how you are considering doing things and get their feedback on it *before* you submit your assignment.

How AV presentations are assessed: What lecturers are looking for

At the very least lecturers use these tasks to measure your level of comprehension of a topic; but, as with any university-level assignment, markers want to see much, much more than basic understanding. Thus, AV assignments are little different from other assignments in that they should demonstrate all the usual things: focus, coherence, clarity, logic, reasoning, critical thinking, analysis, synthesis, evaluation, and so forth.

However, in asking you to create an AV presentation, lecturers are further giving you the opportunity to show how well you can present often difficult and/or complex material in an effective, non-text-based manner. In particular, they will be evaluating the appropriateness of the AV material you have selected to support your point of view; how well you have explained (and therefore demonstrated your understanding of) basic points using images, sound, voice-overs, and such like; how clearly your narrative develops (see above); and, in most cases, the visual and auditory techniques you have used to present your ideas (that is, your level of visual and auditory literacy).

One thing is certain, though, when it comes to lecturers' assessment of AV presentations: you will be flirting with a Fail if you lifelessly read out an essay and record for digital posterity the act of your doing so. AV presentations should be used to interest, excite, energise, invigorate, captivate, and absorb your audience, not lull them to sleep.

 Activity   Analyse documentary audio

Step 1 – Find some documentary-style podcasts. Search podcast directories such as Podbean.com, Podcastalley.com, iTunes, or Podcastdirectory.com. Choose podcasts that you think will try to tell a 'story' – national radio stations often produce such audios and can be accessed from a variety of sources.

Step 2 – Analyse the audios. Listen to the audio not just for its auditory grammar elements, but for all the elements that go into its construction:

(Continued)

(Continued)

- How is the audio structured? Is there a clear narrative?
- Is the content 'just enough'? Or is there too much or too little?
- How effective has the author been as regards getting their point across?
- How have the authors 'cited' their sources?
- What format has been used? What elements are in the mix? Vox pops? Narrations? Interviews?
- Are the style and tone appropriate for the type of content that is presented?
- What elements of auditory grammar can you identify: tempo, speed, pitch, tone, background, modulation, volume, silences, fill-ins, sound effects, music, rate of delivery, slow and fast fades, truncation, echo?

Step 3 – Apply what you've learnt. If you have to make your own audio presentation, be sure to plan it carefully according to the above elements – use what works and eschew what doesn't, and avoid adding sound effects or music or similar just because you can.

SPECIAL CONSIDERATIONS FOR AUDIO-VISUAL PRESENTATIONS

You need to pay particular attention to two main sets of issues when creating an AV presentation: legal issues and production issues. The current section is devoted to production issues; legal issues especially as they relate to copyright and intellectual property for using all social media are covered in the final chapter of the book.

Get started early

You can't do an AV assignment 'the night before' and expect to get a good – or even a passing – grade. AV assignments take planning, and lots of it. And they also require technical production skills that you may not already have and thus need to work on – skills relating to recording, editing, file conversion, publication, etc. Furthermore, there is so much that can go wrong with creating an AV presentation. Some examples include when you

- Forget to hit 'record' and speak for ten minutes before you realise your mistake.
- Have to re-record an item because the quality of the audio or video is poor.
- Encounter a copyright problem, which means you need to find an alternative to what you've already done.
- Need to fix a long, unexplained silence in your recording.

All of these things can occur (and, indeed, I have done all of them – and more), even if you are 'only' adding a voice-over to a slideshow.

It is easy to underestimate the amount of time you need to record an AV presentation.

Time limit

When planning your AV presentation it is essential that you work to the amount of time you have been given and *not* to the number of points you think you want to cover. Over and over again, I come across students who try to cover too much material in their AV presentation. The result is a rushed, often unfocused, confused, and confusing piece of work that leaves the audience staggering under too much information and too little analysis or critique. Sculpt the subject matter to fit the time limit; don't do things the other way around.

Think about the time you have, not the number of points you want to cover.

And, whatever you do, don't go over time! Your lecturer has given you a time limit so stick to it. As indicated earlier, AV presentations often take a long time to mark and this requires good time-management strategies on the part of your lecturer. One such strategy employed by a number of lecturers I know (including myself) is to not view or listen past the set time limit. So, if an assignment is given an 8-minute time limit, then the chances are that your lecturer will stop your presentation at the 8-minute point exactly (or, perhaps, 8 minutes and 15 or 30 seconds, if feeling generous) and not mark past that point. This is yet another reason for considering the amount of time you have to deal with a topic and not the number of points you want to cover: unfocused, rambling assignments will be given short shrift, so get to the point quickly.

Your work might not be marked once it goes past the set time limit.

Narration and scripting

Any narrative or voice-over track that you include in your AV assignment needs to be 1) scripted and 2) competently presented.

In scripting, you can afford to 'tone things down' a bit as regards the level of formality in the language you use. There is nothing more excruciating for a lecturer than having to sit through something that has been written as an essay and is being read out into a voice recorder – even worse if it is being read out in front of a video camera! So, script your work in a more natural style and tone than you would use for a formal piece of writing, and imbue your script with some personality. As regards presentation, be sure to avoid pauses, silences, 'umms and ahs', and any irritating verbal or physical ticks that might annoy your audience when listening to or viewing your presentation. You may also have to modify your accent if it is particularly strong, and you might need to slow down if you have a tendency to speak quickly. Add modulation to your voice and avoid the 'kiss of death' of any AV presentation, the monotone.

Consider whether or not you really need to add a slideshow to your narration and vice versa. When done well, both visual and audio formats can exist quite perfectly on their own.

Conducting expert interviews

Interviewing takes time. Not only do you need to decide upon, research, and develop intelligent questions around a topic, you need also to find a potential interviewee, contact them, and explain why you want to talk to them. Then you need to write up an interview schedule, find a mutually convenient time and place to record the interview, actually conduct the interview, and finally send a thank you note when it's all over. Nevertheless, conducting an interview with an expert often adds interest and a degree of 'intellectual legitimacy' to your AV presentation and the effort can pay off in terms of marks.

Once you have an interview lined up, it is a courtesy to send the interviewee a copy of the interview schedule or list of questions or topics you want to ask them about. This doesn't mean that the interviewee should script their answers – indeed, reading from a script should be avoided, as audiences can always tell when someone is reading something out. Before the interview, tell your guest a little bit about the recording process, how long the interview will go for, and the need to keep strictly to time (you need to bear this last point in mind, too!). Also let them know that you will give them a 'wind up' signal if you need to move on at any stage or if they seem to be deviating from the main point.

Editing your presentation

Students make two main mistakes when it comes to editing their AV presentations: the first is that they don't; the second is that, when they do, they underestimate how long editing can take. On the first point, editing is essential because it helps to 'polish' your work by removing unnecessary clicks, bumps, hisses, pauses, ums and ahs; this makes things sound or look better and can also buy you precious seconds in the time-limit department. Although sound and video recording has been made super-easy these days with the advent of cheap and easy to use digital devices, and although a certain degree of amateurism can be endearing, you should nevertheless try to refine your work somewhat to avoid the appearance of sloppiness or lack of effort on your part.

> Do not read out your AV presentation. Sitting in front of a phone camera and reading something out does not, under normal conditions, interest lecturers to any great extent.

On the second point, you need to schedule more time for editing your recording than you do for actually *making* the recording. This is because of the simple fact that during the editing phase you have to view or listen to the recording again, at least once, in its entirety – and if you add in any edits you have to make, then the process can take at least as long (if not longer) again. So, for an 8-minute recording, you may actually spend 30 minutes in the editing phase – and that's if 1) you know what you're doing to start with and aren't trying to learn technical skills as you go, and, 2) if you are simply editing things *out* and not adding things *in*, such as extra images, voice-overs, sound effects, music, captions, etc. This is why it's also a good idea to try to get a 'clean' first take, where there aren't too many 'ums and ahs' or other distractions that will need later correction.

Finally, when editing your work make sure you edit from a *copy* of the original file and not from the original file itself. Dealing with AV material is a complex task by its very nature, so be sure to keep backups.

Perfectionism

Perfectionism (as with most social media) is a curse and not a blessing when it comes to putting together AV presentations. In the first instance, AV presentations give us the often uncomfortable opportunity to listen to and look at ourselves when we'd really rather not – and to be able to do so over and over again. The only good advice I can give here will sound flippant, but it needs to be said nevertheless: get over yourself. The chances are that you are not an expert presenter, so do not expect yourself to be one and do not compare yourself with those who are. Sure, you can learn from good presenters, but these skills take time to develop and/or accompany a naturally ebullient personality, anyway. Don't be too hard on yourself – you are probably doing a better job than you think you are.

Secondly, AV presentations can become a time trap for the perfectionist who wants to get every single detail of the sound and/or vision absolutely right. It really does not matter if that font is one point too small, or that second image is two pixels wider than the first image, or that spoken sentence ungrammatical. What is more important is the quality of your message and your ability to engage your audience in that message. Get it close and then move on.

That said, slipshod work is more likely to fail than is work done by a perfectionist, so don't assume that your natural charm and charisma will get you over the line: pitching and balancing your effort is vital to producing an effective AV presentation.

SUMMARY □

- AV presentations include slideshows with voice-overs, audio recordings such as podcasts, and video recordings.
- Common audio file formats include .mp3, wav, .flac, and .ogg. Common video formats include avi, .mp4, .mpeg, .mov, .wmv, .swf, and .flv.
- Typical AV tasks set by lecturers include creating a narrated slideshow, interviewing an expert, making a mini-documentary, and producing an ongoing video or audio series.
- AV presentations are used by lecturers to help you develop the higher-order skills of selecting, explaining, interpreting, combining, integrating, assessing, reasoning, and judging. They are also used for developing skills in building a coherent narrative on a subject.
- Using AV media successfully requires you to adopt an appropriate style and tone to your work, be aware of visual and auditory 'grammar', demonstrate creativity, and plan for content and structure.
- AV presentations give you the opportunity to show how well you can present often difficult and/or complex material in an effective, non-text-based manner. You need to be able to interest, excite, energise, invigorate, captivate, and absorb your audience.
- Special considerations for AV presentations include the need to get started early, adhere to time limits, narrate and edit your work competently, and handle any perfectionist tendencies you might have.

FURTHER READING

Bamford, A. (2011) *The Visual Literacy White Paper*, commissioned by Adobe Systems Pty Ltd, Australia. Available at: http://www.adobe.com/au/solutions/white-papers/education-k12.html. Accessed 12 September 2013.

Cohn, N. (2012) 'Visual narrative structure', *Cognitive Science*, 37 (3): 413–52.

Greiffenhagen, C. (2013) 'Visual grammar in practice: Negotiating the arrangement of speech bubbles in storyboards', *Semiotica*, 195: 127–67.

Matusiak, K.K. (2013) 'Image and multimedia resources in an academic environment: A qualitative study of students' experiences and literacy practices', *Journal of the American Society for Information Science and Technology*, 64 (8): 1577–89.

Rogers, D. and Coughlan, P. (2013) 'Digital video as a pedagogical resource in doctoral education', *International Journal of Research & Method in Education*, 36 (3): 295–308.

Social Media for Self-directed Learning, Research and Development

Part III examines the ways in which you can use social media to support your more general scholarly activities, in particular focusing on using social media for building your online profile (Chapter 7), for search and research (Chapter 8), and for improving your productivity (Chapter 9). All of these undertakings go a long way to supporting your self-directed learning and professional development.

7

Building your Online Profile

OVERVIEW

This chapter begins by outlining the contrast between a traditional and a digital academic profile. It considers the difference between an online presence and an online profile before looking at why building an online profile might be important. In particular, different models of online portfolio are described, as well as the value of pre-publishing and self-publishing work online (cautions against these are also sounded, however). Different social media and how they can be used to promote an online profile are discussed and different professional social networks are all covered alongside the advantages and disadvantages of each – including when and why you would use one tool or service over another. Networking via these various media is especially encouraged because they promote collaboration, communication, and knowledge-sharing – all of which are important in building a solid, professional reputation online.

WHY IS YOUR ONLINE PROFILE IMPORTANT?

Having something of a profile has always been important in academic circles. But the pressures to be seen and heard as a scholar are arguably more forceful today than they have ever been. However, before we look at how to build your profile online, we need first to understand how such profiles work according to context.

Traditional vs digital academic profile

Until recently, building your academic profile was a fairly linear (if not always simple) matter based around formal outputs relating to production (of, for example, journal articles and monographs), endorsement (through editors, examiners, and the peer-review process), distribution (via publication, conferences, and seminars), and promotion. This traditional academic profile was established in an economy of scarcity where only a few final works could ever make it to publication, leading necessarily to a focus on a 'finished' *product*. However, the chief problem with such a product-focused environment was that the depth and complexity of scholarly *processes* could never be fully captured. Now, though, in an age of digital abundance of (self-)publishing possibilities, this economy is being challenged (Anderson, 2006): the background processes of scholarship are moving more and more into online view as academics post their initial thoughts in their blogs, produce wikis to collaborate on projects with colleagues in other countries, take part in social media forums where they start describing their research findings, and make available their raw data to anyone who wants to inspect it. Moreover, researchers can now also publish just about any artefact relating to their scholarship: field-based journals, experiments, graphs, tables, databases, ethics committee applications, recordings of interviews or focus group meetings (with permission, of course!), photographs (ditto), references lists, grant applications, letters and emails, and notes on anything and everything. All of this, of course, means that building an academic profile is a much messier, more chaotic, less linear enterprise than it has been in the past.

Sticking with the traditional, 'analogue' profile is becoming less and less an option in the increasingly socially networked world of academe. In the first instance, it doesn't help to increase awareness of your work, especially when a lack of online engagement (or outright non-engagement) on your part shunts you so far down a search engine's results list that no-one will ever find you. Secondly, the less you actively work to build your online profile, the more likely it is that an unwanted or simply useless and incoherent profile will form around you regardless. This is where taking the time to consciously construct an online profile – as opposed to simply having an organically gathered online presence – is essential.

Online presence vs online profile

If you are reading this book, then the chances are that you already have an online presence, that is, you probably have a Facebook account, you might be on Twitter, and you more than likely have some account with a Google-, Yahoo-, or Microsoft-affiliated service. But having an online *presence* – that is, simply being online and interacting with others socially – is different from having an online *profile*.

Your online profile should be deliberately built around a consistent, coherent identity through which you present your professional face to the world. This means that you need to establish a 'narrative' or 'story' that you use to tell the world about yourself, a narrative that brings together your scholarly interests and achievements and that keeps your personal and private lives separate from your public one. Of course, this separation isn't always easy to achieve (not least because the bounds between them are becoming more and more opaque as we 'smoosh' together life and work) but, as with all social media use, it is important to be aware of audience and how you present yourself: people who are interested in your academic accomplishments might not care that you ride horses, play World of Warcraft, or enjoy reading, and, if they are looking to employ you or admit you to a graduate program, they might not appreciate what a totally good time you had at the pub on Saturday night.

> Think of your online presence as a 'private' matter, whereas your online profile is a 'public' matter.

Once you gain some control over the public and private aspects of your online undertakings, you can start to reap the benefits for your academic career.

Benefits for your career

Using social media to build your online profile has numerous benefits, most of which have to do with sharing, networking, and establishing your credibility. In particular, though, using social media:

- *Makes you more visible and searchable.* Perhaps the most obvious and largest benefit of having an online profile is simply that it increases your visibility and searchability across the internet. The aim is to try to make it to the first page of a search engine's results, which increases the chance of people clicking on a link related to you and your work. If people can easily find your material, then they are more likely to read or engage with it, leading to a potential increase in the number of citations of your work. This will also move you up in the search returns on Google Scholar, which, candidly speaking, is the first (but not only) port of call for many academics conducting research, and not just the preserve of undergraduates seeking to put together a quick references list.
- *Increases your public engagement.* Being professionally visible online increases opportunities for distributing your work to a wider audience and not just to fellow academics. A chief form of public engagement is being able to reach the layperson and have them interact with your research and ideas for the public good, perhaps through your blog, wiki, or Twitter feed. You may even find that through such engagement you end up informing policy, or influencing business, industry, or public opinion.
- *Builds your networks.* Finding people who are interested in the exact same research problems as you has become easier as social media link people through their online

profiles into 'niche markets'. This can be explained by digital technology itself, which has, according to Anderson (2006), created a 'long tail', that is, a situation where increased choice is fulfilling unlimited demand. The upshot of all of this is that there is now greater opportunity for you to work on research projects and research topics in teams rather than simply as an individual. This kind of collaboration is highly favoured by funding and grant bodies, so having a robust online profile that allows like-minded scholars to discover and connect with you increases your chances of putting together a solid, group-based research proposal.

- *Refines your ideas.* Your career won't progress unless you have ideas – and good ideas at that. Establishing an online profile and sharing your thoughts via social media as a way of seeking feedback can be a perfect strategy for refining your work. If we accept that scholarship is not simply about product but also about process, then getting this kind of feedback even *before* you send something out for peer-review can save you a lot of time on revisions and re-writes. For special consideration regarding pre-publishing your work in this fashion, see below.

- *Creates a new form of resumé.* Your online profile provides you with a new form of resumé, in which your various digital activities and materials can be drawn together to create a portfolio of your work (see below) that is easily updated. This can be particularly effective (and impressive!) when you provide your personal URL or web address to potential employers, allowing them to learn more about who you are and the type of work you have been doing.

- *Allows you to take your profile with you.* Although your institution may provide you with a personal page on the department or school website that outlines your academic achievements and responsibilities, that page will be removed once you have left your employment there. If you have a more 'distributed' profile, however (that is, if you have intentionally built your profile across a number of platforms), then you have far more control over the type, variety, and amounts of information about yourself that gets uploaded; in fact, you will be able to upload a lot *more* information, which assembles a more nuanced picture of who you really are as a researcher and scholar.

 Activity   Google yourself and clean up your act

'Googling' yourself once used to be a fairly unfashionable thing to do, but it is now essential if you are to know what material exists about you on the internet.

Step 1 – Conduct a search of yourself. Search variants of your name, and don't forget to search nicknames, usernames, previous names, etc. You should also search images and videos and other media. Use not only Google, but also 'people search engines' such as Pipl.com, Zabasearch.com, and 123people.com (search 'people search engines' for more).

Step 2 – What kind of profile is there of you? How do you present to the world? Are the top hits to do with your personal or your professional life? What 'story' does your profile tell the world?

Step 3 – 'Bury' material you would rather people didn't see. If you find something online about yourself that you find embarrassing, untrue, upsetting, unprofessional, compromising, or that will reflect poorly on you, then try to remove or, better still, 'bury' it. Removal is not always easy, especially if you are not the owner of the site on which the material appears; in fact, asking to have material removed, or engaging with material that you don't like about yourself (for example, by getting involved in commenting on it), often simply forces the material higher up a search engine's results. 'Burying', on the other hand, can be more effective, as you add different, 'safer' material about yourself that forces the unwanted material further down the results.

Step 4 – Google yourself regularly and update/curate material accordingly. Building and curating your online profile takes time and effort, but avoiding these things only moves you further and further down the search results. Make sure you keep things as up-to-date as possible.

USING SOCIAL MEDIA TOOLS FOR BUILDING YOUR ONLINE PROFILE

As we have already seen, everything you do online contributes to your online presence; turning that *presence* into a *profile* is another matter, however, and this means that you need to know at least a little bit about the various types of social media tools and services that can help you achieve a professional web outlook. But, more than this, you should use these tools strategically to build your online profile across three main areas: presenting information about yourself, curating content, and developing content.

Presenting information about yourself

The most basic step in building your online professional profile can be achieved through the tendering of static information about yourself. At heart, this means creating a profile on a site and keeping that profile updated. You can extend this, however, by taking advantage of the more active networking opportunities that most such sites offer, not least because this will increase your searchability and visibility across the web (see above).

- *Professional networks and online resumés.* To start building your online profile you should consider opening accounts with professional networking and/or resumé services such as LinkedIn, Academia.edu, Research Gate, and even About.me (but see the caution, below). Here, you can enter information about your educational background, work experience, previous and current employment, awards and nominations, publications, and any other details you think might be of interest to potential employers, colleagues, research partners, etc. Such services will help you connect with other professionals in your field, whether you already know them personally or whether you discover them through the network itself. Do be careful, however, as such services might ask for access to your research or profile information that you find unacceptable, or you might be in breach of copyright if you upload articles to their sites (see Chapter 12), and they may even end up diluting your profile. The chief thing is to keep your profile(s) updated – especially if and when you are looking for employment and/or collaborative research opportunities.

- *Google Scholar Citations.* Many services allow you to upload your publications or to build reference lists (see above) but having a profile with Google Scholar Citations is essential if your professional details are to be readily listed when people search Google Scholar. Google Scholar Citations provides citation metrics, graphs, and ways of tracking who is citing your articles. Some of this is generated automatically by Google (which you can review), but you can also manually input data to keep your Citations profile up-to-date.
- *Expert guides.* Most universities have some kind of expert guide that the institution compiles and publishes on its website. This is helpful, but it doesn't often give you much control over the information that appears on the site. Instead, you should also seek to register with an expert-finding service. In Australia, for example, Expertguide.com.au is the 'go-to' site for journalists, public relations and human resources personnel, and others who are seeking expert commentary or contacts in all manner of research areas. There are similar services in other jurisdictions, but you may need to ask around to find the most effective for your particular field. Again, don't neglect services such as LinkedIn, Academia.edu, and Research Gate, which also act as expert guides.
- *Facebook page.* If you already have a fairly high profile as an academic – or if you are aiming for such a profile in the future – then you might consider creating a Facebook page. A Facebook page is different from your regular Facebook profile in that a page allows you to have 'fans' (and not just 'friends') as a way of 'branding' yourself.

You may choose to end your profile-building activities here; however, there are other things that you can do to enhance your profile, as discussed below.

Curating content

You can also use social media tools and services to curate content, that is, to draw together information from various sources and sift it so that it is accessible to visitors with similar interests to your own. Undertaking this kind of internet-based activity is a step up from simply building a static profile and then networking with others through commenting on their sites or 'liking' what they've posted. With content curation, your profile will increase if you manage to bring together content that is both interesting and useful to visitors so that they come back for more and drive traffic to your site.

There are many content curation tools available online. Search 'Content creation tools' to find comparison charts and top-ten lists to help you decide which tools or services best suit your purposes.

- *Reference and research management systems.* Almost all social media services today come with some form of networking facility, that is, some way of connecting with others to share interests, information, and discoveries and, to this end, even online reference management systems such as Mendeley and Zotero (see Chapter 9) have such provisions. In making your profile public, and in sharing your discoveries, thoughts, and materials, you can network across and within the research groups that inhabit such spaces, alerting new audiences to your work and interests.
- *Twitter.* Twitter is not a content curation service per se, but there is no doubt that a lot of content curation and dissemination occurs via individual tweets, re-tweets, and the sharing of others' content. If you tweet timely and relevant links, images, and other information, then you can build an audience of followers.
- *Social bookmarking.* Social bookmarking services provide a simple way of collecting and sharing your 'favourites' on the web (see Chapter 8). Although most bookmarking services don't have the research-specific functions of online research management tools, some researchers nevertheless prefer the simplicity of social bookmarking and prefer to share their discoveries by compiling favourites lists that others can access.
- *Mashup services.* Services such as Paper.li and Storify are dedicated content curation sites that allow you to create daily 'newspapers' of interesting articles, tweets, blog posts, videos, images, etc. These tools are simple to use and produce good-looking sites, but because they are usually news- as opposed to research-based, they can be time-consuming to maintain: often it is much easier to share high-level, academic content in a service that you are already using to maintain your references list than it is to start an entirely new form of curation that you have to maintain separately.

Developing content

Finally, you can use social media services to develop or create content itself and to build your profile through the materials you produce and share.

- *Slideshow and document-sharing sites.* Perhaps the easiest thing you can do to share content you have created or developed yourself is to put your slideshows (that is your PowerPoint presentations) or documents on a site such as Slideshare.net or Scribd. You are most likely producing slideshows, papers, and other scholarly documents for seminars and lectures, so it is a simple step from there to share your work online. This can be a very effective way of pre-publishing your work and getting feedback (see below); indeed, for myself, I am sure I have gained more readers for papers that I have uploaded to such sites than I have ever gained via formal article-publishing channels.

> The trick is to 'double-up' as much as possible: if you are creating content anyway, see if you can share it via social media.

- *Blogs.* If you have the time and energy to devote to blogging, your online profile can be truly enhanced by sharing your ideas, opinions, discoveries, and thoughts via your own blog. Building your reputation via a blog will help you garner a following as an expert in your field and thus raise awareness of your work. But you don't have to have your own blog: there are many blogs out there with multiple authors – contact the blog owners and suggest yourself as a potential blogger on their site. You might want to include your CV, a link to your own site, and a sample post or two; this can be a great way to develop and contribute content without the pressure of having to blog on a frequent, regular basis.
- *Wikis.* Wikis are perhaps the ultimate content production and collaboration tools. The key word, here, though, is 'collaboration'. Wikis are about communities of users and so do not always provide the quickest path for individuals seeking to raise their online profile. Nonetheless, wiki participation can be successful in this area if you are a site administrator and an enthusiastic contributor to both taking part in the discussion forum and in building wiki content.
- *Photos, audio, and video.* Creating and distributing this kind of rich media content is easier today using digital technologies than it has been in the analogue past. That said, not all rich media content is equal in the creation stakes. For example, it is far easier to take and/or share research-related photographs and upload them to a photo-sharing site such as Flickr or Instagram than it is to create audio or video content that needs scripting, recording, and editing (see Chapter 6). That said, if you can produce some kind of image- or audio-based content that links in with your research interests, then your online profile suddenly becomes far more dynamic than a profile that relies heavily on text-based media.

Table 7.1 suggests some tools you might use for presenting, curating, and developing content.

> Some services require that you have an .edu email address in order to sign up, so sign up now to reserve your account.

ONLINE PORTFOLIOS

So far we've looked at the various tools and services you can use to help establish your online profile. But how should you bring them together? The answer is that you should set up an online portfolio (sometimes called an 'eportfolio') that presents information about you and that collects all your

TABLE 7.1   Tools you might use for presenting, curating, and developing content

Presenting information about yourself	Curating content	Developing content
Resumé services (LinkedIn, About.me)	Mashup services (Storify, Paper.li)	Blogs
Facebook page (for 'brand you')	Reference management systems (Mendeley, Zotero)	Podcasts
Facebook profile (more private)	Twitter	Photo- and videosharing (Flickr, Instagram, YouTube)
Scholarly citations profiles (Google Scholar Citations, Academia.edu)	Social bookmarking services	Document and slideshow sharing (Scribd, Slideshare)

details, writing, research outputs, content, and other work-related materials in the one spot. You can do this either by constructing a standalone portfolio or a centralised portfolio. Whichever format you choose, future employers, colleagues, students, and others should be able to access a single URL (web address) that takes them *to what you want them to see* as regards your professional profile on the web.

Standalone portfolio

If you want to keep things simple you can construct a basic, standalone portfolio in which you use only one service or platform to present your professional profile information. This is a good option if you don't want to spend too much time keeping your portfolio updated and/or if you lack the confidence or skills to develop several profiles across the internet and then draw them all together into the one, main location as you would with a centralised portfolio (see below). Having a standalone portfolio is the low-maintenance alternative but it does limit you to using only the tools that that particular service supplies.

Can't decide between a standalone or a centralised portfolio?

Then you should choose a social media platform that will allow you to expand if you want to. My recommendation is to start with a blogging service such as WordPress; you can use it first off to simply host static information (you will need to set your homepage to a static webpage), but, later, if you want to extend your portfolio, you can use it to write blog posts, aggregate tweets and bookmarks, display videos, etc.

With that in mind, it doesn't matter which or what type of service you use for your standalone portfolio – the main thing is that you choose something that you find easy to use and easy to keep updated. Blogs make for very good standalone portfolio hosts (see box), but you might also consider making your presence on a site such as LinkedIn your standalone portfolio 'home'. Although you are aiming for a streamlined, simple online profile through your standalone portfolio, it is still smart to have a service that can host your publications and similar materials in the one spot.

Centralised portfolio

The other alternative for bringing together your online profile is to create an integrated or centralised portfolio in which you have information and materials distributed across a number of different platforms or services that you then aggregate into one central place that acts as a gateway to your profile. Although this might seem like a lot of hard work, it shouldn't be: most services allow 'embedding' and/or feed aggregation (see Chapter 2) so, if you've got, say, accounts with Flickr, Twitter, Slideshare, and other services, then you should be able to feed them all into your main site: once you have it set up properly, the thing should run itself.

There are several advantages to generating this kind of portfolio. In the first instance, you can use the best tool for the job: a blog is not Twitter and Twitter is not a social bookmarking service (see next chapter) and you will get more out of your social media use if you use the tool for its intended purpose. A related point is that centralised portfolios can access the various kinds of material that you present, curate, or develop across a number of different services and can display them all in the one place, meaning that you are able to embed videos, audios, slideshows, scrollable documents, and similar rich content. All of this makes for a more interesting portfolio. Furthermore, in distributing your materials across various social media services you are increasing your searchability and visibility (see above) as well as adding to the variety of content included in your portfolio.

What to include in your online portfolio

- *Resumé/CV.* The basic timeline of your work experience, to the last ten years. Do not include contact details for referees – you may not have their permission to publish this information online. Publish this as both a PDF and as a webpage, where possible. Do not upload Word documents as they do not always print as you would like them to.
- *Contact details.* Let people know your preferred contact method and keep your details updated. If using email, then use an address you check regularly and that reflects well on you professionally (that is, don't use your 'wanderingstar32@yahoo.com' address).

- *About.* You may wish to use an 'About' section to provide an abridged professional biography.
- *Scholarly works (journal articles, monographs, etc.).* List your scholarly output and, if possible, provide copies of or links to your various pieces. Bear in mind, however, that the company that has published your work may own copyright over it, in which case you should only provide a link to the paper, not an entire copy of it in its published form.
- *Your thesis.* Although your thesis may already be in a digital repository in your institution's library, you should consider also placing a copy with your online portfolio. People are far more likely to read your thesis if they have easy access to it via your site.
- *Presentations, keynotes, conference papers.* Provide a short abstract on your best presentations as well as the date and venue for the presentation. Embed copies of or links to your work if you can. If providing PDFs of slideshows, then save them in 'hand-out' format so that visitors don't have to print out 38 pages of huge slides.
- *Awards.* This includes teaching awards, research grants, scholarships, nominations, and anything else that shows that you have received community recognition for your efforts.
- *Social media engagement.* Include details for any relevant social media you engage in professionally. Include your blog address, Twitter name, and any groups or forums you moderate or take an active role in.

Choosing a service to host your online portfolio

Any form of social media that you use for your professional activities should be robust, reliable, dependable, reputable, and provide an appropriate level of functionality for your needs. But perhaps most importantly, you need a service that allows you to backup or export your content and to take it with you if you decide to switch providers (see Chapter 12 for more information on such issues). It's also smart to choose a platform that allows you to grow if you need to and that allows you to bring together your diverse activities online. In this regard, blogging platforms probably provide you with everything you need to centralise your online exploits: blogs can be static or dynamic (depending on how you set them up), are good for embedding and displaying material that is hosted elsewhere, and allow you to have a distinct profile that you can tailor to your needs.

SUCCESSFUL ENGAGEMENT WITH BUILDING YOUR ONLINE PROFILE

Simply putting stuff up about yourself online is no guarantee that people will find out all they need to about you. You need to be rather more co-ordinated than that, and you need to put some thought into how best to present yourself.

Have a strategy

As with most things you do in professional life, you should have a plan of action to help you build your online profile. You don't have to write up a fancy, ten-page strategy document complete with mission statement, vision statement, and a clear understanding of the difference between the two; but you *do* need to at least jot down some notes around the following questions:

1. *What is my purpose in building my online profile?* Is it to get a job? To publish previously unpublished work? To get my ideas 'out there' for early feedback? To bring together my various professional materials and activities so that others can engage with them? To connect and network with other scholars and experts? To curate or develop content? You might also consider what is your *goal* in building your online profile, that is, are you seeking to engage a whole community of scholars in ongoing debate and commentary on a topic area? Or do you simply want something that you can present to potential employers or clients as a representation of you and your work? Answering these questions will inform how you go about the remainder of the task.

> ## What's the difference between a goal and a purpose?
>
> In most cases, we could argue that the difference is largely semantic. But for our needs, consider a purpose as encompassing the general reasons for which you are building your profile and your goal as the final objective you want to reach.

2. *What kind of portfolio will best support my purpose?* That is, do I need a standalone or a centralised portfolio and what tools or services should I use (see above)? Generally speaking, a simple, standalone portfolio will best suit the 'job-seeking' type of profile, whilst a centralised portfolio is more helpful for the more 'engagement-based' profile.
3. *What resources and skills do I need?* Of course, you need the right digital tools and services in order to build your profile, but don't neglect your ability to use those tools and services effectively. Do you need extra training or assistance to achieve what you want to achieve? Do you have friends or family who can help you or will you have to pay someone else to do things for you? If doing things yourself, do you have the time it takes to keep your profile spruce and the energy to keep your profile updated? Further, think about your communication skills: Are you quite certain, for example, about the correct tone and style you should use in a blog post (see Chapter 3) or do you need to do a bit of professional development in that area?
4. *What limits will I encounter or need to set?* This ranges from the measurable (such as bandwidth or upload quotas) to the inexact (such as effort and energy). You need to think through your technical requirements as well as your emotional and personal limits: be realistic about things such as resources, time, and skills. Know the limits and work within them.

Make it dynamic and visual

Whether you have a standalone portfolio or a centralised one, you should include both static and dynamic content – don't just have screeds and screeds of text taking over the whole screen. Break things up with images, videos, slideshows, bullet points, etc., all of which provide visitors with multiple media pathways into your profile. Moreover, many services allow you to choose 'themes' that help to make your site look good, but you might still need to improve your visual literacy (see Chapter 6) to prevent things from becoming visually cluttered or untidy. Think, too, about your 'branding' – a fairly unattractive marketing-type term that nevertheless describes consistency in look and feel in your site and in your public image.

Be active

You can raise your profile in large part by raising your level of activity across the internet. This doesn't mean you have furiously to create and distribute only your own content, although that is a key part of gaining a following. Rather, it means making sure that you share links via Twitter, that you embed interesting videos in your blog posts, and that you like, rate, recommend, favourite, and comment on worthwhile items. But remember, everything you click on – and, for that matter, *don't* click on – provides data that can be used to build a portrait of your internet usage (see Chapters 5 and 12 for more information).

Identity and audience

We noted earlier that although it can be difficult to keep your personal, private, and professional lives separate in the online sphere you should nevertheless aim at constructing a coherent 'narrative' that describes who you are in the community of scholars. Thus, you should consider your scholarly online 'identity'. For example, do you see yourself as a neutral commentator on current events or as an advocate for social or policy change? This also means that you need to know (or define) your audience: Who do you want to engage with your profile? What information is of value to them? Why would they be interested in you and what you have to say or share? Who are you trying to reach? What news, discoveries, or links would they be interested in? Are you pitching your profile at students, peers and colleagues, the lay person, industry, or government? Are you there to educate the public or influence experts? But don't just consider who you want to include: also think about who you want to exclude or discount as part of your audience – knowing who you are *not* trying to attract can be as important as knowing who you *are*.

127

Stats and analytics

If you are serious about building your online profile, then it's vital that you get to know how traffic works on your site. Most social media services offer some form of site statistics or analytics, but often they are quite basic. More detailed statistics can be provided by certain companies that specialise in a particular service (such as Facebook or Twitter), but you will probably have to pay for them. Google Analytics, on the other hand, allows you for free to collate statistics for any site you administer, although, as with many online services, you can get more if you pay for a premium upgrade. Some of the traffic data you might want to view includes the number of unique visitors to your site, the number of return visits, the length of visit, the visitor's country of origin, the number of referrals from a search engine or from a link from another site, etc. All such data can be used to build a picture of your users and what they find useful or otherwise. Other services, such as ImpactStory, aggregate data from your articles, datasets, blog posts, tweets, and so on in order to measure the impact of your work (via 'altmetrics') across various scholarly formats and genres. As with any online service, however, be sure to carefully read the Terms of Service before signing up for anything – you need to be sure about what, exactly, such services are doing with your information. See Chapter 12 for more information.

SPECIAL CONSIDERATIONS FOR BUILDING YOUR ONLINE PROFILE

As with most uses of social media in the university context, you must take account of the special environment in which you are participating. There are serious matters you need to consider before you post, upload, or share information relating to your online profile.

Reputation management

The information that feeds your online profile also feeds your online reputation: whatever is 'out there' about you contributes to the judgements that others make about you and can affect your career and employment opportunities. You need to be mindful of what you post, share, tweet, blog, link to, comment on, like, recommend, and so forth, and how all of that reflects on you – and not just how it reflects on you now, but how it will reflect on you in ten years' time. To this end, you need to be aware of what danah boyd (2011 [sic]) calls 'invisible audiences'. Such audiences may misread or misinterpret your activities and may even go on to misrepresent them, especially if they are not aware of the full context that surrounds what you are doing. This can leave you subject to attack and unfair scrutiny and can be both personally and professionally damaging. So, take the time to evaluate your online reputation: How might others perceive you based on your current activities? What might they think of your past online exploits? What judgements would they make about you as a person and as a professional? What if people saw your stuff ten years from now? Clean up your profile now by removing (if possible) or 'burying' any material that you feel reflects poorly on you (see the activity, this chapter), and monitor your reputation regularly. Remember: once something goes online, it is very difficult to remove or delete it (see Chapter 12).

Intended audiences

Perhaps the major concern for most professionals wanting to build their online profile centres around audience issues, especially as they pertain to privacy. Rather than focusing on privacy, however (that topic is dealt with in more detail in Chapter 12), I would suggest that it's more useful to think about the different kinds of audience you might be reaching and how you can control for that. In particular, there are four audiences you should bear in mind when developing or contributing to your online profile:

- *Private.* Only those people who you would trust with your most intimate thoughts and feelings. Usually family and best friends.
- *Personal.* Those who you don't mind knowing about you as a person, who you can have a laugh with, but with whom you wouldn't want to share your innermost emotions. Usually friends and close acquaintances.
- *Professional.* People who know you as regards your specific, work-related or academic, undertakings. Usually colleagues, peers, and associates.
- *Public.* Anyone with an operating internet connection and the ability to use it.

Most social media services recognise that you want to give various audiences various levels of access to your online activities, and thus they allow you to control your privacy settings accordingly. You need to think carefully about which audience you are addressing and when.

Your data is never entirely private

It is essential to realise that any audience has the potential to also host an 'invisible audience'. 'Private' is never private when we are online; those with both legitimate (for example, law enforcement officials and technicians, both working under certain conditions) and illegitimate (for example, hackers) intentions can always access your data for different ends.

Pre-publishing and self-publishing

Most academic publishing has traditionally occurred via journals and mono-graphs, and involves editorial processes that present significant lag times between original submission and final 'print' publication. With the advent of social media, however, many scholars are now choosing to 'pre-publish' their work online in order to gather instant feedback and criticism on early drafts and ideas. Such a strategy is most effective if you want to test a controversial thesis or a novel conceptual framework or a new theory before you send some-thing off for formal peer review. You need to be prepared, though, for criti-cism from people who are not experts and who may not be qualified in your field. Nevertheless, it is often better to get feedback at the early stages of putting together a paper than it is after you've written an entire journal arti-cle and sent it off only to have it rejected outright.

Self-publishing, on the other hand, means simply that you avoid formal channels of academic distribution all together and instead disseminate your work via your blog, a wiki, a document-sharing site (such as Slide-share or Scribd), or other online or open-access service. You may choose to do this because you are disenchanted with traditional publication pro-cesses, or because you know you have a paper that is really terrific but which has had difficulty in getting recognised formally. With self-publishing there is also a very high possibility that your work will be seen by more people than if you rely on conventional publication methods, as your work will be easier to access and not obtainable only by paid subscription. Do note, however, that choosing to self-publish will almost certainly not count towards your research and publication output at your yearly performance review, and that any previously self-published papers may have to be removed from the internet if they later appear in a journal if you are to avoid a copyright breach.

One of the chief concerns voiced by people wanting to pre- or self-publish via their online profile is that people will steal their ideas. This is never an unjustified concern, but it is probably over-rated. Having others take your ideas and represent them as your own is not a new phenomenon, and even sending an article off for peer review is no guarantee that a reviewer won't appropriate your most interesting work and use it for themselves before it is published. Thankfully, such occurrences are rare because the academic com-munity generally believes in principles of honesty in scholarship.

In fact, putting your work online arguably gives you an advantage in this area, not least of all because if your material is date-stamped when you upload or post it then you have proof of precedence for your ideas. This allows you to assert your intellectual property early (although it doesn't prevent either you or others from 'backdating' their work, either, for fraudulent purposes).

Handling criticism

A final worry is that exposing your work and ideas through channels relating to your online profile leaves you open to criticism. It is important here to acknowledge that critique and criticism that act as assessment or analysis are essential parts of academic life: they help us develop and refine our ideas and bring us closer to the truth. However, it can no doubt be dispiriting when it seems that others are being unduly harsh, or even disapproving, in their comments. Sadly, not all reviewers (academic or otherwise) have the emotional intelligence to present their intellectual exasperations in ways that distinguish a person from their ideas. In such instances, the best you can do is to control your own reactions by differentiating between the relevant, useful, and legitimate, and the more disparaging and pejorative.

SUMMARY

- Traditional academic profiles tended to focus on the products of academic endeavours; digital academic profiles expose more of the depth and complexity of scholarly processes.
- An online presence means simply being online and interacting with others; having an online profile, on the other hand, means that you deliberately build a consistent, coherent identity through which you present your professional face to the world.
- Having an online profile provides benefits for visibility and searchability, public engagement, building networks, refining your ideas, posting your resumé online, and being able to take your profile with you.
- You should use social media tools strategically to build your online profile by presenting information about yourself, curating content, and developing content.
- A standalone online portfolio uses only one service or platform to present your professional profile information; a centralised portfolio integrates information and materials distributed across a number of different platforms or services that you then aggregate into one central place.
- It is essential that you have a strategy for building your online profile.
- Special considerations for building your online profile include reputation management, accounting for intended audiences, pre- and self-publishing, staking a claim to your ideas, and handling criticism.

FURTHER READING

Duh, K., Hirao, T., Kimura, A., Ishiguro, K., Iwata, T. and Yeung, C.M.A. (2012) *Creating Stories: Social Curation of Twitter Messages*, Sixth International AAAI Conference on Weblogs and Social Media, 4 June, Dublin, Ireland. Available at: http://www.aaai.org/ocs/index.php/ICWSM/ICWSM12/paper/view/4578. Accessed 10 September 2013.

Faktor, S. (2013) *The 10 Types of Twitterers and how to Tame their Tweets*. Available at: http://www.forbes.com/sites/stevefaktor/2013/01/04/the-10-types-of-twitterers-and-how-to-tame-their-tweets-twitter-users/. Accessed 10 September 2013.

Jones, T.D. and Swain, D.E. (2012) 'Managing your online professional identity', *Bulletin of the American Society for Information Science and Technology*, 38 (2): 29–31.

Marwick, A.E. and boyd, d. (2011) 'I tweet honestly, I tweet passionately: Twitter users, context collapse, and the imagined audience', *New Media & Society*, 13 (1): 114–33.

Mounce, R. (2013) 'Open access and altmetrics: Distinct but complementary', *Bulletin of the American Society for Information Science and Technology*, 39 (4): 14–17.

Pochoda, P. (2013) 'The big one: The epistemic system break in scholarly monograph publishing', *New Media & Society*, 15 (3): 359–78.

Zhong, C., Shah, S., Sundaravadivelan, K. and Sastry, N. (2013) *Sharing the Loves: Understanding the How and Why of Online Content Curation*. Available at: http://pub.geekonabicycle.co.uk/icwsm13.pdf. Accessed 10 September 2013.

8

Using Social Media for Search and Research

OVERVIEW

Chapter 8 shows how social media can be effectively harnessed for search and research and demonstrates how, with a little creativity, some quite useful resources can be discovered using social media tools and services. The chapter takes you through the various stages involved in both study and research before describing particular search techniques using hashtags, tags, and other people's bookmarks. Various other sources of useful links and information, including blogs, podcasts, Amazon, and even eBay, are also described. Social media for research are discussed particularly in relation to building networks of researchers in certain fields, and for accessing, producing, and sharing data. The chapter also covers the idea of 'mobile' study and research, which provides both students and researchers with opportunities to extend their learning and data-gathering outside of formal class or meeting times, before discussing successful engagement with social media for study and research. Finally special considerations relating to the finding and saving of relevant materials, as well as a discussion on how to manage habits and distractions, are presented.

WHY SEARCH AND RESEARCH WITH SOCIAL MEDIA?

Accessing information for study and gathering data for research are key – and manifestly related – components of scholarship. As a student, you begin in the 'study' zone of the scholastic enterprise where you chiefly look for materials that describe other people's thoughts, ideas, and findings. As you mature into a researcher, however, you start to generate your own topics for investigation, and, importantly, you develop ways to go about collecting data to support your investigations. Further, as a researcher, you build academic networks and communicate the results of your inquiries.

Social media can assist both activities – that is, study and research – to a large and useful extent. For example, rather than rely solely on journal articles and monographs for study materials, we can now search blog posts, tweets, and even others' online bookmarks or favourites to discover the latest thinking on or discoveries relating to a topic. In the realm of research, tools and services such as RSS and subscriptions (see Chapter 2), social networking services, and infographics can be used to find and manage the literature, collaborate in teams, and disseminate findings. Of course, research necessarily incorporates search, but the opposite does not apply. With this in mind, it should be noted that the current section separates search and research chiefly for simplicity's sake.

Benefits for search

If you have an understanding of the processes you go through when trying to find materials relating to a topic of study then you can start to figure out where social media fit in with your search objectives. Carol Kuhlthau's (1991) work is invaluable here, as she identifies six stages of the Information Search Process (ISP):

1. *Initiation*: You prepare to select a topic and start looking for and/or discussing possible approaches. You are aware that you lack understanding, and that there is a gap in your knowledge (similar to the 'conscious-incompetence' phase of the learning cycle described in Chapter 1).
2. *Selection*: You identify a topic for research and the approach to be taken, and you acknowledge the need for information.
3. *Exploration*: You start gathering (typically) rough information and orienting yourself to the topic, even though you haven't yet nailed the focus; you start investigating the topic, but are still unsure as to exactly what information needs collecting.
4. *Formulation*: You begin evaluating the information you've collected, leading to more focus; you start choosing ideas to work with and gain more clarity on the topic.
5. *Collection*: You collect more relevant and targetted information to support the focus of your search when you have a clear sense of topic. This is the most efficient data-/information-gathering stage as you have better direction to what you are doing.
6. *Presentation* (aka 'search closure'): You conduct summary searches because you are quicker to notice irrelevant and redundant material, and you identify more accurately the need for additional material. This is the stage at which you can start putting it all together for others.

Social media support these stages in different ways. For example, services such as Twitter are useful in the early phases of initiation, selection, and exploration where you are orienting yourself to a topic of study and starting to see what information is out there. At the other end of the search process, both collaboration and productivity tools are helpful in managing the formulation, collection, and presentation stages, whilst Google Scholar, and blogs, podcasts, and video are helpful throughout the entire search process (see Figure 8.1).

Precisely which social media platforms can be used for search – and how they can be used – are detailed in the next section. For now, however, it is enough to recognise the two chief advantages that searching with social media have over more established forms of search. Firstly, and quite simply, social media provide access to a greater variety of materials. Traditional forms of search (such as searching library catalogues, subject-specific databases, or indices of journal articles) limit search results to journal articles, monographs, and similar – of course, this can be an advantage when you are looking for peer-reviewed material. Searching with social media, on the other hand, throws up all manner of items: websites, reports, briefs, media releases, videos, blogs, images, graphs, audios, tweets, bookmarks, and so on, and often in the places where the latest findings are communicated first. Secondly, searching outside traditional catalogues moves you into the realm of 'folksonomy' as opposed to taxonomy. Taxonomic classificatory systems are based on predefined categories where similar items are grouped together according to a formal, hierarchical, expert-directed listing. Folksonomies, however, are user-generated and are commonly tag-based (see Chapter 2), meaning that the online community itself is responsible for classifying objects. This leads to a more quixotic, serendipitous (and often more 'human') kind of search in which the social meaning of an object or item comes to the fore. The upshot of this is that if you find a community of experts in a particular research field, you can search their collections to find relevant, specific, expert-filtered materials and you can easily monitor those materials for updates and changes.

That said, of course, there are advantages and disadvantages to both forms of search, as Table 8.1 makes plain.

Perhaps the most important thing to remember, here, is that search is not limited to library catalogues and the limits set for them. But neither is it limited to Google. You should have all possible tools in your search inventory.

Library databases are important because they have a huge depth and breadth of coverage of academic materials, meaning that anything you might find via such a database is almost guaranteed to be peer-reviewed.

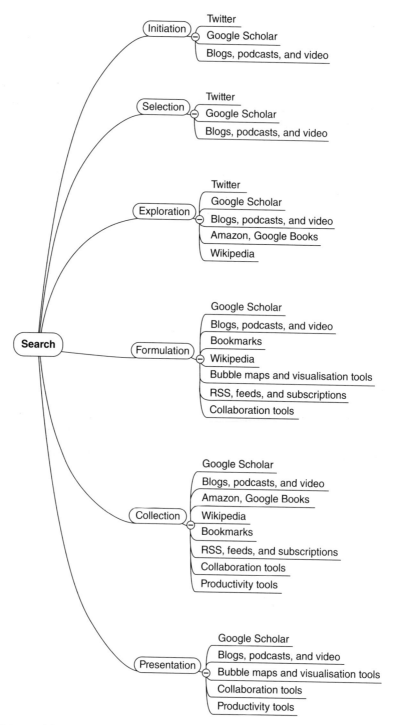

FIGURE 8.1   Kuhlthau's (1991) Information Search Process and social media tools that support it

TABLE 8.1 Advantages and disadvantages of traditional search and searching with social media

Form of search	Advantages	Disadvantages
Traditional search	• Depth • Peer-review • Quality • Fixed categories	• Fixed categories • Social meanings not embedded in search categories • Information may be out of date due to lengthy peer-review processes • Limited types of item are searched
Searching with social media	• Variety • Serendipitous links • Latest thinking • Good starting point • More 'human' search/links • Real-time results • Monitor topics for changes • Flexible • No time-lag for access to latest research • High user-relevance	• Lacks depth • Info overload • Materials not always suitable, not peer-reviewed/difficulty in cutting through the rubbish/need good critical media skills/varying in quality • Can lack efficiency at early stages of search process • Search terms change quickly • Need to find the right tag • More popular items filter to the top

Benefits for research

When we break it down, we find that much, if not most, of the research process is actually about communication: engaging with the findings of others, building research teams, choosing how to best present data, disseminating results – all involve complex communicative processes. Social media are themselves complex communication platforms and can thus be exploited in the research enterprise; in other words, social media and research are pretty much a perfect fit. Under scrutiny, then, research and social media can work together in the following ways:

1. *Finding and reviewing the literature.* As we saw in the previous section, social media provide different and more varied ways of finding the literature and current research on a topic. For example, reading blog posts or checking Twitter feeds and hashtags can be a useful way to encounter new ideas or the most recent developments in a field. Similarly, searching others' online bookmarks might unearth unusual articles, ideas, information, and other sources that get you thinking in different ways.

2. *Building and contributing to research teams.* Social media can be key to bringing researchers together, whether across continents or simply across cities. In the first place, social networking services help us to identify common research interests, find collaborators, and build research clusters. Further, tools such as shared mindmaps and wikis facilitate brainstorming, object sharing, and collaborative knowledge creation.

3. *Gathering data.* For many disciplines, social media allow for the quick collection and sharing of data, whether it be through the implementation, analysis, and distribution of

surveys, the observation of human behaviour or the conducting of focus groups or interviews, or the recording and sharing of fieldwork data via mobile uploads of figures, graphs, photographs, etc. Such data collection and distribution can be fast, large-scale, and occur in real-time.

4. *Analysing and presenting data.* There is a proliferation of social media tools dedicated to data analysis and presentation; importantly, many of these tools have some form of feedback or comment mechanism attached to them. All it takes is an internet search to find the tool that you need for mapping, diagramming, plotting, visualising, graphing, locating, and more. Of course, not all are free, and you may have to decide whether or not to spend some of your research budget on using them.

5. *Disseminating findings.* Formal research products are disseminated via the peer-review process; however, more and more researchers are using informal communication modes – such as blog posts, tweets, social network comments, etc. – to talk about their findings (see Chapter 7) or to tell people about their publications once they appear in a journal. This allows us to get in touch with new audiences, or at least to better reach the ones we are already aiming at.

6. *Managing the research process.* There are many social media tools that help us do the practical, background work required to make research happen. In particular, online meeting, scheduling, conferencing, collaboration, and authoring tools can bring researchers together to share ideas, discuss findings, and even write papers together. See Chapter 9 for more discussion.

7. *Building your research career.* This topic has been covered in detail in Chapter 7. For now, it should be simply noted that social media are essential for building your online profile in what is a highly competitive workforce environment.

Knowing how to use social media to support your research activities will be an 'academic survival tactic' into the future.

SOCIAL MEDIA TOOLS FOR SEARCH AND RESEARCH

So far we have discussed the general principles involved in search and research and how social media can support those principles. This section, however, explores specific social media tools and services and how their particular features might be harnessed in academic work (see Figure 8.2). Some of the information below may sound a bit technical or jargonistic; if so, I suggest you google unfamiliar terms, or, better yet, open an account with a relevant service and explore for yourself how things work.

- *Blogs.* Blogs are good places to find the latest thinking or information on a topic because bloggers often link out to useful materials, write reviews, or provide good summaries or critiques of debates, so you should take the time to find a few good blogs that you visit regularly (you can find blogs either by conducting a general internet search or by using Google's blog search). Once you have found a blog of interest, use the search box or tag cloud to search for relevant content. As a researcher, blogging provides an easy way for

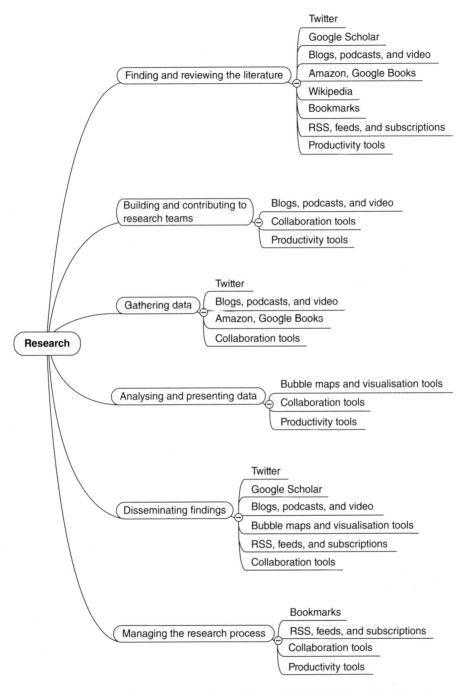

FIGURE 8.2   The research process and social media tools that support it

you to present your early thoughts, findings, and so on, and to get feedback on – and raise the profile of – your research.

- *Twitter*. Good Twitter users are exceptional sharers because they find and link to content and retweet material that is of interest and value to their community. You can use a Twitter manager such as TweetDeck or HootSuite to follow topics and people, to monitor conversations and content via hashtags and direct mentions, or to see what is 'trending'. For research purposes, you can tweet your latest ideas or findings, ask questions, ask for feedback, save and review interactions, engage in chat-style conversations, contact others with similar interests, gather data, find potential collaborators and/or colleagues, and generally raise your research profile.

- *Social bookmarks*. Exploring other people's bookmarks can be an excellent search technique. Social bookmarking gives you 'social' search results as opposed to a search engine's algorithmic ones, meaning that if you hit upon the right users and the right tags, you can find and follow some excellent people and topics because the users or community itself acts as a kind of filter for the most pertinent materials. On the research side of things, social bookmarking can help you with research management as you keep track of useful websites, group your bookmarks, take notes, highlight important points, create 'sticky notes', and generally keep things organised.

- *Bubble maps and visualisation tools*. Bubble or mindmaps help you discover, plot and show relationships between ideas and can be invaluable for presenting data, sharing your work, and getting feedback through comments, likes, or recommendations. Other visualisation tools include infographics, online slideshow and presentation software, image generation services, etc. – basically, any tool, site, or service that allows you to present your work visually.

- *Newsfeeds*. Subscribing to news or RSS feeds (see Chapter 2) allows you to get the latest information on a topic sent directly to your inbox, Facebook profile, or feed reader. You can monitor subjects or sources, set up alerts, group items according to topic, share feeds with others, use filters for more advanced searches, and 'star' or recommend items. As a search and monitoring strategy, such subscriptions can keep you abreast of the latest developments and thinking in a field.

- *Google Scholar*. By no means the only source for finding scholarly articles, Google Scholar is nevertheless useful in that it allows you to search by date and relevance (and to set search other limits) and to create alerts that go directly to your email inbox when a new item fitting your search parameters is published online. Google Scholar also displays related articles and gives a citation measure for each article. For authors and researchers, you can see who has cited your work and you can add your own citations to your Google Scholar Citations profile (see Chapter 7).

- *Wikipedia*. Although it is generally accepted in the academic community that Wikipedia shouldn't be cited as an academic, peer-reviewed source (see Chapter 4), it is nevertheless an excellent starting place for exploring issues or for finding (sometimes quite detailed) information on a topic that is new to you. Note, however, that Wikipedia has a strict policy of 'no original research', meaning that you cannot use the service for distributing your own findings or for building your online profile.

- *Amazon, Google Books, online library sharing*. Don't neglect commercial services such as Amazon and similar online retailers when searching for information. Users of these sites often contribute reviews and provide background information or history on a topic or 'product', which can help you get a sense of the issues. You can also manage your own collections, create your own libraries, find related items and, depending on the service you are using, share and even annotate your own items.

- *Collaboration tools.* Wikis, social networks, collaborative documents, and real-time collaborative tools such as chat, IM, and Skype are pretty much essential for the modern researcher. Not only can they be vital for building research teams and keeping people in touch with each other, they can also be used to solicit and receive feedback on your ideas or methods via comments and discussion forums, to build and publish wikipages on your area of research, to work collaboratively on article writing, and to share information and documents essential to your research project. These tools are also useful in the search process when you are looking for recommendations or advice from others regarding the literature.
- *Productivity tools.* Calendars, to-do lists, dropboxes, note and research management tools, etc., can be used to track study or research tasks, manage your study or research collections, access and share your own materials, and even to annotate the literature. Such tools can also be used to collect, analyse, and share data, to create graphs, and to build infographics, and to tag and sync items across your various digital devices and accounts. Chapter 9 discusses these tools in more detail.

As you can see, there are many and varied tools out there that can support your study and research. Find what suits your purposes: never be afraid to experiment to find new ways of doing things and never be afraid to either retain or discard practices and tools, as required.

USING MOBILE DEVICES FOR STUDY AND RESEARCH

Until now, we have focused solely on online tools services that can be used for study and research; however, certain *devices* – particularly 'mobile' devices – are also valuable additions to the scholarly, digital toolkit. These instruments can extend learning and research outside formal class or meeting times or be used to record ideas, to access information, and to gather and distribute data *in situ*, amongst other things.

Mobile phones

All mobile phones today – regardless of whether they are smartphones or 'dumb' phones – contain powerful learning and research tools in the form of data recording and playback functions. Most notable of these tools are the phone's camera and its audio and video recorders, all of which allow you to record data or notes 'in the field'.

Smartphone applications

Smartphones are basically hand-held computers that allow you to access the web as well as digital tools and services via various 'apps' or programs. In particular, you might want to consider installing productivity apps (see Chapter 9) that allow you to schedule events, meetings and tasks or that let you retrieve documents and files. Specialist guides based on your discipline area can also be useful, as can be dictionaries, grammar and punctuation guides, calculators, protractors, clocks, unit converters, stopwatches, compasses, maps, and atlases – in other words, anything relating to your field of studies or your research area. Apps that link you into various kinds of newsfeed (see Chapter 2) are essential if you need to access the latest information while you are on the go, and you should consider installing any app that is related to the online reference management systems you might be using (for example, Mendeley or Evernote, discussed in Chapter 9).

Tablet devices

That which applies for smartphone apps also generally applies for tablet devices: they are portable, versatile, and 'always on', making them perfect for accessing the internet regardless of location. Where tablets have an advantage over smartphones, however, is in their larger size, allowing you to more painlessly access files, download and read e-books and course texts, and to type up documents or lecture notes, much as you would on a laptop. Tablets mostly work on the principle of 'cloud computing', meaning that a lot of what you do on a tablet is stored not on the local drive of the device itself but on the internet (of course, some apps allow you to store files on the device, but you shouldn't assume this to be a default setting). This means that you can access your materials anywhere that you have a network connection; but it also means that tablets tend not to come supplied with USB ports, so you can't put your files on a 'stick' and use this method to transfer your work between computers or devices. Consequently, many tablets have limited storage and memory capacity so if, for example, you are doing a lot of audio or video recording and editing and need a more powerful computer, then you should invest in a laptop.

Laptops

Although tablets are becoming more and more popular as a portable device, laptops are still the computer of choice for many students as they will do everything that a normal computer will do and yet still be 'mobile'. They are also powerful enough to deal with large file types and sizes and can be easier to use than tablets if you are doing complicated project work that involves working with large amounts of data (whatever those data may look like).

Voice recorders

Although most of the above devices come with voice recording facilities these days (which can be great for taking short voice notes on the fly), you can nevertheless purchase dedicated voice-recording gadgets. Voice recorders usually have more file storage space than a smartphone and will allow you to record for longer. This can be useful if, for example, you need to record lengthy interviews or conversations with, say, research contributors, fellow students, or podcast participants, or if a friend asks you to record a lecture or seminar (which you would only do with the speaker's permission, of course!). If you intend to do a lot of voice recording then such a device will be invaluable, but remember, you get what you pay for: cheap recorders are often of poor quality.

Digital cameras

Video recordings and photographs can be used to document all manner of research- and study-related activity, from lab experiments to performances to field trials. As with voice recordings, if you intend to undertake a lot of this kind of thing – regardless of whether it is for study or research purposes – you should invest in a higher-quality instrument, and, of course, you should first gain people's permission and let them know how you will be using the images before hitting 'rec' on any image-capturing device. Failure to do so may place you in breach of your jurisdiction's privacy laws (see Chapter 12 for further discussion).

Mp3 players

An mp3 player of some description is pretty much essential for students these days. Most universities insist that academics record their lectures, making the audio available for download. This gives you the ability to listen to lectures again if you feel you missed something the first time around. Of course, mp3 players also allow you to listen to podcasts on topics relevant to your study or your research area and podcast directories such as iTunes U, iTunes, Podbean, and Podcast Directory (there are many others, just google them) allow you to subscribe to ongoing podcasts, meaning that you can listen to materials at times that suit you best.

SUCCESSFUL ENGAGEMENT WITH USING SOCIAL MEDIA FOR SEARCH AND RESEARCH

It is one thing to know what tools are out there and how they can support the various processes involved in study and research; it is quite another to use these tools to their full effect.

Go beyond basic search techniques

Many of us neglect to use the full range of options when it comes to searching for materials on the web. For instance, in the majority of disciplines it is important to refer to the most up-to-date publications in the area, so setting date ranges to give search returns from the past few years is a good idea. Moreover, most search engines – and not just those attached to formal library catalogues and databases – also allow you to use search operators to exclude certain terms or items, include similar words, search for an exact phrase, add 'wildcard' (that is, unknown or 'placeholder') terms, and find related pages.

Filters are also useful for helping you to find what you want. Search engines such as Google let you filter by content type (blog, image, file type), reading level (you might want to select 'advanced' under this field), location, and more. For other services, such as blogs or Twitter, you can easily filter material via the use of tags and hashtags.

Inside Google Search

Visit Google's 'Inside Search' pages to learn more about how Google Search works through techniques of crawling, indexing, and algorithms. Use this information not only to improve your search techniques, but also to find out how Google aggregates data relating to your online profile.

Set up alerts

Alert services such as RSS (see Chapter 2), Google Alerts, and Google Scholar Alerts can be used to monitor topics and to have notifications delivered straight to your inbox when new web-based materials are published on those topics. You can choose how often you wish to receive alerts, what types of content you want to be alerted to (for example, blog content, news items, videos, or discussions), and whether or not you wish to receive all results or just the most relevant. Social media management or 'dashboard' services such as TweetDeck and HootSuite also act as alert systems, allowing you to monitor hashtags, users, mentions, etc.

Use services that sync your content

The chances are that, once you start using social media for search and research, you will need to access your materials in different places and on different devices. This is fine if you are simply retrieving work that is hosted on a website, but many social media management services such as Evernote and Mendeley (see Chapter 9) have apps that you install on your mobile phone, desktop or tablet device and that make local copies of your items. This is where you need to make sure you synchronise your content so that all your materials are up-to-date and the same, no matter where and how you access them. You should therefore set any preferences or options so that things synchronise automatically and so that you can access them offline, if necessary.

Make social media central to your research communication

As a researcher you need to be taking full advantage of social media at every stage of the research process. This includes everything from finding new colleagues, building research teams, and developing proposals, to sharing discoveries, collaborating on documents, and publishing findings. It also means creating links with different audiences such as industry, the general public, the media, journalists, not-for-profit organisations, etc. Fundamental to all of this is a good working knowledge of what social media are out there and how they can support research communication. Consequently, you may need to build your digital literacy (see Chapter 10) or at least spend some time 'playing' with different tools and services to see how they work before you choose which ones will best suit your needs.

SPECIAL CONSIDERATIONS FOR USING SOCIAL MEDIA FOR SEARCH AND RESEARCH

Using social media for search and research often requires the transfer of old skills to new contexts. Being able to manage these new contexts is key to the success or otherwise you will have when using social media in academic environments.

Finding relevant and reliable materials

Being able to find good, useful, relevant materials can be a big challenge for students and researchers using social media as part of their scholarly enterprise. Firstly, there is the task of searching through the abundance of information on the internet to find items germane to your work. To manage this 'information overload' it is essential that you have a clear idea about your topic. You should also have a clear set of search terms and even some quite explicit research questions before you begin your search. If you log in and 'just go looking', your searches will remain vague and unfocused and you will waste time, especially if you start going down intellectual 'rabbit holes'. If you succeed in sourcing potentially relevant items, then the next problem comes through figuring out which items are trustworthy. You need to build your skills in identifying the source's authority, accuracy, reputation, currency, and affiliation, amongst other things. And as a complement to this, you also need to be able to analyse and interpret how messages are conveyed across a variety of media. This topic is covered in more detail in Chapter 10, which addresses building your digital literacy.

Managing distractions and habits

It's a common phenomenon: you sit at your computer and start work with the best of intentions but quickly end up hanging out on Facebook or watching cat videos on YouTube. In fact, just sitting in front of a computer can make us feel as if we're being productive, when, really, we are being distracted by email, instant messaging, texts, phone calls, and Twitter, all of which conspire to interrupt a clear run at a task. To manage distractions, you need to 1) examine why you get distracted, 2) understand the habit loop and implement a plan, and 3) be metacognitive.

The reasons you get distracted will vary, but for most people they can be traced to one or a combination of the following:

- Being disorganised
- Not having a clear idea about your task
- Lack of focus
- Inappropriate work environment.

All of these things can feed the 'habit loop', which consists of cue – routine – reward (Duhigg, 2012): a certain *cue* (such as having Facebook open on your desktop or on the homescreen of your device) can set off a *routine* (you log in to Facebook) that furnishes you with a *reward* to satisfy a *craving* (contact with friends). If, for example, your 'routine' is to be disorganised and unclear about what you will be doing today as regards your study or research, you may find yourself craving the reward of contact with friends and thus responding to the cue of the Facebook icon on your laptop before you know it. The trick is to develop and implement a plan that replaces one routine with a better, more productive routine and to adjust your rewards accordingly. Finally, you need to monitor your plan and your progress; this is where being 'metacognitive' – that is, thinking about your thinking – comes into it. If you know about your habits, you can monitor your thinking as regards them and regulate your behaviours as you need to. This might all seem like hard work, but understanding this process and implementing a plan to build and maintain good habits will pay much higher dividends than will a fuzzy commitment to 'try harder in future'.

 Activity   Understand your habit loops

Step 1 – Examine why you get distracted. What factors impact on your productivity? Being disorganised? Not having a clear idea about your task? Lack of focus? Inappropriate work environment? Too many interruptions? Not being able to get a 'straight run' at things? Having too many other things on the go? Having too many devices switched on?

Step 2 – Understand the habit loop. Read the appendix to Duhigg's (2012) *The Habit Loop.* You can find it online if you search 'How habits work Duhigg'. Follow his steps for changing habits:

1 Identify the routine. This is the behaviour you want to change. You also need to identify what rewards you get for sticking to this routine, and you need to identify the cue that sets the routine off.
2 Experiment with rewards. Change your routine so you get different rewards, ones that still give you what you need, but which help you change the behaviour you want to change.
3 Isolate the cue. What triggers or sets off the behaviour? Duhigg suggests you look at time, location, other people, your emotional state, and your preceding actions.
4 Have a plan and implement it. This means writing out – and sticking to – a new set of actions that help you change the habit.

Step 3 – Be metacognitive. Continually monitor your habits, behaviours, and actions. Throughout this process, you need to be continually aware of what 'cravings' your habits are satisfying and how they keep you stuck in a routine. Perhaps you are 'craving' being connected with others? Or you have a 'craving' for procrastination? Or for stimulation? For a break? A craving for distraction itself? Also monitor your cues. What sets all this off? Boredom? Lack of sleep? Too many distractions? Too much noise? And replace your rewards: instead of seeking the reward of a quick distraction, instead replace it with a reward or craving for achievement, or for success, or for sense of completion.

Ephemerality and archiving

Social media isn't forever. Despite the fact that once something is put into digital format it can potentially be replicated innumerable times, websites and bookmarks nevertheless disappear, pages are updated, blog posts are deleted, and threads expire. That said, Google's cache of the web allows us – in theory, at least – to access previous versions of webpages; but good luck remembering an expired URL or finding the exact cached link to what you need amongst the one million hits returned for your search. You need a way of archiving and accessing *for yourself* the material you need offline. For example, if being able to go back over a particular Twitter stream is central to your data collection, then you should use a Twitter archiving tool to help you save, organise, and access your materials offline. Alternatively, website copying software such as HTTrack for PC or SiteSucker for Mac will allow you to download html pages that can then be saved to a safe place on your hard drive that is itself backed up (see Chapter 2, but also see Chapter 12 for copyright considerations). In any case, you need to come up with ways of dealing with important, web-based materials that may disappear on you.

Controlling the impulse to find (and save) everything

One thing that many of us struggle with when it comes to being online is the feeling that we need to find *everything* on a topic before we can begin reading, writing, or whatever. We saw in Chapter 2 that perfectionism is not your friend in social media environments because it can quickly lead to your feeling overwhelmed. Remember: it is impossible to know, find, or read everything online that is related to your topic. Again, we come back to the point that you must set limits around your search and research topics. This may seem difficult in the early stages of initiation, selection, and exploration discussed earlier in the chapter, but the quicker you arrive at a clear sense of what it is that you are trying to do – *and the quicker you commit to it* – the more control you will have over your social media study and research activities. It can also be good to remember that sometimes we don't need to get too hung up on archiving and saving: be selective in what you choose to save 'for real' – the other stuff may only have been useful in getting you to a certain point in your thinking and understanding and it can thus probably safely go by the wayside.

Library catalogues and databases are still essential for search

Social media and online, commercial search engines won't provide everything you need to support your search endeavours. Library catalogues and databases are still the go-to places for finding peer-reviewed scholarly materials and thus provide quality, in-depth search results for both students and researchers.

SUMMARY

- Using social media for search provides both access to a variety of study and research materials and for serendipitous search results.
- Using social media for research benefits all stages of the research cycle, including engaging with the findings of others, building research teams, choosing how to best present data, and disseminating results.
- Social media tools that you can use for search and research include blogs, Twitter, social bookmarks, bubble maps and visualisation tools, news feeds, Google Scholar, Wikipedia, shared online libraries, and collaboration and productivity tools.
- Mobile devices extend learning and research outside formal class or meeting times and can be used to record ideas, to access information, and to gather and distribute data *in situ*.
- To engage successfully with social media for study and research you need to go beyond basic search, set up alerts, sync your content, and make social media central to your study and work practices.
- Special considerations for using social media for search and research include finding relevant and reliable materials, managing distractions and habits, ephemerality and archiving, and controlling the impulse to find (and save) everything.

FURTHER READING

Boase, J. (2013) 'Implications of software-based mobile media for social research', *Mobile Media & Communication*, 1 (1): 57–62.

Chretien, K.C., Azar, J. and Kind, T. (2011) 'Physicians on Twitter', *Journal of the American Medical Association*, 305: 566–8.

Duhigg, C. (2012) *The Power of Habit*. London: William Heinemann.

Gikas, J. and Grant, M.M. (2013) 'Mobile computing devices in higher education: Student perspectives on learning with cellphones, smartphones and social media', *The Internet and Higher Education*, 19: 10–17.

Kayam, O. and Hirsch, T. (2012) 'Using social media networks to conduct questionnaire-based research in social studies case study: Family language policy', *Journal of Sociological Research*, 3 (2): 57–67.

Kuhlthau, C.C. (1991) 'Inside the search process: Information seeking from the user's perspective', *Journal of the American Society for Information Science*, 42 (5): 361–71.

Pearce, N., Weller, M., Scanlon, E. and Kinsley, S. (2010) 'Digital scholarship considered: How new technologies could transform academic work', *In Education*, 16 (1): 33–44.

Rowlands, I., Nicholas, D., Russell, B., Canty, N. and Watkinson, A. (2011) 'Social media use in the research workflow', *Learned Publishing*, 24: 183–95.

Zimmer, M. (2010) '"But the data is already public": On the ethics of research in Facebook', *Ethics and Information Technology*, 12 (4): 313–25.

9

Productivity in Study and Research

OVERVIEW

The final chapter of this part of *Studying and Researching with Social Media* covers online productivity tools and techniques that can improve your skills for gathering, storing, retrieving, and managing information. Productivity tools such as folders, online documents, dropboxes, mind-mapping tools (for conceptualising and visualising the relationships between ideas), to-do lists, bookmarking, and calendars are covered, as are online services that specifically support note and research management. Perhaps more significantly, however, issues relating to time management, information management, staying motivated, and maintaining focus are discussed. Finally, this chapter offers a different way of thinking about productivity. It argues that sharing with others is a productivity measure because the quicker we get feedback from others on our ideas, the more quickly, effectively, and efficiently we can distribute the products of our work.

WHY USE PRODUCTIVITY TOOLS FOR STUDY AND RESEARCH?

We have seen so far how social media tools can support the more intellectual, conceptual and educational elements of your study and research endeavours, most simply because they allow you to find, create, and share things with others via the internet. But social media tools can also be used to improve your workflow and, thus, your productivity (they can also become time-traps, but this issue is addressed later on). Some of the benefits that accrue from using such tools can be explained by the very features of social media themselves (the two most significant being, perhaps, sharing and syncing), whilst others come through the activities they enable, such as the building of digital resource repositories.

Sharing and syncing

By now, you should understand the huge and important role that sharing plays – has always played – in scholarship and in the development of what we know about the world. Nevertheless, traditional notions of the monolithic learner and the isolated scholar still pervade many academic cultures, even though such notions have never really properly described either 1) how things *actually work* as regards study or research, or 2) sound academic practice. In the first instance, learning and scholarship have only ever advanced through the dissemination and critique of ideas and findings; and, in the second, we know that both learning and research for most people best happens when it happens in groups (see Chapter 1).

It might seem counter-intuitive that sharing with others could possibly be a productivity measure, but the reason I am spending a bit of time on setting up the above point is this: although as students and researchers we might think we prefer to work alone – without the hassle of other people – in fact, our work is diminished without ongoing interaction with and feedback from others. And as scholars, we seek to produce good work that is of value to the world. Such altruistic goals do not mean that we have to be always online or always in someone else's office or always at the coffee shop: of course, we all need quiet time to get some thinking, writing, or creating done. But once we've done the thinking, writing, or creating we need to expose our work to others; in fact, with social media, we can even share our processes with others as we go – we don't have to wait until we've got a 'draft'. The bottom line is that you can produce better papers, write better essays, and create better sculptures more quickly, effectively, and efficiently if you share your development processes with, and get feedback from, others. Social media aids this process infinitely. More obviously, perhaps, social media also helps improve productivity through sharing on more collaborative assignments, such as group writing, editing, project management, and similar tasks, and it is these such tasks that the remainder of the chapter will focus on. The purpose here, however, has been to stress the point that sharing – even as an individual scholar – is essential to scholarship, and that that scholarship can be conducted more productively through the common-sense use of social media.

> ## Getting feedback as a 'rejection management' strategy
> Having a paper rejected is a waste of time so you should always get feedback from colleagues on any paper you want to submit to a journal. The sooner you get feedback, the sooner you can incorporate it into your paper and the less chance there is of getting a rejection when you send the work off for publication. Use social media to get feedback as part of your rejection management – and thus, productivity – strategy.

Moving away from the more social aspects of the design of shared online architectures, a more mundane, technical feature of social media that supports productivity in study and research is the ability to 'sync' or 'synchronise' your materials across your various work appliances. Syncing ensures that the version of a file or object you are currently working on will be the same when you open it on another computer or device: it is a form of 'version control', if you will. It means that you can work in two or more locations and still have access to identical versions of your mail, contacts, documents, calendars, notes, bookmarks, lists, etc. It additionally means that you can dispense with a USB stick and also avoid the inelegant (and, these days, embarrassingly anachronistic) practice of emailing files to yourself so that you can collect them on another computer.

Services that offer synchronisation typically host your data – your notes, documents, photos, whatever – 'in the cloud' (generally speaking, on the internet) and allow you to download and install 'client' software that accesses your data and helps keep everything updated. Sync is such a powerful social media feature that, really, you should not be signing up for any file-hosting or -sharing service that does not offer sync functionality.

> Sync is king. Try to choose tools and services that have sync functionality.

Resource management

So far, we've focused on the technical and social architecture of social media and how they can enhance productivity in study and research, but a further benefit is described by the outcomes they support, chiefly, digital resource management. Being able to manage all the various 'stuff' you collect as a scholar is a major challenge in this age of information abundance. There are journal articles, images, bookmarks, calendars, email, documents, slideshows, websites, graphs, images, videos – all manner of resource that either informs or goes into your scholarly products. You need to be able to locate your materials quickly, so it is vital that you develop systems that help you do this if you want to avoid the digital equivalent of piles of journal articles strewn around the floor. There are many social media tools that help you save, organise, categorise, tag, archive, and retrieve exactly what it is that you are looking for, and the next section outlines some of the most useful, whether they be for group or individual projects, or for both.

SOCIAL MEDIA TOOLS FOR PRODUCTIVITY MANAGEMENT

'Productivity' tools need not be limited to Microsoft Word, PowerPoint, Outlook, and Excel, which usually come standard on your desktop, laptop, or university-supplied workstation: there are other tools that can help you do your work.

Dropboxes and folders

Online 'dropbox' services such as Dropbox and Box.net mimic 'traditional' office software folder systems in that they allow you to 'drop' files into folders – but the advantage with online folder systems is, of course, that 1) they sync your files across your devices so you can access them anywhere, and 2) you can share your files with others. You can keep your files and folders private or make them public.

Online documents

Some social media services allow you to write, store, share, and manage 'office' documents online, meaning that there is no need for you to have separate software installed on your computer; all you need to do is to get an account with a service such as Google Drive or Zoho.com and you can log in and access your documents from any internet-connected device. These services do more than simply store your files, however: they also allow you to create text documents, spreadsheets, and slideshows from scratch, much as you would if you were using Microsoft products. In addition, they will also convert other formats into their own: for example, if you create a document on your local hard drive in Word, you can upload it to Google Drive where it will be converted into Google Docs format (it also works the other way around). A further advantage comes with the ability to share and joint-edit documents, where you can track the contributions of others, leave comments about changes you have made, and even restore documents to a previous version (much as you can with a wiki – see Chapter 4), all of which is excellent for collaborative authoring and version control (syncing). As with many social media tools and services, you can control access to your files by either keeping them entirely private or by sharing them with selected others or by opening them up to the world.

What about Endnote?

Endnote was one of the first digital reference managers to gain popularity in the Academy. Although it organises your lists of references for you, it doesn't have quite the functionality that some other, newer reference management systems have. Some users describe it as old-fashioned or clunky and I have known more than one student to have lost entire lists of Endnote references just before they were about to submit their PhD thesis. That said, other users swear by it and wouldn't work without it. In keeping with most of the other advice in this book, I suggest you try out a number of different tools and services and find what suits you best. Search for 'reference management comparison' to find tables and charts that give you a run-down on the features of the various systems.

Calendars

Online calendars or diaries can be accessed anywhere, unlike paper or desktop-based calendars. Services such as Google Calendar allow you to add diary items, schedule things with others, invite people to meetings, create multiple calendars and colour-code them, and receive notifications of upcoming appointments, events, lectures, etc. Calendars can be shared, kept private or opened up to the public. This can be useful for team-based activities, as it means you can allow others to subscribe to your calendar or you can create a group calendar for managing projects. However, you do need to consider what level of information you provide; if you choose to let others see your calendar, then consider – for personal security reasons – displaying only a 'busy' message rather than the details of your schedule. Calendars can be added as an app to your mobile device and can be synced.

To-do lists

To-do lists can be kept on a piece of paper, of course, but they can also be kept on the internet – and it is much easier to remember where the internet 'is'. Online to-do lists span the spectrum from simple widgets (see Chapter 2) that you add to a service you already use (such as Google Docs or a calendar) to fully blown, fully featured time-management systems that host checklists, folders, and sub-folders, that set reminders and due dates, and that attach importance ratings and colour-codings to items and categories. Naturally, you can share your to-do list if you choose to, and you can sync your list across your devices; in fact, there are many, many mobile to-do apps available on the market – choose one that suits you best.

Reference managers

One of the chief things any scholar wants to do as regards their productivity is to organise all their study and research materials – most notably, PDFs of journal articles. Of course, you can keep files in a dropbox, as described above, but this is a fairly static reference management technique. Dedicated reference management services such as Zotero.org and Mendeley.com, on the other hand, allow you to

- Collect and store PDFs.
- Tag, annotate, highlight, and take notes on articles.
- Search your collection.
- Create bibliographies and reference lists.
- Generally organise your reading materials.

If you sync your collection across your devices you can build repositories of journal articles, websites, and useful references that you can access anywhere. Finally, you can share your collection if you wish and you can search others' collections (see Chapter 8) for materials related to your own interests and projects. Note that each service offers slightly different features, so you should explore and compare them carefully before settling on which one would suit you best.

Note managers

Sometimes, you just want a note manager that will 'do everything'. In this case, Evernote is probably your best bet. Unlike the reference managers just mentioned, which are largely targetted at an academic market, Evernote is aimed at a general audience and allows users to decide how they want to use the service. Evernote is based on 'notebooks' (fundamentally, a pseudo-folder system) within which you create notes. Notes are basic text documents but they also allow you to drop all manner of file into the note: PDFs, Word docs, PowerPoints, text files, images, videos, audios, etc. Moreover, you can search your notes – including the text of your PDFs, and even photographs of hand-written notes, if you have them. You can tag up your items, share them with others, and sync them across your devices so that you always have digital access to them.

Bookmarking

A simple way of keeping track of useful websites is through bookmarking or social bookmarks, as described in Chapter 8. Bookmarks allow you to collect, organise, share, and sync links to websites so that you can access them regardless of location (and as long as you have an internet connection, of course!). Some services allow you to take notes, edit, annotate, and highlight bookmarks and websites, or to just clip the most useful parts of a site and save it to your account. Again, you can tag up your materials and share what you want, depending on your privacy settings. You can also subscribe to different users' bookmarks or to tags, both of which can act as a form of search.

Online bookshelves

Online bookshelves help you create catalogues and collections of books – whether they be books you want to read, books you already own, or ebooks. Services such as Shelfari, LibraryThing, and Goodreads are available on the web, but there are also many, many library management apps available for mobile and tablet devices and through various app stores. Online bookshelves also have sharing and social elements to them: you can write reviews, share your collection, get recommendations, keep notes, build references lists and bibliographies, and search others' tags.

SUCCESSFUL ENGAGEMENT WITH PRODUCTIVITY TOOLS

To make the most of productivity tools, you need to do more than simply use tags, make to-do lists, and share calendars; rather, you need to consider how these tools can work together to form a structured, coherent, and effective workflow.

Share your ideas to get feedback and improve focus

As mentioned in the very first section of this chapter, sharing your ideas with others and getting feedback on those ideas is essential if your work is to develop quickly, effectively, and efficiently. Sharing ideas through the standard academic feedback loop usually involves writing and sending a draft paper to someone else and waiting for them to read it and to get back to you – a process that can take some time. Social media, however, expand the formats for sharing to include images, tweets, soundbites, videos, discussion forums, libraries, notes, data, websites, digital sketches, etc. And with this expansion in formats comes also the potential for an expansion in audience. Extending your sharing repertoire in such ways can be especially useful for eliciting feedback at the nascent stages of a study or research undertaking as you receive comments and suggestions that help you sort out the good ideas from the bad. The point is this: sharing ideas and materials and getting feedback on them improves your focus, which, in turn, increases your productivity.

Choosing the right tool for the job

As with any social media tool or service, you need to choose the right one for the task at hand. To this end, you need to be very clear about what a particular tool is used for and how you expect it to support your work. For example, a research team might choose to use a Google Doc for collaborative writing, but a wiki for building a resource repository or recording the minutes of meetings. In any case, you must take time to explore a variety of tools and how they work before settling on the ones that best suit your purposes. If something better comes along, then you can always switch, but only do this if switching has clear benefits and can be undertaken fairly easily.

If you are stuck in the belief that spending time on the internet checking out different apps is a frivolous activity undertaken only by geeks and teenagers, then try thinking of it as professional development (PD). PD does not have to involve sitting around a piece of butcher's paper with some super-chunky textas (marker pens) and a handful of strangers. If you want to be mercenary about it, then understand that knowing about social media is important for your career: it makes you far more employable than the person who can only describe the depth of their academic engagement as being limited to presenting at departmental seminars. Getting to understand social media and how it can support your work is legitimate, professional activity.

Choosing the right tool for you

Choosing the right tool for the job is only half the problem: you also need to choose the right tool for *you*. There are so many productivity tools out there that you can quickly become overwhelmed by the choice; in this situation, the maxim 'know thyself' is particularly appropriate: take some time to examine not only your productivity needs, but also your work habits and tendencies, and ask yourself which ones you want to preserve and which you could safely dispense with. Use this information to make sure that the productivity tools you choose don't only give you the functionality you think you need, but also support the way you want to work.

Put some thought into your systems and workflow

Productivity is usually enhanced when you are organised and when things are systematised in some way – that is, when you have some kind of 'workflow'. But getting the balance right between being organised and being flexible is not always easy – whether it be in virtual or real-life environments! We saw in Chapter 2 that perfectionism is not a helpful quality when it comes to using social media for study and research; but neither is carelessness. And although it can be good just to 'jump in' and start playing around with a new tool to see how it works, eventually you will need to take a bit of time to figure out how, exactly, you will use that tool to organise yourself online. For example, you might find that you really need a to-do list to get you through the academic day – so, how should that list work alongside your calendar? And should you set your list up on your phone? Or would that be more of a distraction than anything else? Would it be best to add it to Facebook, or, again, would that just prove distracting? Or perhaps you want to use a reference management system to keep track of articles you need for your literature review: Will the service you are using allow you to take notes or to highlight PDFs? If so, is the functionality adequate or do you need to find an add-on that allows you to quickly and easily annotate documents? Can you set up a feed so that the latest articles on a topic are sent straight to your reference manager as soon as they are published online? Or will an email notification via Google Alerts (see Chapter 8) fit better with your workflow? It's OK to 'just start' as part of exploring a new productivity tool, but, eventually, you will need to make considered choices about how these tools work together as a way of keeping you working effectively and efficiently. Thus, it is also a good idea to centralise your productivity efforts as much as possible.

Use break-scheduling software to give you regular 'time-outs' from computer work. Such software will 'lock' your computer for a certain period (which you specify) so that you have an enforced break, during which you can get up from your chair, stretch, walk around, etc. Search 'computer rest break programs'.

Shift to cloud-based tools

Storing things 'in the cloud' means that you can access them anywhere you have an internet connection; in other words, you don't need to be sitting at the same machine on which you created an item in order to access that item. If you are currently using tools (such as Word or an email program) that are solely hosted on your local computer, then consider shifting them to cloud-based tools or services. Even better, shift to cloud-based tools that allow you to download or install client software.

What is client software?

Client software is simply software that you install on your local device and that accesses your data on the internet to keep everything synchronised and updated, regardless of which device you are using – as long as you have the client installed.

Why should I install client software?

Client software can access and display data quicker than if you were working straight off the internet and is specially developed to display and work well on your device's operating system.

So, even if you are supplied with a university-based email program, consider getting all your mail forwarded to a single account, for example, your Gmail, Yahoo, or Hotmail account, and then accessing your email there and not on your work machine. Similarly, start to wean yourself off Word and begin to write documents in Google Drive or Zoho Docs or Scrivener – or at least know when to use one over the other. For example, for larger projects, such as writing a book or thesis, you might want to stick with Word – it is still one of the most powerful word-processing tools available and the chances are that you are familiar and comfortable with using it. But for smaller works, such as journal articles or essays, or for collaborative writing projects, you might want to switch to a cloud-based solution.

 Activity How are you spending your time?

It's one thing to *think* you know how you spend your time, and another thing to know for certain. If you are always feeling overwhelmed by everything you have to do, then you need to figure out how you are using your time. And even though it might seem, in this

(Continued)

(Continued)

situation, that you have better or more important things to do, you don't. You must prioritise this activity if you are to improve your productivity and feel better about what you have achieved by the end of the working day.

Step 1 – Record how you spend your time. Take an activity log for a week in which you record what you do for each and every half hour of the day. Make sure your log is as detailed as it needs to be; for example, don't just write, 'Made handout' if in one half hour you also wrote emails, sent texts and made a cup of tea. Instead, write, 'Made handout for class; made cuppa; finished work emails; emailed Upul; texted Fiona'.

Step 2 – Analyse how you spend your time. You might be surprised by where, exactly, your time is going. On the above example, making a handout and a cup of tea, and attending to work emails are probably legitimate work-hour activities. Emailing Upul and texting Fiona are OK if they're limited, but if a pattern emerges where you are in contact with your friends for a lot of the day, then the chances are that you are not being as productive as you could be.

Step 3 – Analyse your digital activity. You need to do a number of things to figure out what your digital activity actually consists of.

- Look at your web or browser history. What sites do you visit? (Categorise your site visits: work, play, social, friends, research, study materials, banking, admin, entertainment, etc.) How often do you visit these sites? How long do you spend on them? What other pages are you visiting whilst you are there? What links are you following?
- Figure out how much time you spend using different programs or apps. Include email, IM, Facebook, Twitter, Google, YouTube, writing, reading, mobile phone – anything to do with your digital activity. Programs such as Toggl, SlimTimer, and RescueTime track your internet and app use (search 'internet time logging apps' or 'web based time tracking tools' or similar) and can generate reports relating to your online usage. How often do you use particular programs? How long do you spend on them? What other apps are you using at the same time?
- Place a 'productivity value' (high, medium or low) on the website or on the activity to help you figure out where you should be spending more time and where you should be spending less time.

Step 4 – Make a plan and implement changes. Once you have the data above, begin to re-schedule your activities so that they better support the productivity outcomes you want. Refer to the exercise on the 'habit loop' in the previous chapter to help you make positive changes not only to your behaviour but also to your daily work activities.

SPECIAL CONSIDERATIONS FOR PRODUCTIVITY TOOLS

Although productivity tools can save time – when used well – they can also, ironically, become 'time traps' themselves. The normal rules of good information and time management must still be applied.

Information management issues

There is no doubt that using productivity tools to manage your materials and workflow can lead to information overload. As we saw in Chapter 2, you can easily feel overwhelmed by all the 'stuff' that is out there and, if you have bit of a perfectionistic streak, you may even delay making a start on a project until you have 'everything' on a topic. You thus need some method of attaching value to or filtering the information you gather before you begin. Using some kind of rating or ranking system can get you off to a good start: for example, use a three-star or three-level system to classify the importance or usefulness of things as being either 'high', 'moderate', or 'negligible'. Applying tags to saved or recorded items is also essential to any information management strategy you might develop – make sure you do this as you go.

Staying motivated: 'Just do 5'

Experiencing difficulty in motivation is not, of course, unique to working online. So here is my best tip both for getting things done and for staying motivated. It's simple: 'Just do 5'. Whenever you 'don't feel like' doing something and you know that procrastination is not too far away, then 'Just do 5': just read five pages, just find five articles, just contact five people, just write five lines (or paragraphs, or sentences, or whatever). Similarly, if you 'don't feel like' doing any exercise but you know that you should because it will keep you fit and thus able to work more effectively, then just swim five laps, just run for five minutes, just walk five blocks, just ride five kilometres. The point is this: once you 'Just do 5' you tend not to stop. How, exactly, this works, I'm not sure, but I suspect it can be explained in either of two ways: either you 'Just do 5' and you find out it wasn't so bad after all and so you keep on going or you 'Just do 5' and it was such a hassle to get going that it's not worth stopping now! Regardless, the technique seems to work.

Scheduling activities for your 'smart time'

Despite the fact that the working day is '9 to 5', most of us cannot work at full throttle for eight hours straight. In fact, you probably only have, on average, four hours or so of 'smart time' in you – and that includes regular breaks. 'Smart time' is what I call the period in which you are working at your intellectual and cognitive best; 'dumb time' (for want of a better term) is the period in which your brain is still 'switched on', but not quite as receptive to higher-order thinking activities. You, yourself, know when your best time of day is: are you a morning person ready to start at 7 am? Or do you take a while to wake up and get oriented to the day and so you're not really ready

161

until noon? Perhaps you are an evening person and prefer to work late into the night when things are quiet and there are no distractions. Regardless of your preferred pattern, it is crucial that you schedule the most difficult intellectual exercises for the four or so hours in the day of 'smart time', when you are really firing; this includes tasks such as reading, planning a paper, writing, or working out a line of reasoning. This, however, doesn't mean that you need only do four hours of work a day! There are plenty of other things you can be doing in your 'dumb time', such as searching for journal articles, compiling bibliographies, writing up and double-checking your list of references, contacting research participants, cleaning test tubes, setting up and streamlining your use of productivity tools … . In other words, all the fiddly, boring – but necessary – chores that go into the successful execution of your study and research. If you can get five hours of hard, intellectual work done in a day, then you are doing exceptionally well. Again, the advice here is not specific to working online, but it should certainly inform how you use social media in your study and research.

Keeping it real

If you see people around you working 14 hours a day and you marvel at their application, diligence, and industry, then marvel no more. Only about a third of their work time is likely to be intellectually profitable and another third only moderately profitable. The final third would probably have been most profitably spent getting some exercise, devoting themselves to their family, making a nutritious meal, or volunteering at the local animal shelter – in other words, taking time nurturing interests, activities, and relationships outside of work or study that help maintain life balance and thus feed back into more effective work and study patterns overall.

Avoiding online distractions

You probably know that you are only ever one or two clicks away from a major time vacuum: websites, applications, Facebook, instant messaging, texting, and email all take us down rabbit holes we know we should avoid. Thankfully, there are ways for you to manage the technology before it manages you:

- Log out of your accounts. This includes Facebook, Twitter, email, and similar.
- Close tabs in your browser. Keep open only tabs to those websites essential to your current activities.
- Close down applications you aren't using. As well as removing a potential distraction, this will also improve your computer speed.

- Don't open a website unless you have to.
- Turn off 'push' notifications.
- Work offline for set periods. Turn off your internet connection temporarily if it helps.
- Group similar activities together and handle them all at once.
- Find and install software that prevents you from accessing a website for a set period of time.
- Watch for self-sabotaging behaviours. None of the above is any good if you deliberately find ways to get around the distraction-avoidance techniques you put in place for yourself!

Of course, productivity tools themselves can be a major source of distraction: you need to integrate them into your workflow rather than see them as exciting, 'cool' things to play with. If a tool does not completely support you in improving your productivity, then don't use it.

Sharing location information

Be wary of sharing location information, both your own and others'. Having a group calendar, for example, can be a great way to schedule meetings and to check people's availability – but it can also present a security risk because telling people that you will be in a meeting is the same as telling them that you will *not* be in your office or at home – which could be the same as telling them that they can rob you. Also be careful that you don't compromise the security of others by giving away *their* location information. For example, never tweet or put on Facebook a message such as, 'At Café Innimmitabel with Anton Andronikidis' – and especially don't do it with the addition of links to personal names or with a dropped 'pin' on a map! By the same token, recognise that others might give away your own location information – either unwittingly or simply without thinking through the implications.

Set your public calendars to 'busy'

Never put specific information about your meetings or movements into a public calendar. *Always* set such calendars to 'Show only busy information' or similar.

SUMMARY

- Sharing with others is a productivity measure because you can produce better work more quickly, effectively, and efficiently if you share your development processes with, and get feedback from, others via social media.
- Social media tools can be used to improve your workflow via sharing and syncing, resource management, and to help you save, organise, categorise, tag, archive, and retrieve information and materials.

- Productivity tools include dropboxes and online folder systems, online documents, calendars, to-do lists, reference and note managers, bookmarking systems, and online bookshelves.
- Successful engagement with productivity tools for study and research includes sharing your ideas to get feedback and improve focus, choosing the right tool for the job and for you, putting some thought into your systems and workflow, and shifting to cloud-based tools.
- Special considerations for using productivity tools for study and research include information management issues, motivation, scheduling activities for your 'smart time', avoiding online distractions, and not sharing location information.

FURTHER READING

Bentley, P.J. and Kyvik, S. (2013) 'Individual differences in faculty research time allocations across 13 countries', *Research in Higher Education*, 54 (3): 329–48.

Dennison, G.M. (2012) 'Faculty workload: An analytical approach', *Innovative Higher Education*, 37 (4): 297–305.

Hrastinski, S. and Aghaee, N.M. (2012) 'How are campus students using social media to support their studies? An explorative interview study', *Education and Information Technologies*, 17 (4): 451–64.

Quimbo, M.A.T. and Sulabo, E.C. (2013) 'Research productivity and its policy implications in higher education institutions', *Studies in Higher Education*, August: 1–17.

IV

The Social and Legal Contexts of Using Social Media for Study and Research

The final part of *Studying and Researching with Social Media* deals with three of the chief issues raised by using social media – in any context. Chapter 10 explores the various elements of digital literacy and includes a discussion of the factors impacting on your digital literacy. Chapter 11 deals with the sometimes tricky issue of online communication and in particular encourages you to develop an ethical communication framework that will help you handle both yourself and others online, especially if you find yourself involved in instances of cyberbullying or cyberaggression. The final chapter (Chapter 12) examines the legalities and practicalities of the online environment, in particular focusing on what it means when you sign up for a Terms of Service, on legal and quasi-legal issues, on issues relating to general use, and on issues for assessment.

10

Building your Digital Literacy

OVERVIEW

This chapter describes the three 'tiers' of digital literacy. Firstly, functional digital literacy, which, in the age of social media, doesn't mean knowing how to write code, or how to program, or how to write javascript; instead, it means knowing how to sign up for a service and what happens after that; it means knowing how to find and add and invite friends; it means knowing how to upload a profile photo, and so forth. Secondly, network digital literacy, which refers to understanding what it means to be a networked citizen. That means knowing how to manage your profiles and identities online; knowing what happens to the material you upload; knowing about data management, etc. Arguably, this is the most ignored of the three components of digital literacy, but it is a component that is covered in depth in this and other chapters. And finally, critical digital literacy, which is about how to find, validate, interpret, communicate, analyse, critique, evaluate, synthesise, and transform information and how to then use skills learnt in this area for informed online participation. But before looking at these three tiers of digital literacy, it is important to understand the current historical and technological moment in which we find ourselves. And to do that, we must explore the nature of revolutions.

THE DIGITAL REVOLUTION

It would be neglectful to embark on a discussion of digital literacy without first examining some of the historical processes that have deposited us at this point in time, that is, at a time when digital technologies are forcing us to question what we know and how we know it. The point, here, is that we need to understand the history and complexity of our current situation – and the uncommonness of the current historical moment – if we are to understand how vitally important it is to be a digitally literate person in the modern world. It may also help explain various attitudes or feelings about new technologies (both your own and other people's), whether they be characterised by a sense of discomfort or trepidation or by an acritical embrace of all that is new and shiny.

Technological revolutions

Revolutions are about shifts in consciousness. They can be recognised when a sudden break occurs in *what we think and what we think about*, which in turn changes how we understand the world and ourselves. Revolutions thus transform the social, political, cultural, and economic structures that affect our everyday lives. A technological revolution is characterised by all these things but finds its expression in dramatic transformations in the tools (products) and techniques (processes) – that is, in the technologies, for technology is a combination of product and process – we use to structure our systems of production, our society and civilisation, and our social and political relations.

The notion, then, that we are experiencing a 'Digital' or 'Knowledge' or 'Information' Revolution is not just a media beat-up or an example of evangelistic hyperbole: it is an identifiable, historically precedented circumstance. The Agricultural Revolution, which occurred around 10,000 years ago, is perhaps the earliest example we can cite of such a revolution. It was characterised, of course, by tools and techniques that aided the domestication of animals and the cultivation of crops, and by notions of sedentarism and boundedness. The subsequent Industrial Revolution of the late eighteenth century introduced technologies of machinery (tools) and manufacturing (processes), which supported operations of mass production and ideas about different forms of social and economic order – in particular capitalism and socialism. It also saw the opening up of markets, the development of commodities, and changes in the concept of labour. Both revolutions saw shifts in consciousness at the societal level. So, too, is it with the impact that digital technology is having on our current ways of thinking and current ways of doing things – again, because our social conditions structure, and are structured by, influence, and are influenced by, technological developments (Shaw, 2008: 2–3). As previously stated, how we think and what we think about is changing – this time thanks to the emergence of digital computing and the internet, to the proliferation of new modes of communication, and to an almost limitless access to data and information. Digital technologies are thus extending our world beyond the scarcity that distinguishes the analogue and the physical, and beyond the world of atoms, into the world of 'bytes' where there is the potential for infinite durability, replicability, and abundance of goods and ideas, and for the creation of different forms of sociality.

> The dialectical relationship between humans and technology can perhaps be most clearly seen in the invention of the printing press. As Neil Postman famously pointed out in his book *Technopoly*, 'A new technology does not add or subtract something. It changes everything. In the year 1500, fifty years after the printing press was invented, we did not have old Europe plus the printing press. We had a different Europe' (1993: 18).

Old practices and new technologies

If you can grasp not just the practical impact that digital technologies are having on our lives but also the impact that these technologies are having on our ways of thinking, then you can appreciate why old, industrial-style approaches to study and research do not serve us well in the digital or knowledge era.

Industrial-model study and research practices were developed in the nineteenth century and have changed little since then. They are characterised by inflexibility, passivity, one-to-many communication, the notion of the 'monolithic' learner or researcher, competition, memorisation, and separation (Churches, n.d.). These practices (which you may notice in your own study and research experiences) emphasise standardisation, homogeneity, uniformity, structure, regimentation, and sequencing, which, in turn, reinforce industrial-style systems based on mass production and continuous flow. In other words, such operations sustain people as useful contributors to industry-based economies but come at the expense of creativity, collaboration, fluidity, distribution, participation, interactivity, networking, customisation, and all those things that we know support effective, socially constructivist communication (see Chapter 1). At this point, it is important to recognise the crucial part that industrial practices have played in improving standards of living, providing better health care, increasing life expectancy, ensuring a regulated juridical environment, and building a literate and educated populace. Nonetheless, we are seeing dramatic societal and social shifts in which digital technologies are taking a central role. This means that the skills an individual needs to succeed in a knowledge society are very different from those needed to succeed in an industrial one, leading us to interrogate what it means to be knowledgeable in the twenty-first century and how technology can support that (Yelland, 2007: 23). The skills you need today are those for discovering, accessing, evaluating, applying, and creating new knowledge;

skills for fostering community, demanding critique, encouraging collaboration, inspiring experimentation, and stimulating creativity; skills for learning
how to learn. All of this means that you need to be digitally literate.

> David Loader, in *Jousting for the New Generation*, states simply that '[t]he capacity to learn
> something new has become more critical than knowing what is currently known' (2007: 13).
> Unless we become experts at learning how to learn, and learning how to learn new things,
> we risk becoming disenfranchised from participating in important aspects of modern social,
> cultural, and economic life.

WHAT IS DIGITAL LITERACY?

So we find ourselves at a revolutionary moment in history when society and
culture are in flux – a moment encountered in the unique products and processes of digital technology. The concurrent shifts in consciousness we are
experiencing mean that we need new ways of understanding – of 'reading' –
our conditions, that is, ways that help us make sense of the world, that help
us draw meaning from it, and that prepare us to participate fully and ethically in the new environment.

Forms of literacy

Traditionally, the idea of literacy has described the ability to read and write.
In recent years, however, the notion of literacy has expanded: as Julia Davies
asserts, '[l]iteracy is not just about decoding marks on a page; it is also about
performing social acts of meaning, where meanings and practices vary
according to context' (2009: 29). It thus now becomes possible to talk about

- Visual literacy: understanding and interpreting images and graphical symbols.
- Financial literacy: understanding how money works.
- Scientific literacy: understanding and applying scientific concepts and procedures.
- Emotional literacy: understanding and explaining people's feelings and reactions.
- Cultural literacy: understanding and participating in sociocultural practices.
- Information literacy: understanding and evaluating what, how, and when to use information.
- ICT (information and communications technology) literacy: understanding and using
  digital tools and devices.
- Media literacy or new media literacy: understanding and critiquing how media producers
  (whether from the mass media or from popular culture) use media to influence socio-
  cultural processes.

'Digital literacy' is one of these new forms of literacy.

So, what makes you digitally literate? As we saw in Chapter 1 in relation to the 'digital natives' debates, just because you may have grown up surrounded by digital technologies it doesn't mean that you automatically know how to engage usefully with them; similarly, if you grew up in a more analogue world, it doesn't automatically mean that you are a lost cause to digital literacy efforts. There is nothing innate about any form of literacy: just as we must learn to read and write – and to read and write well – so, too, must we learn how to meaningfully engage with and usefully apply digital technologies to our everyday lives. This means firstly figuring out what constitutes digital literacy.

Definitions of digital literacy

Numerous definitions of digital literacy exist, but almost all agree that being digitally literate means more than knowing simply how to use a mouse to point and click. Hague and Williamson state that digital literacy means 'knowing how technology and media affect the ways in which we go about finding things out, communicating with one another, and gaining knowledge and understanding' (2009: 5). This includes the ability to find, select, organise, process, review, and make judgements about information; the ability to create, and share new products (2009: 8–9).

> Success today depends more on declarative knowledge than it does on procedural knowledge. In other words, it's more important to know *that* you can do something, than it is to remember the steps for *how* to do it.

Similar features are listed by MCEECDYA (Australia's Ministerial Council for Education, Early Childhood Development and Youth Affairs) in their detailed reports of young people's digital literacy levels. In particular, MCEECDYA defines 'ICT' literacy as 'the ability of individuals to use ICT appropriately to access, manage, integrate and evaluate information, develop new understandings, and communicate with others in order to participate effectively in society' (2010: viii). This is characterised by knowing how to

1. Access information through appropriate identification and retrieval methods.
2. Manage, organise, and store information.
3. Evaluate information for its integrity, relevance, and usefulness.

4. Develop new understandings by creating knowledge and authoring new products.
5. Communicate and share with others.
6. Use ICT appropriately, that is, critically, reflectively, strategically, ethically, and legally (MCEECDYA, 2010: 7).

Hague and Payton are perhaps the most successful in defining digital literacy in that they draw together the social, critical, and functional elements of these definitions. They describe digital literacy as

> the ability to make, represent and share meaning in different modes and formats; to create, collaborate and communicate effectively; and to understand how and when digital technologies can best be used to support these processes. Digital literacy involves critically engaging with technology and developing a social awareness of how a number of factors, including commercial agendas and cultural understandings, can shape the ways in which technology is used to convey information and meaning. (2010: 4)

Useful and insightful as these definitions are, they nevertheless all tend to focus on the procedural (that is, functional, the 'how to') and conditional (that is, critical, the 'when') elements of digital literacy. These elements are, of course, essential to any understanding of digital literacy, but they neglect a third element, that is, the declarative, or the 'what' (or, even, 'that') element, that is, you know 'what' you need to do or 'that' you need to do it. In particular, such definitions fail to incorporate an understanding of what being a 'networked citizen' involves in this digital age, especially in terms of knowing what happens to your data once it goes online. To make this all a little clearer, let me propose that digital literacy can be broken down into three literacy 'strata':

1. *Functional digital literacy – knowing **how** to do things.* In the early days of computers and programming, being functionally literate in the use of digital tools meant knowing how to write code, how to develop software, how to use html or javascript. Today, however, all of this hard work happens in the background of whatever social media site or service you are using; in other words, it's done for you. When you think about it, this is a pretty amazing technological achievement and it basically came about because people saw the huge potential of the internet as a communication tool and they wanted to 'democratise' it by allowing anyone to use it without the need for special 'techie' knowledge. From a practical standpoint, then, being functionally digitally literate today means that you know how to sign up for a service and how to activate your account; how to find, add, and invite friends; how to upload photos, how to change your profile information; and how and where to log in and sign out.

2. *Network digital literacy – knowing **what** the implications are of being online.* Knowing what it means to be a 'networked citizen' is crucial to anyone who claims to be digitally literate. It requires understanding what happens to your data once it gets uploaded and how to manage that data, how to negotiate your various online profiles and identities, how to manage your online risk, and how to read and interpret Terms of Service and Privacy Policies. boyd [sic] helps us think about our online data by identifying four properties of networked publics. They are (1) persistence: what you put online will stay there forever because it is automatically cached and archived, (2) replicability: what you put online can be infinitely reproduced because there are no material limits on digitally expressed bits and bytes as there are on physically bound atoms, (3) scalability: what you put online is potentially visible to anyone, (4) searchability: what you put online can be searched for and accessed (boyd, 2011: 46). Possessing network digital literacy means you can answer the question, 'Do you know what it means when a service asks for a transferable, worldwide, royalty-free, sub-licensable licence to any of the intellectual property that you post on or in connection with the service?' Most people probably cannot answer questions such as these and therefore cannot properly appreciate their implications. This chapter, and the final chapter, will help you understand such issues.

3. *Critical digital literacy – knowing **when and why** we should use digital technologies.* Knowing how to access and find information in digital form is not enough to be called digitally literate: you must also know how to validate, interpret, evaluate, communicate, analyse, critique, synthesise, and transform information so that new meanings can be created from old ones. Of course, being able to use such high-order skills to further cognition is not unique to digital environments; indeed, such skills are central to the kinds of thinking demanded of anyone involved in a higher education enterprise. What is different, however, is knowing under what conditions we should use digital technologies and social media to engage with social, cultural, political, and intellectual life in a networked world. It also means understanding the influencing factors that impact how we create, build, and distribute knowledge in online environments.

Understanding the functional, networked, and critical strata that comprise digital elements that make up digital literacy helps us work towards systematically building our skills in this area.

 Activity   How digitally literate are you?

Complete the three following questionnaires (in Tables 10.1, 10.2, and 10.3) and rate yourself according to the 'conscious competence' (see Chapter 1) scale given for each questionnaire. The scale works like this:

(Continued)

(Continued)

1 **No idea at all:** 'I don't know what I don't know'. This means that you probably don't even understand what the activity in the list refers to. Give yourself 1 point for each answer. A total of less than 12 on any of the questionnaires indicates that you are in the unconscious incompetence category for that type of digital literacy.

2 **Not competent:** 'I know what I don't know'. This means that you explicitly realise that there are things you don't know about online. Give yourself 2 points for each answer. A total between 12 and 24 on any of the questionnaires indicates that you are in the conscious incompetence category for that type of digital literacy.

3 **Competent:** 'I can do it but need to think about it'. This equates to conscious competence and means that you can complete the activity at a reliable level. Give yourself 3 points for each answer. A total of between 24 and 36 on any of the questionnaires indicates that you are in the conscious competence category for that type of digital literacy.

4 **Expert:** 'I don't even think about it'. This equates to unconscious competence and means that the activity has become second nature. Give yourself 4 points for each answer. A total of more than 36 on any of the questionnaires indicates that you are in the unconscious competence category for that type of digital literacy.

TABLE 10.1 Functional digital literacy questionnaire

Activity	No idea at all 1	Not competent 2	Competent 3	Expert 4
1. Type in a URL	☐	☐	☐	☐
2. Sign up for and activate an account	☐	☐	☐	☐
3. Problem-solve technical issues	☐	☐	☐	☐
4. Invite friends	☐	☐	☐	☐
5. Upload photos and documents	☐	☐	☐	☐
6. Embed videos and audios	☐	☐	☐	☐
7. Create hyperlinks	☐	☐	☐	☐
8. Write code, script, stylesheets	☐	☐	☐	☐
9. Change my password and manage my profile	☐	☐	☐	☐
10. Control access to my site	☐	☐	☐	☐
11. Find cached information	☐	☐	☐	☐
12. Install software	☐	☐	☐	☐

TABLE 10.2   Network digital literacy questionnaire

Activity	No idea at all 1	Not competent 2	Competent 3	Expert 4
1. Understand online copyright, IP and licensing arrangements	☐	☐	☐	☐
2. Interpret and comply with Terms of Service and Privacy Policies	☐	☐	☐	☐
3. Manage different online identities	☐	☐	☐	☐
4. Know about data security and control arrangements and third-party data access	☐	☐	☐	☐
5. Apply user permissions and roles and manage privacy settings	☐	☐	☐	☐
6. Recognise Creative Commons options	☐	☐	☐	☐
7. Turn off cookies and monitoring	☐	☐	☐	☐
8. Account for archiving and caching	☐	☐	☐	☐
9. Create backups	☐	☐	☐	☐
10. Check date stamping	☐	☐	☐	☐
11. Control advertising	☐	☐	☐	☐
12. Understand cross-platform functionality	☐	☐	☐	☐

TABLE 10.3   Critical digital literacy questionnaire

Activity	No idea at all 1	Not competent 2	Competent 3	Expert 4
1. Assess relevance, usefulness, authority, and integrity	☐	☐	☐	☐
2. Validate information	☐	☐	☐	☐
3. Determine intended audience	☐	☐	☐	☐
4. Assess reliability	☐	☐	☐	☐
5. Synthesise different sources	☐	☐	☐	☐
6. Assess currency	☐	☐	☐	☐
7. Conduct advanced searches	☐	☐	☐	☐
8. Control information flows	☐	☐	☐	☐
9. Store and retrieve information	☐	☐	☐	☐
10. Create and communicate new scholarly products	☐	☐	☐	☐
11. Strategically communicate online	☐	☐	☐	☐
12. Convey meaning online	☐	☐	☐	☐

A HOLISTIC UNDERSTANDING OF DIGITAL LITERACY

It should be clear by now that being digitally literate is essential if you are to succeed in your study and research endeavours in higher education. But more than this, digital literacy (indeed, literacy of any form) is essential to your success in the modern world more generally. If you are not digitally literate, you will find it increasingly difficult to participate in the social, economic, and cultural routines and practices that are defining our culture. Thus, without a degree of 'digital capital' – that is, access to the digital knowledge, skills, networks, resources, and connections that are valued by our society – you will struggle to meaningfully take part in important social and societal relations.

This takes us back to the very philosophical and human basis of why literacy is important. Literacy is important because it is the key to unlocking an individual's potential, it is about building citizens, it is about intellectual and ethical wealth, and it is about dignity. Literacy helps us recognise and respond to the human condition, and it helps us contribute to a greater knowledge of ourselves and to a shared knowledge of others. Literacy is a right and it is important because it is essential to human flourishing (Poore, 2011). The opposite of literacy is ignorance, and being ignorant – digitally or otherwise – should neither be relied upon as a survival tactic nor seen as something to embrace. Being a digitally literate, educated person in today's world thus means more than knowing which buttons to point at and click on when stationed in front of a screen. Instead, and on a much more holistic view, being digitally literate means being aware of how we are socially constructed, how we construct ourselves, and how we construct others through digital technologies; it entails a realisation of the social forces that act upon us and how we ourselves contribute to them and can shape them in the digital realm; and it means that we need to think carefully about how we should develop amongst and for ourselves a literacy that will help us navigate the unfolding digital space. This means you need to know how to produce – as well as consume – digital artefacts and culture and how to critique (which is not the same as 'to criticise') digital media messages. You need to know how to make the most of electronic and digital media – not the least of them (Hartley, 2009: 20).

BUILDING YOUR DIGITAL LITERACY

In common with the general approach of this book, I am not going to provide you with a step-by-step, 'how to' guide to building your digital literacy, not least because developing a literacy of any kind cannot be reduced to a checklist that once completed will ensure your digital success. Instead, I want to concentrate on how you can mature into the right mindset for building your digital literacy because that is where I see most digitally *illiterate* people come unstuck.

Perhaps the most important thing to recognise up front is that becoming 'literate' in anything is not a process that can be fast-tracked; neither is it something that can be done all at once, nor something that should be left to chance. As with learning to read and write, and as with learning to do sums, learning to navigate digital spaces is most effective when you start at a level appropriate to your current skill set and build from there. All of this is straight-out common sense and surely few would argue that these principles are not sound. For example, if I said that you had to learn Norwegian and you had never spoken Norwegian before then you would expect to start from a low base, learn the language according to some kind of structure (starting with basic grammar, pronunciation, and vocabulary), and take several months of full-time study before you reached a professional proficiency level in speaking, listening to, and writing Norwegian. Moreover, you would expect to make mistakes and have them corrected as an ongoing part of the learning process.

However, something strange sometimes comes over people when they enter digital environments and it is something I have noticed in both the students and the academics who I have worked with when instructing them in the use of social media. Often, any concession that using digital technologies and social media effectively and meaningfully might require time, structure, practice, mistakes, and patience disappears. In these situations, there is almost an expectation that either things should 'come naturally' or that the tools and systems people are working with should somehow be aware of each and every little idiosyncrasy that this particular user brings to the interface. In the first instance, there is the feeling that, because it does not come 'naturally' to you, then you are 'stupid', and, in the second instance, there is the affirmation that it is not you who is stupid (which is true) but the computer that is 'stupid' (which is not true). Neither perspective is realistic, of course, and each can lead to immense frustration.

So, then, what is the kind of mindset you need to build your digital literacy? And who are the most successful at building the kind of literacy that serves them well in navigating digital spaces?

Functional digital literacy

People who exhibit excellent functional digital literacy know how to do things using social media, know how things work in a functional sense, and exhibit certain qualities that allow them to learn more about how digital spaces operate. They

177

- *Know that most sites and services work along similar lines.* They understand the basic principles for creating accounts, uploading items, creating hyperlinks, sharing information, etc. They don't try to remember the 'exact steps' for doing things but instead realise that each tool or service provides instructions when they are needed. They know where to look for things on a screen, in an app, or on a system.
- *Exhibit playfulness, curiosity, and openness.* They tend to jump in and try things without waiting for someone else to show them. They tend *not* to read instructions or to only read them when they can't figure out something for themselves. They learn as they go rather than attempt to do things all at once.
- *Are good problem-solvers.* They know that if they want to do something using a social media tool or service, then they probably can – they just need to figure out how. They find their own solutions using Google, FAQs, YouTube tutorials, and discussion forums and are both tenacious and patient in finding answers. They trust their own judgement and increase their competency by continually building on their previously gained knowledge. They are methodical and think things through according to cause-and-effect rather than take a trial-and-error approach (although they also know that that might work as a last resort) and transfer the skills that they have from elsewhere to help them in their problem solving.
- *Don't worry about making mistakes.* Related to all of the above, people with excellent digital literacy know that – generally speaking – you can't break things in digital environments, so they are not afraid to slip up occasionally. They know that learning about how something functions means they are bound to make errors along the way and they take the attitude that if there is a fault, then it is more likely with them than it is with 'the computer'.

Network digital literacy

Those with good network digital literacy know what happens once they go online and they have a good working knowledge of the interplay between the technical, legal, and social elements that characterise being networked. They

- *Understand how data works.* They know that digital data is fundamentally different from other forms of data in that it is (as boyd [sic] reminds us above) persistent, replicable, searchable, and scalable. They know that anything they put online can be found or hacked – no matter how careful they are – and they make accommodations for this as best they can by being careful about the digital trail they leave: they know that everything they upload, download, click on, don't click on, like, don't like, recommend, save, share, post, comment on, view, and ignore all contributes to an online profile that can be attributed to them personally.
- *Can interpret the legal and quasi-legal conditions of being online.* They have a good working knowledge of copyright, intellectual property, and Creative Commons (see Chapter 12), and can interpret how they relate to licensing and sub-licensing arrangements. They read and understand Terms of Service before signing up for anything, knowing which are the most important clauses to look out for. They are conscious of adhering to privacy legislation and Privacy Policies and they maintain their own privacy and do not breach the privacy of others.

- *Manage multiple identities.* People with good network digital literacy understand that profiles and identities online change according to audience and they know how to switch between these identities. They have a good sense of 'online genre' and know what is appropriate in which space, that is, they know what makes a good tweet as opposed to a blog post as opposed to a Facebook comment. They are always aware of audience in that they know *who* they are addressing but, at the same time, know that there may be unknown and unidentified others also taking note.
- *Actively manage risk online.* They understand *levels* of risk and know about the relationship between probability and impact – that means that they consciously decide on what sites, tools, and services to engage with and how to engage with them. They are constantly on the look-out for risks to their online security and act immediately to address any possible breaches. They practise cybersafety as a matter of course.

Critical digital literacy

A person with good critical digital literacy knows when and why they should and can do things online, using higher cognitive and critical skills relating to analysis, synthesis, and evaluation. They

- *Know how to validate and evaluate online information.* They don't take things at face-value, even if a site or service looks 'professional'. They know how to cross-check information and don't rely on one source. They are aware of internet scams, and not just those relating to 'Nigerian bank scams', either, because they know about phishing, banking scams, loan scams, PayPal and eBay scams, credit card scams, and so forth.
- *Know which communication channels to use for what and when.* They have an excellent understanding of genre and how to write or create for different media and they know under what conditions to use which media.
- *Use social media to engage in social, cultural, intellectual, and political life.* They have access to knowledge and networks and know how to build both by using social media.
- *Can think with the technology.* They use the technology as a way to enhance cognition and can deal with epistemological questions relating to social media. They know how social media help us build and distribute, create and transform knowledge, and can create new ideas from disparate sources and types of media.

Spending time on getting yourself skilled up in these areas is not an 'added extra' to your study and research: it is a key component of your professional development and, as such, you need to devote time to it.

FACTORS IMPACTING ON YOUR DIGITAL LITERACY

So far, we have examined some of the 'big picture' factors relating to digital literacy. But there are also more mundane influences on our ability to engage with and participate fully in the digital space.

Experiences of digital technology in the classroom

We can safely say that the use of digital technology in the classroom is now commonplace in higher education: most courses have a presence in some kind of virtual learning environment (VLE, see Chapter 1), even if that presence is only there to host the course outline and the lecturer's contact details. Most lecturers, however, at least upload lecture notes and slideshow presentations to their VLE so that students can access course materials online. But for most, the use of such technology stops here. Few lecturers really push the VLE to its socially constructivist, pedagogical limits (again, see Chapter 1) and only a few others choose to work outside the confines of the VLE to set up their own teaching and learning environments in a blog or wiki or elsewhere. This means that often the VLE is used little more than as an 'advanced photocopier' and that internet technologies are favoured in higher education for reasons of convenience and control and as platforms for administration and content delivery (Allen and Seaman, 2012; EDUCAUSE, 2012; JISC, 2007, 2008).

That said, both students and lecturers believe that digital technologies can benefit the learning experience – it's just that there exists a degree of uncertainty on both sides about how current pedagogies and classroom practices can be mapped onto the technology; in other words, it's not always clear how digital technologies and education can work together. This might be because we are trying to do old things in new ways, rather than trying to develop new ways to do new things – things that are better suited to realities of the unfolding digital space – but in any case it means that the use of digital technologies in higher education is often poorly executed.

Beliefs in proficiency

As we noted in Chapter 1 as regards the conscious competence learning cycle, confidence does not equal competence. Studies show that both students and young people, regardless of actual skill, tend to place themselves in the 'very skilled' or 'expert' category when it comes to using digital technologies to efficiently and effectively search for information, evaluating sources for credibility, and understanding the legal issues associated with accessing digital information (EDUCAUSE, 2012; Salaway et al., 2008). This kind of self-assessment can be dangerous, however:

> Many educators believe that students' perceptions about their net savviness are questionable. It is a do-it-yourself approach to information literacy; students rely on peers (*and may perpetuate misinformation from peers*) rather than on library staff or faculty; and students may have excessive confidence because they are unaware of the complexities involved or just because they have grown up with technology. (Salaway et al., 2008: 52, emphasis added)

The point about relying on peers rather than experts is a good one: although peer learning can be important – especially in socially constructivist educational environments (again, see Chapter 1) – the input of experts is essential if you are going to make the most of social media and if you are to keep safe online. And, of course, this applies regardless of whether you are using social media for study or for research.

Information behaviour and skills gaps

From the above, it may sound as though there is a lot of misplaced confidence out there amongst students. In some instances this is probably true but, at the same time, many students acknowledge the difficulties they have with using social media in educational settings. For starters, many student web users are concerned about the unmanageable scale of the web (CIBER, 2008) and can often feel overwhelmed by the sheer volume of information available online. This frequently leads to surface-level search habits that, in turn, means we then have difficulty in evaluating and hierarchising search results (CIBER, 2008; EDUCAUSE, 2012). Another common problem occurs when there is a skills gap between using social media to create content and using social media to create *meaningful* content (New Media Consortium and EDUCAUSE Learning Initiative, 2008). In fact, it is in developing this latter skill – creating worthwhile, meaningful, relevant content – that students are seeking most guidance: as various studies tell us, students don't want endless workshops on how to use the technology itself, but, rather, direction on how to *think with* information and how to *think with* technology (Green and Hannon, 2007; JISC, 2008).

The digital divide

A final but important factor that impacts on your digital literacy is your place on the so-called 'digital divide'. Originally, the term 'digital divide' described the gap between the 'haves' and the 'have nots' particularly in relation to access to the hardware and software systems that supported computers: on one side of the digital divide were those who had access to PCs, laptops, printers, email, servers, and the internet, and on the other side were those who did not. But today the digital divide is not 'simply' about having access to computing hardware and software; instead, the divide has become rather more complicated. As both hardware and software have become cheaper, and as broadband and wireless internet connectivity has become semi-ubiquitous (in the developed world, at least), the problem of the divide has shifted from one relating to patterns of *ownership* to one relating to patterns of *use*. Put differently, the digital divide is today characterised not so much by access to devices and the technical systems that support those devices, but, rather, it is characterised by access to the kinds of knowledge and sociocultural and communication skills that enable one to make the most of digital technologies in daily life. In other words, being on the right side of the digital divide means that you have the sociocultural capital (as well as the 'functional' skills) to perform meaningfully in digital environments – and it means that you are properly digitally literate.

SUMMARY

- We are currently experiencing a digital technological revolution. This means that we need to learn new ways of thinking and new ways of doing things.
- Being digitally literate means having the functional, network, and critical skills to participate fully in modern cultural, social, and economic routines and practices.
- Becoming digitally literate takes time: you need to be patient and to treat it as if you were becoming literate in any other area of life and learning.
- Having functional digital literacy means being curious and playful, being a good problem-solver, and not being worried about making mistakes.
- Having network digital literacy means knowing how data works, understanding the legal environment online, and being able to manage risk.
- Having critical digital literacy means knowing how to validate and evaluate online information, how to use social media to engage in social, cultural, intellectual and political life, and being able to think with the technology.
- Factors impacting on your digital literacy include your experiences of digital technology in the classroom, beliefs in your own proficiency, your information behaviour and skills gaps, and the digital divide.

FURTHER READING

Churches, A. (n.d.) *21st Century Learning Spaces*. Available at: http://edorigami.wikispaces .com/21st+Century+Learning+Spaces. Accessed 10 September 2013.

Jones, H., Johnson, P. and Gruszczynska, A. (2012) 'Digital literacy: Digital maturity or digital bravery?', *Enhancing Learning in the Social Sciences*, 4 (2).

Lin, C., Kuo, F., Tseng, F. and Tang, W. (2012) *Motivating and Sustaining Women's Digital Literacy through ICT Learning*, AMCIS 2012 Proceedings, Paper 20. Available at: http://aisel.aisnet.org/amcis2012/proceedings/AdoptionDiffusionIT/20. Accessed 10 September 2013.

Ng, W. (2012) 'Can we teach digital natives digital literacy?', *Computers & Education*, 59 (3): 1065–78.

Park, Y.J. (2013) 'Digital literacy and privacy behavior online', *Communication Research*, 40 (2): 215–36.

11

Handling Yourself (and Others) Online

OVERVIEW

This chapter explores online communication practices and helps you to develop your own communication framework for handling yourself – and others – online. It does not seek to tell you what to think or how to act towards others but rather asks that you reflect on these things as a way of helping you to develop resilience and coping skills in difficult online situations. It covers both theory and philosophy as a way of dealing with the 'bigger picture' elements of communication, but it also takes a look at cyberbullying and cyberaggression. This might be a difficult chapter, not because it is overly intellectually challenging (although you might have to read some sections again in order to understand some of the finer points), but rather because it asks you to reflect on your values, beliefs, and behaviours, and to be honest about how you relate to others in the online environment.

DEVELOPING A COMMUNICATION FRAMEWORK

This section is designed to give you an outline of the principles of dialogical communication as they apply to everyday communication and to communication online. The aim is to help you develop a communication framework so you can decide what to do – or what not to do – in the difficult situations you might encounter when using social media.

I believe that developing such a framework for yourself – one that is personal to you – is far more effective than simply giving you a list of bullet points that tells you how to act and what to do when confronted with a specific, tricky online situation. Although bullet points are helpful in many circumstances (and we will still refer to them later in the chapter) they do not cope well with nuance – and effective communication requires nuance. If you can develop for yourself an understanding of what constitutes for you a right and a good communicative act, then you will be working from your own personal first principles rather than a list of elements designed by someone else, a list that might not fit with your own beliefs and values. This approach, therefore, seeks to provide you with an intellectual framework for developing (and continuing to develop) your own core principles, values, and ideals for living a 'good' life – however that might look for you. The reasoning behind this is that if you are aware of the principles, values, and ideals that govern your life, then you can decide on how you want to interact with and influence others both online and off. The ultimate aim is to build self-understanding and (in the words of the famous Brazilian philosopher and educator Paolo Freire) to raise your critical consciousness as an historical actor who can intervene in and change the world – both your own and that of others. This will help you become an acting, self-constituting person, one who *acts deliberately* in the online space, as opposed to one who *reacts* involuntarily and feels blown about by the apparent fickleness of others and of the world. In the final analysis, this means that you should be able to prevent potentially difficult situations from happening in the first place, rather than trying to control a mess once it has occurred.

In order to do all this, however, we first need to touch a little bit on the field of philosophy and to understand how it can help us build the kind of rigorous, intellectual framework that will help us handle difficult online situations.

Philosophy versus theory

Philosophy can be described as the study of central and fundamental problems, especially those connected with knowledge, concepts, values, and reason. It is about the nature of things and it is about asking why things are as they are. There are various branches of philosophy, including aesthetics (which deals with the nature of art and beauty), epistemology (which deals with the nature of knowledge), metaphysics (which deals with the nature of existence), and logic (which deals with the nature of reason). What concerns us here, though, is ethics (sometimes called 'moral philosophy'), which is a branch of philosophy that explores right and wrong, good and evil, virtue and vice, and asks how we ought to live and act.

Why is this important for you as a user of social media? Why don't we just look at various theories of communication as they relate to social media? There is certainly a huge body of literature regarding communication and social

184

media – wouldn't this be more practical than philosophy? I would argue, 'No'. Theory is simply a way of explaining 'reality' in an abstract way through the use of general concepts: it is a proposition, abstraction, or hypothesis that seeks to explain the concrete. We can use theory to *understand* how communication works in social media environments, but it does not provide us with a *framework* for handling communicative acts at the everyday level. Philosophy, on the other hand, causes us to ask fundamental questions about the very nature of communication – questions that can inform and influence our very actions. And inasmuch as using social media is a communicative act (see Chapter 1), then communication itself is an ethical act and you will continually be presented with ethical dilemmas in your online explorations. Using philosophy to create an intellectual framework to handle these dilemmas will, in the end, give you better coping skills, help you build your emotional and personal resilience, and generally improve your well-being because you will have something rigorous and personally valuable to check yourself against. Finally, ethical philosophy is common sense and has common-sense applications because it helps us ask *useful* questions and to find the 'best' answers. It forces us to ask,

- How should I act?
- What should I do?
- Did I act wisely?
- Did I act well?
- What are my motivations?
- Are my feelings morally justified?
- What could be done better?
- What do I need to do to fix the situation?
- Have I learnt anything from you?

Having the courage to confront such questions – and to answer them truthfully – gives you control over yourself in difficult situations instead of making you feel at the whim of the world.

Dialogical communication

Now that we have set up an argument for why ethical philosophy is useful in handling ourselves and others when communicating online, we can explore a particular form of communication – and its uses – in more detail, namely, dialogical communication. I will be drawing, here, on the work of Paolo Freire, the aforementioned Brazilian educator and philosopher who spent much of his life developing a 'critical pedagogy', which is a way of educating so that people become aware of the sociocultural, political, economic, and historical forces that shape their lives and their life situations. Once we understand these forces, Freire argued, we are in a position to intervene in and change the world (Freire, 1996 [1970]).

Freire spends much of his work talking about how we relate to and communicate with others. He says that rather than being simply reactive and responsive to others and to the world, we instead need to 'enter into the situation' of those whom we encounter in order to fully understand them and in order to transform the situation (Freire, 1996 [1970]: 31). In doing so, Freire says we have to create new situations through 'transforming action' in the pursuit of a 'fuller humanity'. Someone who can do this, who can enter into the experience of another, 'is not afraid to confront, to listen, to see the world unveiled. This person is not afraid to meet the people or to enter into dialogue with them' (Freire, 1996 [1970]: 21). People must therefore be free to 'speak their own words' and to 'name the world' – we need to be free to speak 'true words' in order to create and re-create the world for ourselves, says Freire. But – and this is the key point – this cannot happen in isolation: people can only transform the world in communication with others.

This may seem like difficult language, but what Freire is talking about is, in many ways, similar to John Dewey's (2004 [1916]) notion of democratic social environments, that is, environments that uphold free interaction, the uncovering of mutual interests, and communication through conjoint experience. (We have to be careful not to confuse this understanding with 'democratic' forms of politics and government because, for Dewey, democracy cannot be present when there is an external authority – democracy is thus 'voluntary'.) These environments are founded on dialogical, democratic principles that can be summarised by the following statements:

- Dialogical communication is about true, open, honest, authentic communication between people.
- Dialogical communication is about entering into the experience of others so that we can understand the world and transform it.
- It is only through true, open, honest dialogue that we can transform the world.
- Only dialogue creates critical thinking.
- Only dialogue sustains communication.
- True communication only happens through dialogue.

Finally, there are certain conditions that need to exist for dialogical communication to occur (Freire, 1996 [1970]: 70–73):

- Love (for the world and for people)
- Humility (a perception of our own ignorance)
- Faith (in humans)
- Trust (by being consistent in our engagement with others)
- Hope (the expectation of success for effort)
- Critical thinking (the continuing transformation of our intellectual world).

Barriers to effective communication

Sometimes, before we know it, we can find ourselves in a situation involving a communication breakdown, with things spiralling out of control. It requires maturity and skill to recognise what is happening at the time or to recognise that what is happening is part of an ongoing pattern of thought or behaviour. In any case, here are some of the things that can get in the way of effective communication:

- Ego
- Feeling that you are always right
- Feeling aggrieved
- Believing that your (maybe poor) behaviour is justified
- Being too willing or too quick to take offence
- Having a sense that you can never be wrong
- Believing that you should not be 'called' on your bad behaviour
- Shifting blame to someone or something else
- Thinking that your position should not be questioned
- Being oversensitive to criticism.

Again, the language may seem difficult, but here it is not because the concepts are expressed uniquely (as they are by Freire, above), but because they are concepts that we often do not discuss in secular, public forums. In my experience, however, people often crave conversations that help us understand ourselves and our situations better because one of the things we want most desperately is to communicate more deeply with others. By simply invoking this kind of language, I hope I am giving you permission to be *with* others, to enter into their situations, and to transform the world, as Freire would want.

A final note for this quick investigation of the current topic: it is a terrible mistake to think that this kind of deep, dialogical communication does not or cannot occur in social media environments. Communication is what we make it. We can either oppress others (and thus ourselves) with anti-dialogical words and actions or we can use our words and actions to take control over how we view the world and others and how we choose to engage with them. Mode of communication does not come into it.

Relating well to others: Becoming a critically conscious person

Arguably, you could skip the rest of the current section and jump straight into the next, which is about bullying and aggression. So, if you feel you have had enough of the philosophy we've studied so far, then please go ahead.

However, if you are serious about developing your own principles-led, personal communication framework – a framework that will help you both online and off – then you will need to read on, as we will now situate our discussion of dialogical communication within the broader notion of 'critical consciousness'. Doing this will move us beyond a fairly simple examination of what dialogical communication 'is' into a far more complex understanding of why dialogical communication is so important to our essential humanity – and to our relations with others.

Consciousness

Truly dialogical communication cannot occur simply by following a set of rules; instead, says Freire, it requires a shift in consciousness on the part of the individual in which we come to understand the 'true' nature of how the world works and in which we also come to understand the part we ourselves play in it. This could mean understanding the social forces that impact on our relations with one another, recognising our own contribution to a situation, or being able to trace our own personal predispositions that might cause us to act or speak in particular ways. The more we can diagnose or define a situation, the more we can 'critically recognise its causes' (Freire, 1996 [1970]: 29), the better we can create a new situation for ourselves and for others.

So, let's try to get at this idea of 'consciousness' a little more clearly. We can say that consciousness, at its most basic, is about 'awareness'. Karl Mannheim, a sociologist who lived through and was greatly influenced by World War II, both personally and intellectually, describes consciousness as an 'attitude of the mind' (Mannheim, 1943: 64–65) in which we are aware of the social, cultural, political, and other forces that affect our situation or our circumstances. It is, says Mannheim (and which is echoed by Freire), an awareness of, and readiness to see, the 'whole situation' and the capacity to grasp the 'uniqueness of our situation' (1943: 62, 63). This comes about, according to Mannheim, through the correct diagnosis or defining of the situation – and that, too, means seeing our part in it. Already we can see resonances with Freire's position, stated above, in which we must understand the 'true' nature of the world and how it works. Once we apprehend such things, the argument goes, we can act to change them.

Our ontological vocation

But, really, why should any of this matter? You could be saying to yourself, 'Why should I bother with all this stuff about consciousness and critical consciousness? I'm just trying my hardest to get along in a complex world by navigating relationships and online environments as best I can. How can this possibly be of relevance to me?' The answer is this, according to Freire, and it is perhaps one of the most cardinal points that can be made about the importance of engaging fully with other people: Freire says that it is our 'ontological vocation' to become more 'fully human' and that if we lack critical consciousness then we negate our very humanity and that of others; without critical consciousness, we can never engage in true dialogue with the world.

By 'ontological vocation' Freire is referring to that branch of philosophy that deals with questions of existence (sometimes known as 'metaphysics'). If it is our 'ontological vocation' to become more 'fully human', then Freire is saying that it is in our very nature to be human and only human – not a cog in an economic machine, not an instrument of totalitarianism, not an example of laissez-faire indulgence or relativism, all of which seek to treat some humans as different from others and which thus dehumanise everyone in the process. Our 'ontological vocation' is, instead, entirely about our significance as human beings. Without critical consciousness, Freire stresses, we deny our own and others' purpose, that is, to become more fully human, and we instead engage in relations that only serve to dehumanise ourselves and others, and that serve structures of oppression. Becoming fully human, then, means actively participating in our ontological vocation.

Historicity

To achieve this ontological vocation, we must be 'with' the world and others and not just 'in' the world, as we have already seen; that is, we need to create the world and not just 'spectate'. This is what Freire calls our 'historicity', which is not to be confused with 'history' as a discipline of study that seeks to understand past events. When we see ourselves as 'historical' beings, we recognise, accept, and act upon our (inter-) subjectivity as human beings. Through this, we acknowledge that people are not just 'objects' or 'repositories' of knowledge, but that we are all sources of it and that we can continually discover ourselves through reflection and action (a process called 'praxis'). Historicity is a process of becoming; it recognises people as unfinished and it leads to transformation, creation, and re-creation; it can never, by its very nature, dehumanise others or be anti-dialogical. Freire puts this all together when he says, 'A deepened consciousness of their situation leads people to apprehend that situation as an historical reality susceptible of transformation' (Freire, 1996 [1970]: 66). This is human, not anti-human; it is dialogical, not anti-dialogical; it is historical, not ahistorical; it is democratic, not anti-democratic; and it is liberating because it allows for change, variety, transformation, novelty, free interaction, and the 'spontaneous integration of consensus on different levels' (Mannheim, 1943: 29). When we are critically conscious, historical human beings seeking to realise our ontological vocation to become more fully human, then we know that we can and must intervene in and change the world, and that trying to change others' consciousness to suit our agenda is not morally permissible. Because those who have gained a level of critical consciousness and an awareness of their own self-constitutive actions (Korsgaard, 2009) have an inner life that continually questions their actions, the reasons for their actions, the outcomes of their actions, whether they acted well or badly, and how they may have acted better. The very practical outcome of nurturing such an inner life is, quite simply, better communication and relationships with others, online and off.

BULLYING AND AGGRESSION

In this section we first take a quick look at what constitutes 'traditional' bullying before examining how cyberbullying is different. But this is only to set up the point that what I am calling 'cyberaggression' is different again, and much more likely to occur in the university study and research context.

Bullying and cyberbullying

Bullying is an insidious phenomenon that can occur to anyone – and be carried out by anyone – regardless of age, social status, or background. Researcher and educator Shaheen Shariff (2008: 16) describes bullying as a form of abuse that is characterised by the following:

- A power imbalance that favours perpetrators over victims
- Peer support (from 'assistants' or 'reinforcers') for perpetrators, or at least a situation in which bystanders do not intervene to stop the bullying
- The isolation of victims from the peer group
- Uninvited and unwanted behaviour
- Deliberate, repeated, relentless actions on the part of the bully.

Bullying can be physical or verbal and it occurs in face-to-face situations.

Cyberbullying, on the other hand, is slightly different; although it retains most of the elements described above, it is mostly verbal or text-based as opposed to physical. Further, cyberbullying may not always be 'repeated' or 'ongoing' (although it often is) simply because of the very nature of digital technology: one instance of cyberbullying can be reproduced infinitely because of the persistence and replicability of digital information. Thus, we can define cyberbullying as being any hostile act specifically directed towards another person that occurs using digital technology.

An additional dividing line between 'traditional' bullying and cyberbullying can be identified in the 24-hour nature of digital communication, which means that hostility and bullying are no longer confined to a particular location: in other words, this kind of bullying can follow you into your home. It can also be replicated infinitely because it is virtually impossible to delete data once it takes digital form. Moreover, with cyberbullying the potential audience is infinite and can run into the millions and, again because it is largely non-physical, there is greater potential for anonymity on the part of perpetrators.

> If you are the victim of bullying or cyberbullying at university, then do not suffer in silence. As well as following the advice given here, you must tell someone about your situation and get advice on it. Talk to a fellow student or colleague, a trusted mentor or lecturer, someone in Human Resources, the Dean of Students or similar, your boss, student services, a counsellor – anyone. You can then work together towards solving the problem.

Cyberbullying can happen to people of any age and in any environment – not just to kids who are still at school. That said, it is probably less likely that you will be *cyberbullied* in the university environment than be the recipient of *cyberaggression*. So, without in anyway diminishing the devastating impact of bullying and cyberbullying, we now quickly move on to discuss cyberaggression, as it is arguably the most common form of belligerence that you will encounter when using social media in your study and research.

Cyberaggression

A very great deal has been written on bullying and cyberbullying amongst schoolchildren of all ages, but little has been written on cyberaggression or cyberbullying amongst adults. In fact, there is almost a sense that adults should either know how to handle these things themselves or just toughen up and stop making such a big deal of it. Further, university environments are largely – if not mostly – competitive environments in which both students and academics contend for limited grades, limited assistance, limited funding, limited time, limited publications, and limited jobs. It's no wonder that under such conditions qualities such as civility, courtesy, respect, patience, and empathy are sometimes neglected as being unimportant. Additionally, there is occasionally the belief that because there are anti-bullying and anti-harassment policies in place people will somehow bear these in mind all day, every day, as they go about their routine study and research business. But this is to paint too bleak and too extreme a picture. Most university environments function well most of the time; it is only at those times when communication breaks down that we become aware of the certain workplace structures and cultures that can vitalise the bad behaviour we see in cyberaggression.

So, how is cyberaggression different from cyberbullying? Perhaps the most important distinction occurs in the targetting of victims. Cyberbullying, like traditional bullying, singles out individuals for one-on-one malicious attention through the use of direct messaging or texting, or through the online posting of vindictive comments about a person. Cyberaggression, however, is not normally so directed; in fact, quite often a cyberaggressor will frequently use a relatively open online space (such as a discussion forum or the comments section on a blog) to have a general 'spray' about an issue – the unfortunate thing is that anyone who gainsays the aggressor in that space could be in the firing line. In other words, where cyberbullying is personal, cyberaggression need not be (although, of course, it can easily *become* personal, in which case the line between bullying and aggression might be traversed).

Furthermore, bystanders to cyberaggressive acts are usually not present – at least not in the sense of those who encourage the bully or who do not intervene to stop bullying from happening. Typically, other members of the forum or of the online community where the aggression is occurring will often step in to put a stop to things, or the community moderator will delete inappropriate, confrontational, or antagonistic conversations. But even though you may not have been specifically targeted for abuse, nasty incidents can nevertheless lead to distress (as opposed to stress), withdrawal, depression, lack of appetite, and sleeplessness, amongst other things. There can also be accompanying feelings of injustice (especially if you feel you have been misrepresented, misinterpreted, or misunderstood) and frustration at being unable to reply in a way that makes you feel heard and appreciated.

Without proper research, it is impossible to state what might be motivating cyberaggressive behaviour. But we can surmise a couple of things. It does seem to be easier to be aggressive towards others when we are online and thus not engaging with someone face-to-face; the many vicious and vitriolic comments that can be found on sites such as YouTube perhaps attest to this. Related to this, and for some reason that again needs proper research attention, some people seem to believe that the normal rules of civility need not apply in discussion forums and the like, maybe because communicating through a keyboard can be time-consuming and cumbersome when compared to communicating in person. A further explanation might be found in the fact that online we see revealed the whole spectrum of human social behaviour: in other words, it's not that people are 'changing' or that they are somehow 'different' online – it's just that we are seeing the true diversity of human behaviour and human social skills exposed, and, if we are not used to aggressiveness, then it can be confronting. Finally – and it's something that I believe explains a lot about human interaction and communication, which is why I spent so long setting the point up earlier in the chapter – perhaps we just find it difficult to enter into each other's experience and to show compassion or understanding for another's viewpoint, which leads us to think that others are stupid or to use intimidation as a way of making ourselves heard.

To end this section, and as a way of amplifying the very last point, I want to make some comments on keeping perspective online because it is essential that we look realistically at our various interactions online and that we not take offence too easily. It is particularly important not to confuse abuse with bullying with aggression with conflict with disagreement. All represent different levels of interaction. To this end, we need to distinguish between behaviour that is rude, churlish, brusque, impolite, obnoxious, or offhand, and that that is derogatory, insulting, hostile, abusive, disparaging, pejorative, or defamatory. Remember, you have a right to be offended, but you also have a right to *not* be offended. If we feel we have a right to never being made to feel uncomfortable, to never being questioned, it can be all too easy for even a small difference of opinion to make us feel greatly aggrieved. This means that we can quickly lose perspective over a perceived initial 'fault' and it can lead us to respond in over-the-top ways by blowing things out of all proportion. My own 'quick check' is to ask, 'Does this behaviour diminish, or seek to diminish, others?' If the answer is 'no', then the chances are that I should not be too affronted; if the answer is 'yes', however, then I should either intervene appropriately to secure the rights of people to be treated as equal human beings, or desist from behaving in such a way myself.

HANDLING CYBERAGGRESSION

Most texts provide a list of bullet points describing what to do in cases of bullying or harassment online, and, indeed, I also provide such a list below. However, because cyberbullying and cyberaggression are different phenomena, I also discuss what it means to be aware of our own potentially aggressive behaviours online. The section ends by considering how we might enter into open conversation with others so that we work towards rational, reasonable, and compassionate solutions to difficult emotional issues.

Dealing with the immediate situation

When you are the victim of online aggression it can be very hard to disengage from the difficult circumstances in which you find yourself – but disengage

193

you must. By this, I mean you must *not* respond to aggressive, hostile, quarrelsome, antagonistic, or similar comments made by the combative party: to do so frequently only inflames the situation. This may seem exceedingly difficult to do because we may feel (rightly) aggrieved, unfairly treated, hurt, maligned, or misrepresented and we just want to put our side of the story across. But, if the belligerent is, as pointed out above, having a general 'spray' about an issue, and if you are not being personally targetted but, rather, find yourself unfortunately in the firing line, then step back and do not retaliate. Nevertheless, you should consider reporting your concerns to your lecturer or to your supervisor so they are aware of what's going on and can take action if it is warranted. It may be that the aggressor needs to be reminded of their obligations under university codes of conduct or behaviour; in other cases, some form of mediation might be required. But be aware that such things can, in themselves, sometimes provoke matters further when it would have been better simply to monitor a situation that will quickly die down. This is why it is imperative that you discuss the situation sensibly and rationally so that the best way of handling it is alighted upon.

If, however, the aggression spills over into behaviour that is bullying, harassing, or otherwise threatening, it becomes an entirely different case. As in instances of aggression described above, the rule of disengagement immediately applies: *never* respond to or engage with someone who is intimidating you. But this is *not* the same as saying you should ignore such communications. In fact, in such situations it is essential that you *do not* ignore what is going on but, rather, that you take measures to protect yourself and to stop the intimidation from escalating. To this end, you should

- Never engage with or respond to someone who is intimidating or bullying you online. This will only inflame and escalate the situation.
- Block all contact from the tormentor. You should be able to either block or filter out their IP address, number, email address, etc. At the same time, however, you need to consider the following point, which is to …
- Keep all communications. These may be needed as evidence to prove that you are the victim of aggression, bullying, or harassment. But *do not* distress yourself by reading through things again and again; put them in a folder and otherwise disregard them.
- Tell someone. It is imperative that you do not try to handle things alone: tell a friend, a trusted lecturer, or a colleague. They may not know immediately what to do, but they will in all likelihood support you in finding ways to stop the malicious behaviour.
- Report illegal and/or criminal activity to the police. In many jurisdictions, this includes threats, extortion, bullying, stalking, and harassment. Again, this is why you need the support of someone you trust. Talking to the police can seem daunting, not least because you are afraid of retaliation, but the police really are the best placed to prevent you from further harm.

An unfortunate fact of online search is that the more you engage with an aggressor, the more chance there is that, firstly, things will escalate, and, secondly, the more chance there is that the 'conversation' will work its way up search results – sometimes, keeping quiet can be the hardest, but most necessary, thing to do.

Having the correct perspective on any aggressive situation is essential to its successful resolution. Especially, this means that you need to weigh up the level and type of injustice with the level and type of infraction; you need to take account of both yours and others' actions, reactions, emotional states, motivations, and intentions; and you need to know when to either let things lie or when to take measures to keep yourself safe.

Avoiding being aggressive yourself online

One thing that is almost never discussed is the situation in which you find yourself an actual perpetrator of cyberaggression. Perhaps this is because it is somehow easier to identify as a victim of malicious behaviour than it is to admit to our own poor behaviour online. But if so many of us are victims of online aggression and bullying, then so too must many of us be perpetrators. Indeed, surely we can be both, for few of us are ever either wholly good or wholly bad in 'real life'. We have almost all unexpectedly found ourselves in situations online (and this includes via email) where we felt frustrated, angry, or irritated with someone else. And we have almost all unexpectedly found ourselves responding to such situations with unfair or disproportionate comments, quips, observations, or criticisms about others.

One of the 'traps' of online communication is its immediacy coupled with its distancing effects: it allows us to communicate instantly with others but without necessarily standing next to them so that we can monitor their non-verbal feedback on how we are coming across to them. For some reason, we will tend to say things online to or about someone that we would never say to their face. Social media are thus requiring us to find new norms of communication and civility and to apply them online; but while that is happening, we need to, perhaps, be more metacognitive than ever. As we saw in Chapter 8, being metacognitive means simply 'thinking about your thinking' so that you can monitor and regulate your behaviour. It means being aware of things that might annoy or exasperate you, of your typical reactions to specific types of behaviour or comment, and of your automatic thoughts when confronted with certain situations; it means identifying, being honest about, and accepting the more disagreeable parts of your behaviour and then acting to correct things; and it means building your emotional intelligence. Do note, here, that there is a difference between being a 'bad person' and being a normal person who sometimes acts badly. Most of us fall into the latter category.

The first step in preventing yourself from acting inappropriately online is to immediately recognise when you are feeling irate: you must learn to recognise when someone or something is pushing your 'hot buttons' or when you are feeling angry, frustrated, irritated, annoyed, exasperated, aggrieved, or anything else that is likely to 'set you off'. You may or may not have a right to such feelings but in either case, and in the first instance, *don't do anything*: don't *ever* send, post, tweet, comment on, or otherwise upload anything whatsoever when you are in a heightened, negative emotional state. In other words, it is imperative that you try to break the emotional circuit that might lead you to do something you could very shortly regret. When you have calmed down, try to look at things rationally. Ask yourself some of the following questions: What is going on here? Why do I feel this way? Do I have a right to feel like this? What if I had acted as I initially wanted to? Would my actions have been warranted? Or would they have been out of all proportion? How would my actions have appeared to others? Would I have acted this way in a face-to-face situation? Hopefully, through being metacognitive, you will have short-circuited any inappropriate actions and therefore you won't have anything to feel remorseful about later on. On the other hand, if you realise that you have done or said something improper, unmerited, or just plain rude, then you should do two things. Firstly, and if possible, delete the offending item and any links to it; this may or may not be technically possible, depending on the system or service you are using. Secondly – and this may be more or less difficult, depending on less measurable elements relating to qualities such as pride, vanity, and humility – you should apologise for the transgression in an appropriate fashion. Of course, not all misbehaviour requires an apology; you need to consider what is called for under the circumstances. If you can manage to do this, well done. If, however, you have analysed the situation and your feelings and you have decided that the matter really does warrant action as you initially thought it did, then you need to think about talking to the other party and having what may initially seem like a difficult conversation but which, in the long run, will help press the 'reset' button on the communication problems you are having.

Don't even *think* about saying anything nasty about someone 'behind their back' via email – it can get forwarded!

Having a difficult conversation

I am convinced that many instances of cyberaggression and/or misunderstanding occur simply because people don't have the skills to undertake difficult conversations: if you are upset, it then becomes easier to fire off an outraged email or to write a nettling post in a discussion forum than it is to talk rationally, reasonably, and compassionately with someone else about a troublesome issue that concerns you both. Having a difficult conversation is most difficult if 1) you enter into the conversation in bad faith, that is, if you don't truly want to resolve the problem in a fair, honest, and open way that respects the thoughts, feelings, and experiences of both parties, and 2) if you don't have the communication skills and emotional literacy to conduct such a conversation. There are, of course, entire books and websites dedicated to this topic, so if you need skilling up in this area, I suggest you conduct some internet searches, buy or borrow some texts, or talk to someone you know who is good with this kind of thing. For the moment, though, and in keeping with the general approach in this book (and especially in this chapter), I am going to provide you with some conceptual ground on which to build these types of conversation. I believe that these conversations happen best face-to-face, primarily because you can pick up on the other person's body language; failing that, a Skype conversation or telephone call can be almost as effective because at least you have your interlocutor's vocal inflections to help guide you. Instant messaging can be used as a substitute as it at least occurs in real time, but it lacks a certain physical embeddedness; email also lacks this and further suffers from being asynchronous and prone to massive 'dumps' of emotion without the moderating influence of real-time interjections and feedback.

What would Darryl do?

If you are unsure how to confront a difficult state of affairs, it can help tremendously to draw on the examples of respected friends and family. To do this, choose someone you admire and respect for the way they handle themselves and others and do a quick, mental check: ask, simply, 'What would they do?' For myself, when I'm faced with a tricky situation, I ask, 'What would Darryl do?' or 'What would Kerrie do?' Because I hold these two people in such esteem, I can determine quite rapidly the first step I need to take in trying to resolve a delicate set of circumstances.

In any communicative act, Dewey tells us, both the recipient and giver of communication are affected (Dewey, 2004 [1916]: 5). To receive a communication, he says that we need to 'get outside' of our own experience and see the world as another sees it, that we need to consider what 'points of contact' exist if we are 'to have an enlarged and changed experience' (Dewey, 2004 [1916]: 5). It means setting aside our ego and finding and feeling a true empathy with the other person – with what they are feeling and with how they experience the world. So, start here:

1. *Enter into the other person's experience of the situation.* Truly *listen* to them, give them time to talk, and don't be crafting your response in your head while you are meant to be listening (this is a common phenomenon). Moreover, don't be tempted to talk over them or to interject with your own perspective on things. What you need to do here is to detach yourself and your own emotions from the situation as much as possible. You also need to find out exactly what is going on in a way that validates the other party's experience but which still gives you a chance later on to put forwards your own. You could start with something like, 'We seem to be having some difficulties in communicating. Do you want to tell me what's happening from your perspective?' or 'You sounded pretty upset on the discussion forum. Something must have gone on that you felt uncomfortable about. Can you tell me about it so I can understand it better?' The essential thing is that you step back and try to grasp the situation as it is when looked at from an outsider's perspective – not as it is in your head. If it helps, think of this as a data-gathering exercise. You can prompt further conversation by asking, 'What else is there?', 'What other things do I need to know?'

2. *Show empathy and understanding.* Rephrase and repeat what the other person is saying and say it back to them. Confirm your understanding of their perspective and seek clarification on anything you are unsure about: 'So you're saying that when I do this, you feel like that' or 'I'm not sure what you mean by that. Can you tell me a bit more?' Again, you are seeking a full comprehension of the situation, but you are also showing good faith in wanting to understand how the other person sees things.

3. *State your own perspective.* When it's your turn, talk about your own concerns and needs but try to link them to the other party's concerns – not in a defensive way, but rather in a way that gently points to the common ground of the issue. Be specific: don't just say, 'What you said was unfair and you should apologise'. Rather, say, 'When you wrote that stuff in the forum I was confused because I didn't know what I had said that might have made you angry. I felt embarrassed, because it looked as if I'd criticised you personally in my previous post, when that wasn't what I thought I'd done at all. And then I couldn't sleep because I was worried that I'd upset you so much and because I felt misrepresented and a bit humiliated.' Notice that this kind of talk is about the speaker's feelings and perceptions only: it doesn't seek to lay blame on the other person.

4. *Identify issues of common concern and work towards a solution – or give an apology.* Once you both have an understanding and appreciation of each other's experience of the situation, you can identify the areas of common concern and problem-solve some solutions: 'So, it seems that the real problem is that we each have different expectations of how discussion should work in the forum. I'd be happy to get a gentle text or private chat message from you as a reminder that I might be getting a bit hot under the collar

about a topic. This would really help short-circuit a possible blow-up on my part!' 'And I'll make sure to read and re-read any post I write and to sit on it for at least ten minutes before I hit "send", just as a way of making sure that it doesn't come across all wrong.'

If, however, you are clearly in the wrong, admit it: apologise and mean it. A true apology does not provide an excuse for why you acted as you did; a true apology recognises the hurt you have caused someone and seeks to repair that hurt, without condition.

Getting perspective on your thoughts and emotions

Cognitive Behavioural Therapy (CBT) is a clinically proven, drug-free treatment for depression. But you don't need to be depressed in order to benefit from it. CBT is a process for recognising the thoughts and feelings that influence our behaviours, and it helps us to see the world from a more realistic perspective. To this end, CBT addresses our negative behaviours through the identification of a number of 'cognitive distortions'. Here is the basic list, but if you are interested in learning more about CBT, then I suggest you explore some of the many excellent materials available online.

- *All-or-nothing thinking*. Things fall into black-or-white categories; if your performance is less than perfect, you see it as a total failure.
- *Overgeneralisation*. A single event is seen as a never-ending pattern of negativity.
- *Mental filter*. One negative detail is singled out for endless scrutiny.
- *Discounting the positive*. Positive events 'don't count'.
- *Jumping to conclusions*. You interpret things negatively, despite the absence of facts.
- *Magnification*. You inflate your faults and problems or minimise the positive.
- *Emotional reasoning*. You feel it therefore it must be 'true'.
- *'Should' statements*. You base your expectations on what you or others 'should' or 'ought to' do or be like.
- *Labelling*. You call yourself or others names.
- *Personalisation*. You blame yourself for something that you can't control.

Learning to deal with these distortions will help you achieve realistic expectations of your own and others' behaviour online.

CONCLUDING REMARK: THERE ARE FORMAL BOUNDS ON OUR BEHAVIOURS

This chapter has focused on what you, as a person and as an individual, can do to handle yourself and others online. The central concern has been to give you an understanding of the power you have to create how you act and react in difficult online situations and an appreciation of the power you have to shape the framework within which you communicate with others. However, we are still bound by rules that are not of our own making. By this, I mean that we are bound by university codes of conduct to act in certain ways that recognise the rights of others and we are bound as well by the laws of the land in which you live. Rules, codes, policies, guidelines, and laws are there to keep us safe in the case that we can't get along with others on our own account.

 Activity   Reflect on a difficult online communication situation

Think about a difficult situation you found yourself in online – one in which you and the other party just couldn't communicate properly, and in which you felt things went badly. You might want to do this activity in discussion with someone else, or you might just want to reflect on it yourself, personally. In either case, the structure of the reflection, below, is important, so be sure to follow it carefully.

Step 1 – Who was this other person? Were they a colleague, a family member, a friend, a neighbour? Provide some context if you need to.

Step 2 – Recount the situation. Avoid using emotive language – just report the 'facts' as if you were a police officer giving evidence in court.

Step 3 – Describe the feelings and thoughts you had about the situation at the time. What was it that the other person did or said that you didn't like? What was it that irritated or angered or upset you about what they did or said? What would you have preferred them to do or say? What did you think they 'should' have done or said? How often did you think or say the following about them:

- If only they didn't do/say ...
- I wish they didn't act like ...
- I wish I could somehow make them see that ...
- I don't understand why they have to ...
- 'Why can't they just ...?'
- They must be stupid if they ...

Step 4 – Using the insights into communication that you have hopefully gained from this chapter, try to rationally consider why you couldn't or didn't understand each other. Where did the communication break down? Why couldn't you retrieve things? What got in the way? To what extent were either or each of you trying to fix how the other thought about things, rather than trying to fix the situation? Was one party trying to lock the other into certain ways of being that best suited them? Did you each need the other to act or speak in particular ways? Were either of you trying to determine a future for the other? Did each of you ignore what you might learn from the other?

Step 5 – Do a final evaluation of your own actions (not those of the other party):

- Did I act wisely?
- Did I act well?
- What were the outcomes of my actions – both for myself and others?
- Was I truly the author of my own actions?
- What were my motivations?
- Was I conscious of the beliefs that informed my actions?
- Were my feelings morally justified?
- How could I have acted better?
- What have I learnt from this?

Conducting this kind of reflection is not simple 'soul searching' – it is structured, pedagogically informed, and philosophically rigorous. If you can develop your own framework for communicating and communicating better, you will be less likely to find yourself in situations over which you feel you have little control.

SUMMARY

- Developing a framework in which you build for yourself an understanding of what constitutes for you ethical communication will equip you with your strongest defence against cyberaggression.
- Cyberbullying can happen to anyone. Like other forms of bullying it involves power imbalances, the isolation of the victim, and uninvited and unwanted behaviour. It is different, however, in that it occurs 24/7, does not need to be confined to a particular location, and can be replicated infinitely.
- Cyberaggression is not usually personally directed but can nevertheless lead to distress, withdrawal, depression, lack of appetite, and sleeplessness.
- Never respond to or engage with someone who is intimidating, bullying, or being aggressive towards you.
- Watch out for your own potentially aggressive behaviours online.
- Sometimes you need to have a difficult conversation in order to sort out online misunderstandings or cyberaggressive behaviours.
- Your behaviour is bound in degree by the criminal and civil laws in your jurisdiction. Do not transgress those laws.

FURTHER READING

France, K., Danesh, A. and Jirard, S. (2013) 'Informing aggression-prevention efforts by comparing perpetrators of brief vs. extended cyber aggression', *Computers in Human Behavior*, 29 (6): 2143–9.

Giumetti, G.W., McKibben, E.S., Hatfield, A.L., Schroeder, A.N. and Kowalski, R.M. (2012) 'Cyber incivility @ work: The new age of interpersonal deviance', *Cyberpsychology, Behavior, and Social Networking*, 15(3): 148–54.

Goodfellow, R. and Lea, M.R. (eds) (2013) *Literacy in the Digital University. Critical Perspectives on Learning, Scholarship and Technology*. London: Routledge.

Hartz Søraker, J. (2012) 'How shall I compare thee? Comparing the prudential value of actual virtual friendship', *Ethics and Information Technology*, 14 (3): 209–19.

Hughes, M. and Louw, J. (2013) 'Playing games: The salience of social cues and group norms in eliciting aggressive behaviour', *South African Journal of Psychology*, 43 (2): 252–62.

Minor, M.A., Smith, G.S. and Brashen, H. (2013) 'Cyberbullying in higher education', *Journal of Educational Research and Practice*, 3 (1): 15–29.

Spence, E.H. (2011) 'Information, knowledge and wisdom: Groundwork for the normative evaluation of digital information and its relation to the good life', *Ethics and Information Technology*, 13 (3): 261–75.

Vallor, S. (2012) 'Flourishing on Facebook: Virtue friendship and new social media', *Ethics and Information Technology*, 14 (3): 185–99.

Xiao, B.S. and Wong, Y.M. (2013) 'Cyber-bullying among university students: An empirical investigation from the social cognitive perspective', *International Journal of Business and Information*, 8 (1): 34–69.

12

Legalities and Practicalities of the Online Environment

OVERVIEW

The final chapter of *Studying and Researching with Social Media* deals with the important topic of keeping safe online through understanding the legal and practical aspects of being online. Practical considerations such as how to make your work more or less visible according to need, turning on or off cookies and monitoring, controlling notifications, and making sure you know how material is archived and cached are all covered. Also covered are understanding legal and policy considerations (including institutional regulations, copyright, intellectual property, and privacy and confidentiality issues); what it means to sign up for a Terms of Service; and what you should particularly look out for when signing up (for example, provisions relating to copyright and IP, content distribution, data security, and changes to the terms of service). The idea behind this chapter – and, indeed, the book as a whole – is to make sure that you understand what it means when you sign up for any social media service as part of your study or research projects.

SIGNING UP FOR A SERVICE

There are a few things that you need to know before signing up for any social media service for study or research purposes, not least of all because the service you are signing up for is usually provided by an externally hosted web service, that is, a service that is not supplied by the university. This section will help you make informed decisions about the type and amount of information that you supply to any particular service. Responsible lecturers and team leaders will give you a run-down of these issues before they ask you to sign up, and will encourage you to raise any questions or concerns you might have about the use of the service. The crux of the matter, though, is that you should never sign up if you are unsure about something; instead, ask around, get advice, or conduct a web search before you sign up.

Entering into an agreement with a service provider

You may be asked to sign up for certain web services as part of your studies or as part of the activities undertaken by your research team. When you sign up for a service, you will be entering into an individual agreement with that service provider, and not with the university, which means that you should read carefully and understand the service provider's Terms of Service before you sign up. You must decide the extent to which you establish your own relationship with the service provider, and you may choose to either disclose or withhold whatever information you wish, or to not sign up at all.

> When you sign up for a service, you will be entering into an individual agreement with that service provider, and not with the university.

Being required to sign up

No-one can compel you to sign up for a social media service if you don't want to. For students, this is especially the case if 1) you are under 18 (or whatever age constitutes duty of care in your jurisdiction), or if 2) you are being asked to sign up as part of your class's assessment activities (see also the discussion on Facebook groups in Chapter 5). In the first case, lecturers should seek permission from your parents when they ask you to sign up for a social media service (although this rarely happens in practice, as lecturers often forget that they might have under-18s in their classes), and in the second, your lecturer may have to find other ways for you to complete the assessment but still meet the class's learning outcomes. However, be aware that in *not* joining a site you might be missing out on access to rich conversations, useful networks, helpful links, etc. Furthermore, you cannot refuse to join a site simply because you don't feel like doing the set assessment tasks and would prefer to do something else: your lecturer has every right to ask if you are on Facebook or if you use Hotmail or if you have an account with Google – and if you do, then there is little argument you can present that would support your not wanting to sign up (unless, of course, there is something very, very wrong with the Terms of Service – see below). If, however, you have been (cyber)stalked for the past two years and wish to mitigate your digital footprint as best as possible, then that is a different matter entirely.

In any case, a generic login should be provided by your lecturer or team leader to be used by those who do not want to sign up for a particular service. Having a generic login tends to get around the above problems.

> No-one can compel you to sign up for a social media service if you don't want to.

Minimum information required on signup

In order to create an account for you, a service provider needs a place to put your data – in other words, when you sign up, you are basically creating your own folder on the site. This means that the minimum information you should be required to give away on signup should be a username, an email address (for verification; sometimes your email address also acts as your username), and a password (so no-one else can access your folder/data). Sometimes you are asked to include your date of birth – this can be for legal reasons, to make sure that you are of the right age to use the service. You should be careful about the information you disclose to a service provider. For the purposes of using a service for study or research, you should not provide information that reveals personal details about you, such as your address, postcode, telephone numbers, ethnicity, occupation, hobbies, religion, sexual orientation, relationship status, or similar information. Remember, too, that information you provide to a service provider will also include – after signup – any material you generate and upload or post as part of the class's or research team's day-to-day workings.

> The minimum information you should be required to give away on signup should be a username, an email address, and a password.

Choosing a username or publicly displayed name

This topic has already been partly covered in Chapter 2. For now, though, you should consider whether or not choosing a username or publicly displayed name based on your real name is a good idea or not in terms of managing risk online and in terms of practical considerations. As regards managing risk, you need to consider the types of things you will be doing online and whether or not they may impact negatively on your future career or reputation once you get out into the workforce or change jobs; this might lead you to choose a pseudonym. Alternatively, the type of things you will be doing online may, indeed, enhance your future career or reputation and may send you on your way to a successful career, in which case you might wish to use your real name.

Choosing a username based on your student or staff number might seem a good option, but, in fact, normally it is not. People will not be able to recognise you as 's4256689' and it is important that other users (whether they be lecturers, classmates, or colleagues) know who is contributing in what ways. Of course, some lecturers may insist that you use your student number, in which case follow their directives and leave it to them to figure out how to distinguish between users when assessment time comes around. A happy medium – that allows you to maintain a little bit of security around your username but at the same time allows the rest of the group to know who they are talking to – can be found by using your first name and last initial to make up your username or publicly displayed name: Chris C or Pat K would work well enough in most cases. Note that similar issues arise when you are asked to choose a web address, not just a username.

> Choose your username or publicly displayed name carefully.

User roles

Users have different 'roles' (or levels of access) on a social media site or service: they may be site admins (administrators) who have control over the entire site, or they may be contributors, authors, editors, or simply guests. Make sure that you know what role you are meant to play on a site and what the expectations are of that role. If you are working in a research team, it may be smart to make you a site admin or it may be smart to keep you at the contributor level – it will depend on your confidence and expertise. In any case, do not take on anything that you aren't sure about. As a student, never, *ever* take on, or volunteer for, an administrator role for a site that a lecturer has set up: there is simply too much risk of your accidentally deleting or losing or otherwise unintentionally changing material that has been posted by other students. And if that material was to be assessed, then you could be in big trouble. So, no matter how skilful, keen, or dependable you are, no matter that you want to contribute in a large way to the running of the class, never be a site admin for a lecturer's class site. Naturally, if you have started your own Facebook group or wiki or similar for your class – independent of your lecturer and independent of assessment activities – then you will, of course, be an admin for that group. In this case you should promote two or three other, trusted group members to admin roles, also, just in case something untoward happens to you.

> Make sure that you know what role you are meant to play on a site. If you are a student, never take on an administrator role for a site that a lecturer has set up.

TERMS OF SERVICE

Most of us click 'accept' to a service provider's Terms of Service without giving it a second thought – or if we *do* give it a second thought, it's only to feel guilty for not reading the Terms when we know we should have. So, we click happily away, often not knowing or caring what rights we retain or give away, what responsibilities we might have, or how our data might be used according to the agreement we've just made. This section introduces you to some of the more important elements that can be found in most Terms of Service agreements you sign. The first thing you should note, however, is that the university usually has no control over a service provider, or how a service provider uses the data it gathers. This means that once you enter into an agreement with a service provider, you are bound by that service provider's Terms of Service – not by university policies or guidelines. Thus, you should read the Terms of Service very, very carefully before you click 'accept'.

Content distribution, intellectual property, and sub-licences

A typical Terms of Service states that you give the service provider the right to display, publish, reproduce, modify, alter, translate, and adapt any content you post to the service. This is usually acceptable as the service provider simply cannot put your work on the internet if you don't give them such permission; they are not asking you to give away your copyright, and they are not claiming ownership of your content.

Potential problems occur, however, when the Terms of Service require you to give away a world-wide, perpetual, irrevocable, sub-licensable licence to your intellectual property. Such a licence means that, once given away, it can never be recalled (that is, it is perpetual and irrevocable) and that others may be authorised to access or distribute your content (that is, it may be sub-licensed), even though you continue to own it. Matters are further complicated when you license the service to do all of this with any content that you post 'in relation to the service' – which is quite a vague pledge you are making. Under these

207

conditions, you should either be very, very careful about what you upload (knowing that it may appear on a billboard or the side of bus because, remember, you have granted a sub-licence to your content), or you should find another service.

> Some licenses are better than others: avoid services that require a sub-licensable license to your content.

Third party access to your data

Knowing who has access to your data – and under what circumstances – is essential if you are to make informed decisions about what you post online. Some services will sell or otherwise provide your data (including your personal information) to third parties, meaning that you do not have control over how your data are used. Reputable services will not do this. That said, things become hazy when intellectual property considerations and sub-licences, such as those outlined above, come into play. It is reasonable, however, if a company gives contractors and agents access to your data, but only for the purposes of developing, operating, repairing, or improving the service. These individuals are bound by confidentiality agreements and liable to criminal prosecution if they breach such agreements.

> Know who has access to your data and under what conditions.

Changes to the Terms of Service

Service providers normally retain the right to make alterations to the Terms of Service at any time. This means that how the service handles important things such as copyright, privacy, data security, and data collection are all subject to change. Services can be sold or completely re-vamped and you don't need to be informed because continued use of a service usually constitutes acceptance of the Terms of Service. It is your responsibility to make sure that you keep on top of the content of the Terms you have signed up for. That said, some services will let you know about any changes to the Terms of Service, so make sure that you read all notifications to a Terms of Service that you receive – they affect you!

> Service providers can make alterations to the Terms of Service at any time.

Pricing

Social media companies are able to provide many of their services for free because they either make their money through advertising on their site or because they charge for 'premium' services or 'upgrades' that provide enhanced functionality. Nevertheless, a previously free service may decide to start charging users – even for basic service provision. As a student, you should not be asked to pay to use a service in order to complete a course of study. If, however, you choose yourself to use a service for your own purposes (either as a student or as a researcher), then that is up to you: there is nothing wrong with paying for a service if you are happy with what you get from it. Moreover, you might be able to claim your use of the service as a tax deduction if it constitutes a work-related expense.

> Service providers can change their pricing structure at any time.

Public and private sites

Most social media services recognise that users may want to keep certain information or data private from others and thus they allow for various 'permissions' or privacy settings to be applied to your account or site. Some sites you will want to be viewable by anyone, but others you will want to keep closed. As a site user, make sure that you are clear about whether the site your class or research team is using is open to the public or whether it is visible only to your colleagues.

If your work is being publicly displayed, be aware that you will be exposing your work to being stolen, plagiarised, or 'ripped off' by others. Even though most services allow you to retain copyright over your material (see section, this chapter), this does not stop disreputable persons from taking your work and using or displaying it on their own website (or in any other form) unacknowledged.

Finally, always bear in mind that anything you post on the internet is liable to being seen by others, regardless of whether you think the site is 'private' or not. This applies even if a site administrator has made a site 'invisible' to search engines because, firstly, the site may be visible to visitors who have a direct link to the site (which is a fair and acceptable way of making a site 'fairly private' without having to make it 'private by invitation only') and, secondly, your information may be intercepted by hackers (which is rare and, besides, hackers are usually going after different targets).

With all of this said, however, do not become unreasonable or irrational as regards your use of the internet for study or research: recognise that some risk is involved but that, if you manage that risk sensibly and with a proper understanding of how things work, you can usually navigate a safe path across the net.

> Know what privacy settings have been applied to the site you are using.

Posting of offensive material

Most Terms of Service have lengthy sections devoted to user conduct and the posting of user content. When you enter into a Terms of Service, you are usually agreeing to not post any material that is offensive, abusive, hateful, obscene, racially or ethnically vilifying, harassing, discriminatory, threatening, defamatory, libellous, or in any other manner objectionable. You are also agreeing not to breach copyright or privacy provisions. Note that these things are not just covered by Terms of Service: in most developed countries, they are illegal and come under various laws relating to discrimination, harassment, privacy, and vilification. Often, the fairly liberal university environment makes us feel that we can say or get away with many things that we might not say or get away with elsewhere; but if you break these laws, you may be subject to criminal prosecution.

If you believe that someone has posted something that is offensive, defamatory, hateful, breaches copyright, discloses personal information about you, or is cause for other concern, then you must notify the site administrator immediately, and they should act to remove the content. Failing that, you can notify the service provider. If, on the other hand, *you* post something offensive and you suddenly realise it, remove it straight away or have the site administrator remove it: it is OK (even advisable!) to make a mistake, admit it, and move to address it.

Finally, do not post anything that brings you, your class or team mates, or your institution into disrepute.

> Do not post offensive material: you may be in breach not only of the Terms of Service but you might also be acting illegally and thus subject to criminal prosecution in your jurisdiction.

LEGAL AND QUASI-LEGAL ISSUES

Legal and quasi-legal issues abound on the internet, making for a very complex – and sometimes complicated – research, work, and study environment. Laws relating to copyright and intellectual property vary from jurisdiction to jurisdiction, so, firstly, you need to understand these things as they apply to the country(-ies) you are living and working in. Secondly, you need to know how they relate to the conditions of your employment or study, and, finally, you need to know how they relate to the specific arrangements you are entering into when you sign up with a certain service.

Copyright and intellectual property (IP)

Owners of copyright and intellectual property (IP) rights have the exclusive legal right to publish, distribute, and reproduce original works as they see fit. They can sell or license out the work for others to use, and they can control how it gets reproduced. Typically, the creator of the work automatically owns the rights to that work: copyright for tangible works (for example, a painting, a photograph, a podcast, a written text, a video) and intellectual property rights for intangible works (such as ideas and designs). However, in a good number of instances, the creator of the work does not hold copyright or IP rights to that work – for example, a record company might hold copyright in a band's work because the band has assigned copyright to the company in return for publishing and distributing the band's music. In the university environment, the institution you work for might claim copyright over any work you produce whilst employed there; after all, they have paid you to produce it, so they claim ownership over it. In such cases, your institution might grant you a non-exclusive IP licence that allows you certain uses of the work, or they might not. Alternatively, the institution might allow you to keep your copyright, but insist that you provide the university with an exclusive (or otherwise) sub-licence to the IP rights in the work.

The kinds of rights that you may or may not have over work that you produce in a university will probably depend on your 'status' at the institution. If you are an academic, the terms of your employment usually allow you to retain copyright over your work, even though the same terms might stipulate that you grant the university an exclusive (or non-exclusive) IP licence to your work. If you are a non-academic staff member, the chances are that the university owns copyright in the work you produce whilst in their employ – and you might or might not be granted an IP licence to that work. Students, on the other hand, normally retain their copyright and IP in their entirety, meaning that the university normally lays no claim to either – but this, too, might depend, especially if you are working on an invention that could attract licensing fees payable to the institution.

As you can see, there are many different copyright/IP ownership and licensing combinations, so you need to know exactly what you do and do not own – and under what conditions – if you are to avoid a breach of copyright.

> Copyright is complicated: know whether or not you own copyright in the work you produce.

Copyright, IP, and Terms of Service

If it transpires that you *do* own copyright in the material you produce, then under the Terms of Service or similar that you sign up for you should retain that copyright; in other words, when you sign up, the service you are entering into an agreement with should not insist that you hand over your copyright to them. At the same time, you should also retain any intellectual property rights you own in the material you supply to a service. However, because a service is hosting what you create, the service will probably require a licence to your IP in order to publicly display, reproduce, translate, publish, and distribute your work; if you do not grant this licence, the service cannot put your work on the internet – it is that simple. It also means that you cannot sue the service for displaying, reproducing, translating, publishing, distributing, and so on, material in which you hold the copyright. Again, if you don't give this licence, the service provider cannot display your work.

The type of IP licence the service requires is important. Ideally, all you should be asked to grant is a non-exclusive licence to your IP so that the service can put your work on the internet. However, if the service asks for a sub-licensable licence to your IP (as certain large social networks do), then think carefully either about what you post or about signing up in the first place: once a company has a sub-licensable licence to your IP, it can sell your material on to third parties without asking and without your knowing it. If a service asks for an exclusive licence to your IP, then it could mean that even you are prevented from distributing your work elsewhere (exactly what 'exclusive' covers will depend on jurisdiction, so be sure to check). To be safe, do not sign up to any service that requires an exclusive licence to your IP.

Finally, you will be in breach of your conditions of employment if you upload material that your institution owns copyright in or that you have granted the institution an exclusive licence to. Reputable services will include a clause in their Terms of Service that requires you to agree that you will not upload any material that breaches the copyright or IP rights of others. If you have any questions or concerns, you should get legal advice from your institution *before* signing up.

> A service should allow you to retain copyright and intellectual property rights over material that you own. Avoid services that require a sub-licensable licence to your content.

Third-party copyright and IP

Generally, and quite plainly, speaking, you cannot post other people's stuff without their permission. This, however, is easier said than done. The very nature of social media means that it is super-easy to breach copyright without knowing or meaning to, as the entire social media world is predicated upon sharing. The safest thing, of course, is to just not post or upload anything in which you do not own copyright – but, as we have seen above, whether or not you own copyright in the material you produce, and the conditions under which you might or might not distribute such material, might be unclear to you. Here are some best practices you can adopt in this area:

- Never download and then upload to your own site images, artworks, audios, videos, journal articles, and so on, that you do not own.
- Always embed or link out to non-infringing material so that the material is not hosted on your site.
- Always credit any work that is not your own.
- Never bypass any protection measures.

If you are found to be in breach, then the first step in any redress process is usually to ask you to remove the infringing material via a 'take-down notice' and to destroy any further copies you might have. Failure to do this could leave you vulnerable to legal action.

> Never post other people's material without their permission.

Creative Commons

We can see from the above that copyright and intellectual property raise many complex issues, especially as regards the distribution of material via the internet. In an effort to cut through some of this complexity, a simpler, more streamlined and practical form of licensing called 'Creative Commons' (CC) has arisen. Creative Commons licensing lets you change your copyright from 'all rights reserved' to 'some rights reserved'. Depending on the type of Creative Commons licence you decide to distribute your work under, this may mean that other people may share your work as long as they attribute the work to you, do not use the work for commercial purposes, and/or agree to share your work under the same licence – you decide. You don't have to apply for a licence or register it anywhere: you simply put a note on your work telling people under what conditions they can use it.

You need to know about Creative Commons because under the Terms of Service your work could be automatically sub-licensed under a Creative Commons licence. For many individuals this is acceptable but for some it is not – and besides, the conditions of your employment may exclude you from granting a CC sub-licence to the service provider anyway. Again, you need to understand how these things work so that you can make informed choices about the Terms of Service you are agreeing to. Visit CreativeCommons.org for more information.

> Your work could be automatically sub-licensed under a Creative Commons licence.

Privacy and confidentiality

Breaches of privacy are treated very seriously in many jurisdictions, and breaching privacy laws may make you liable to prosecution. Reputable services have a Privacy Policy that is compatible with the privacy laws for the country in which it operates – but this doesn't mean that the service's Privacy Policy is automatically compatible with the privacy laws in your own country. Of course, privacy issues relate both to the protection of your privacy and the protection of others' privacy. As regards your own privacy, you need to know who, under a service's Privacy Policy, might access your private information. Frequently, third parties are allowed to access your data under the following conditions: for auditing, research, and analysis in order to maintain, protect, and improve the services; for ensuring the technical functioning of the network; or for developing new services. As regards other's privacy, you must at least never provide information to a service about other people without their express consent and you must never upload database files that contain people's names and addresses to a service. Check the service's Privacy Policy for full details. If you have any questions or concerns, contact your lecturer or team leader *before* you sign up.

> Do not breach others' privacy and confidentiality and be sure to protect your own.

Jurisdictional issues

Terms of Service are governed by the laws of the country in which the service legally operates (this is the 'jurisdiction'), and although laws in many countries might appear quite similar, they are nevertheless not the same. If a breach of privacy or copyright or similar occurs but occurs via a service located outside your jurisdiction, you may not be able to seek legal redress. On the other hand, if you yourself breach another country's laws – inadvertently or not – you may be liable to legal action in that country. Although these issues are far from sorted in a legal sense, you need to be aware of them as they currently stand.

> Different laws apply in different countries. If you breach another country's laws, you may be liable to legal action in that country.

Accessibility

You have a right to accessible websites and should not be disadvantaged in class or research work because a lecturer or colleague has chosen to use a particular social media site or service for your group's activities. In fact, in many developed countries there are laws against discriminating against people with disabilities, so the use of social media services that inhibit, for example, vision or hearing-impaired people from participating fully in group pursuits could well be illegal. If you experience any difficulties in this area, talk to your lecturer or colleagues about how to make the site or service compliant with W3C's web accessibility standards; if it can't be made compliant, then request use of a different service. By the same token, be sure not to create sites or use services that do not meet accessibility standards: you may be in breach of discrimination or similar laws in your jurisdiction.

> You have a right to accessible websites. At the same time, be sure not to create sites or use services that do not meet accessibility standards.

GENERAL USE ISSUES

Regardless of whether you are using social media for study or research, there are some general issues that will arise and that relate to your daily use of a service. Be sure you can deal with the following everyday practicalities.

Monitoring

Most of our web travels are monitored by what are called 'cookies', that is, small packets of data that are collected and then re-used each time you log into a website. When you type in your username or email or other details into a field and they are 'autocompleted', there is a cookie lying behind the field, finishing off your request so that you don't have to keep re-entering the same information over and over again. Cookies, as their name suggest, leave a trail of your internet use, which some users find helpful and others find discomfiting or unnecessary. You can turn cookies off in your browser's privacy settings or preferences.

> Know how to turn off cookies and monitoring.

Notifications

When you sign up for a service you may receive marketing or other service-related email messages (such as, 'A page has been updated') in your inbox. Some people find these messages annoying, so most developed countries now have laws that require there to be an 'unsubscribe' link that with one click allows you to opt out of such notifications. You can also turn off these messages via your account or profile settings or preferences: just navigate your way to 'email notifications' or similar and switch them off.

> Know how to turn off notifications.

Archiving and caching

Search engines may find, index, and cache the information you provide to a service. This should only occur with your openly accessible information, but, as we all know, accidents and breaches can happen. It could also be the case that you have posted something publicly and then changed your mind and either deleted it or subsequently made it private; in any case, it might not matter for in the intervening period a search engine may have trawled your site or page, downloaded it and archived it, which means that it may still be visible to a public audience via the engine's cache (search engines make their cached material publicly accessible). So, even if you posted something that you later thought better of and deleted two minutes later, there is every chance that the search engine, *in those two minutes*, cached your site – meaning that the material is still out there, somewhere, visible on the web. The implications of this for you, personally, can be enormous, especially if you posted something that breached copyright, privacy, or anti-discrimination laws and that can no longer be erased. There are procedures that you can follow for removing material from a search engine's cache, but they are often laborious or tricky and you would need to go through each and every search engine individually to make sure the material is no longer on the internet – an impossible task. Much better in the first instance to avoid posting material that you might later want to remove.

> Search engines find, index, and cache the information you provide. Once you have posted something, it is virtually impossible to remove it.

Help desk support

Universities have been very slow in adopting IT helpdesk models that accommodate the use of non-university-supplied social media services. In many instances, IT and training staff are tasked with servicing only those systems that the university has paid for or has chosen as part of its enterprise network. This means that if something goes wrong with the social media service that you are using, then you could have difficulty in finding someone who can help you. By the same token, there may not be any university-supported or -supplied training in the service you are using in class, in which case either your lecturer, colleagues, or fellow students might have to fill the breach. Alternatively, you will have to rely on the help provided via the social media service itself through things such as FAQs, video tutorials, and discussion forums. See Chapter 2 for further discussion around problem solving and helping yourself.

> Do not rely on university IT services to support non-university-supplied sites or services.

ISSUES FOR ASSESSMENT

A number of quite specific issues arise when a lecturer chooses to use social media for assignments. As a student, make sure you understand the conditions under which your work is being assessed. If you aren't sure about anything, ask your lecturer.

Visibility of your work

Lecturers who use social media for assessment purposes often think long and hard about how visible your work should be – both to other students and to the outside world more generally. Make sure you know who can and who cannot see your work and under what conditions. For example, maybe your site is entirely protected from non-course participants but enrolled students can nevertheless see each other's work. Or perhaps you are working in small groups, in which case maybe only members of your group can see what's going on, whilst others – even if they are in the same course as you – cannot. Or maybe the entire site is public and anyone and everyone with access to an internet connection comprises your potential audience. In any instance, you need to be clear about who can and cannot see your work, and under what circumstances.

> Be clear about who can and cannot see your work.

Backing up your work

If a social media service is being used for assignment purposes, then you are responsible for backing up your work: just as you are supposed to have a spare copy of any essay or report you write, so, too, are you supposed to have a spare copy of any blog posts, wikipages, videos, audios, and so on, that you produce for assessment. You cannot claim that your work 'disappeared' from the site, as your lecturer will simply ask you to submit what you had already done in a format that can be read by them. You should back up your work on a regular basis, whenever you make significant additions, contributions, or alterations to the site, and at the point where you submit the work for marking. In fact, it is good practice to backup your work on any site you use, even if it is not being assessed. If you aren't sure how to backup your work, ask your lecturer and see Chapter 2 in the current volume.

> It is your responsibility to back up your own work.

Date stamping

Work or material posted to a social media service is almost always date stamped. If your lecturer owns and administers the site, this means that any changes made to your site after the due date will be noted. If, however, you are the owner of your own site, then you are responsible for ensuring that your account's time zone is correct. Do not hand in work late and backdate it – that is dishonest. Similarly, do not make changes to your work after the due date and claim that they were made before the due date. That is also dishonest.

> Your work must be accurately datestamped.

Attribution of work under your login and group work

Work generated under any particular login will be attributed to that login by your lecturer. For example, if you are working with another student and your work appears under that student's login, then the chances are that you will not be recognised as the author of that work. You need to make sure that your work appears under your own login, as you would have difficulty in claiming to be the author of work done under another student's login. You are responsible for anything that occurs under your account login. If you are taking part in group work, then make sure the lecturer can track who has made which contributions.

> You are responsible for anything that occurs under your account login.

Minimum period your work will be kept for

There is a likelihood that, upon completion of a course of study, university regulations, procedures, or policies might require that work that you complete as part of your assessment might need to be kept for a minimum period – sometimes six months, sometimes a year, or some other time frame. This is so that, if a grade or marking process is questioned, then the original piece of work can be viewed and re-assessed. The same rules apply if you are using a social media service. So, if you wish to add to or develop your site or similar after the assessment due date, then you should consider providing your lecturer with a dated electronic backup of the site as it appeared on the due date. This will allow you to continue to work on your site upon completion of the course. If you don't do this, then you could be prevented from working on your site until after the proscribed period unless a dated 'restore to previous version' function is available on the site.

Find out how long assessment items need to be retained.

ASSURANCES YOU NEED IN THE USE OF SOCIAL MEDIA SERVICES

Regardless of whether you are a student using social media for assessment or whether you are contributing to the social media activities of your research team, there are certain assurances that you need from those who have made the decision on your behalf to use this form of communication in the first place. You need to know that every effort has been made to choose service providers that

- Provide fair Terms of Service that are likely to be acceptable to you.
- Allow you retain both copyright and rights to your intellectual property.
- Do not sub-license your intellectual property to third parties.
- Give you a large degree of control over how much and what type of your personal information is displayed.
- Allow you to backup your material to your hard-drive in one form or another.
- Permit you to switch off notifications.
- Are normally stable, reliable, and available.
- Have a good reputation.
- Have strong online communities built around them.
- Allow you to switch off advertising.
- Provide services that work across platforms (PC, Mac, Linux) and across browsers (Firefox, Internet Explorer).
- Do not expose you to potential violations of institutional policies or, indeed, legislation in your jurisdiction.

Of course, you should take some responsibility for looking into these things yourself. You should also find out whether or not a risk assessment has been conducted as regards the use of the service or tool in your context. If not, then suggest that one be conducted and contribute to it yourself.

SUMMARY ☐

- Before signing up for a social media service you need to read, understand, and agree to the Terms of Service. Don't just click 'accept'. You should never be required to sign up for a Terms of Service if you do not agree with those Terms of Service.
- Choose your username carefully.
- Service providers may change the Terms of Service at any time without notifying you.
- Know what levels of privacy are applied to your site.
- Do not post offensive material.

- Understand who has access to your data, and how your content is distributed.
- Understand copyright, intellectual property, Creative Commons, privacy, and confidentiality as they pertain to your use of a social media service.
- You should be able to turn off monitoring and notifications relating to your use of a social media service.
- Search engines will archive your work. Do not post anything that you might later want to remove.
- If social media are being used for assessment, you need to consider issues relating to backing up your work, date stamping, the minimum period your work will be kept for, and attribution for and visibility of your work.
- You need certain assurances about how a social media service is being used in your study or research environment if you are to keep safe online.

FURTHER READING

Bozdag, E. (2013) 'Bias in algorithmic filtering and personalization', *Ethics and Information Technology*, 15 (3): 209–27.

Child, J.T., Haridakis, P.M. and Petronio, S. (2012) 'Blogging privacy rule orientations, privacy management, and content deletion practices: The variability of online privacy management activity at different stages of social media use', *Computers in Human Behavior*, 28 (5): 1859–72.

Hugenholtz, P.B. and Okediji, R. (2012) *Conceiving an International Instrument on Limitations and Exceptions to Copyright*, study supported by the Open Society Institute (OSI); Amsterdam Law School Research Paper No. 2012–43; Institute for Information Law Research Paper No. 2012-37. Available at SSRN: http://ssrn.com/abstract=2017629 or http://dx.doi.org/10.2139/ssrn.2017629. Accessed 10 September 2013.

Jacobson, D., Rursch, J. and Idziorek, J. (2012) *Security Across the Curriculum and Beyond*, FIE '12 Proceedings of the 2012 IEEE Frontiers in Education Conference (FIE). Pp. 1–6. Available at: http://ieeexplore.ieee.org/xpl/articleDetails.jsp?arnumber=6462297. Accessed 10 September 2013.

Karjala, D.S., Brown, J.E. and Day O'Connor, D. (2013) 'International convergence on the need for third parties to become internet copyright police (but why?)', *Richmond Journal of Global Law and Business*, 189, Spring.

Madden, M. (2012) *Privacy Management on Social Media Sites*, Pew Research Center's Internet and American Life Project. Available at: http://pewinternet.org/Reports/2012/Privacy-management-on-social-media.aspx. Accessed 9 September 2013.

Martin, K. (2012) 'Information technology and privacy: Conceptual muddles or privacy vacuums?', *Ethics and Information Technology*, 14 (4): 267–84.

Pearson, M. (2012) *Blogging and Tweeting Without Getting Sued*. Sydney: Allen & Unwin.

Rheingold, H. and Weeks, A. (2012) *Net Smart: How to Thrive Online*. Cambridge, MA: The MIT Press.

Stutzman, F., Vitak, J., Ellison, N.B., Gray, R. and Lampe, C. (2012) *Privacy in Interaction: Exploring Disclosure and Social Capital in Facebook*, Sixth International AAAI Conference on Weblogs and Social Media. Available at: http://www.aaai.org/ocs/index.php/ICWSM/ICWSM12/paper/view/4666. Accessed 10 September 2013.

University of Edinburgh (2007) *Guidelines for Using External Web 2.0 Services*. Available at: https://www.wiki.ed.ac.uk/display/Web2wiki/Web+2.0+Guidelines. Accessed 9 September 2013.

Afterword

If you have made your way to this afterword, you should now have a good sense of how social media can be used to support your study and research activities. But more than this, you should now have a sense of the complexity of the social media environment as it applies to the modern Academy. Not only must scholars learn how to write and produce materials outside the parameters of traditional academic genres, we must also learn new forms of engagement outside the university campus. We need to understand the intricacies of the social, policy, and legal contexts that constitute being digitally networked, and we need to figure out how to best use social media to communicate all the good work we are doing – if we don't, then we are in danger of being swamped by the many other voices that inhabit online spaces.

One thing is certain: social media are here to stay. In the space of only a few years, social media have become central to our everyday communication practices, and, inasmuch as study and research are about communication, then the visibility of social media within higher education can only continue to increase. It is imperative – whether you are a first-year undergraduate just starting on your first course of study or an experienced research academic – that you grasp both the broad conceptual implications of this fact as well as the intricacies of how social media work in your particular scholarly context. I hope this book has given you something of what you need, not only in terms of information, but also in terms of an appreciation of the complexity of social media as it applies to study and research. I hope I have explained things at least well enough that you might be encouraged to try something new or be able to extend your expertise. If you were feeling lost I hope that you now have found a place to start, and if you were feeling confused or overwhelmed I hope things are now a little clearer and more manageable.

In the final analysis, though, being online is perhaps not so different from other aspects of our lives: caution must be balanced with curiosity, and excitement tempered by prudence; ambivalence is generally not a survival tactic but enterprise is, and courage and compassion can get us far. So, be intrepid, discover new ways of doing things, and rethink old ones. Embrace all these qualities and you will only ever be successful in your academic – and other – endeavours.

Bibliography

Allen, E. and Seaman, J. (2012) *Conflicted: Faculty and Online Education, 2012*, a joint project of the Babson Survey Research Group and *Inside Higher Ed*. Available at: http://www.insidehighered.com/sites/default/server_files/survey/conflicted.html. Accessed 4 July 2013.

Anderson, C. (2006) *The Long Tail. How Endless Choice is Creating Unlimited Demand*. London: Random House.

Arazy, O., Yeo, L. and Nov, O. (2013) 'Stay on the Wikipedia task: When task-related disagreements slip into personal and procedural conflicts', *Journal of the American Society for Information Science and Technology*, 64 (8): 1634–48.

Arnold, N., Ducate, L. and Kost, C. (2012) 'Collaboration or cooperation? Analyzing group dynamics and revision processes in wikis', *CALICO Journal*, 29 (3): 431–48.

Attwell, G. (2007) *Web 2.0 and the Changing Ways We Are Using Computers for Learning: What are the Implications for Pedagogy and Curriculum?* Available at: www.elearningeuropa.info/files/media/media13018.pdf. Accessed 10 September 2013.

Bamford, A. (2011) *The Visual Literacy White Paper*, commissioned by Adobe Systems Pty Ltd, Australia. Available at: http://www.adobe.com/au/solutions/white-papers/education-k12.html. Accessed 12 September 2013.

Bentley, P.J. and Kyvik, S. (2013) 'Individual differences in faculty research time allocations across 13 countries', *Research in Higher Education*, 54 (3): 329–48.

Boase, J. (2013) 'Implications of software-based mobile media for social research', *Mobile Media & Communication*, 1 (1): 57–62.

boyd, d. (2011) 'Social network sites as networked publics: Affordances, dynamics, and implications', in Z. Papacharissi (ed.), *Networked Self: Identity, Community, and Culture on Social Network Sites*. New York: Routledge. pp. 39–58.

Bozdag, E. (2013) 'Bias in algorithmic filtering and personalization', *Ethics and Information Technology*, 15 (3): 209–27.

Cao, Q., Lu, Y., Dong, D., Tang, Z. and Li, Y. (2013) 'The roles of bridging and bonding in social media communities', *Journal of the American Society for Information Science and Technology*, 64 (8): 1671–81.

Child, J.T., Haridakis, P.M. and Petronio, S. (2012) 'Blogging privacy rule orientations, privacy management, and content deletion practices: The variability of online privacy management activity at different stages of social media use', *Computers in Human Behavior*, 28 (5): 1859–72.

Chretien, K.C., Azar, J. and Kind, T. (2011) 'Physicians on Twitter', *Journal of the American Medical Association*, 305: 566–8.

Churches, A. (n.d.) *21st Century Learning Spaces*. Available at: http://edorigami.wikispaces.com/21st+Century+Learning+Spaces. Accessed 10 September 2013.

CIBER (2008) *Information Behaviour of the Researcher of the Future.* Available at: http://www.jisc.ac.uk/media/documents/programmes/reppres/gg_final_keynote_11012008.pdf. Accessed 13 September 2013.

Cohn, N. (2012) 'Visual narrative structure', *Cognitive Science*, 37 (3): 413–52.

Curşeu, P.L., Janssen, S.E.A. and Raab, J. (2012) 'Connecting the dots: Social network structure, conflict, and group cognitive complexity', *Higher Education*, 63 (5): 621–9.

Dabbagh, N. and Kitsantas, A. (2012) 'Personal Learning Environments, social media, and self-regulated learning: A natural formula for connecting formal and informal learning', *The Internet and Higher Education*, 15 (1): 3–8.

Davies, J. (2004) *Wiki Brainstorming and Problems with Wiki*, MSc Project submitted September. Available at: http://www.jonathan-davies.co.uk/portfolio/wiki.php. Accessed 13 September 2013.

Davies, J. (2009) 'A space for play: Crossing boundaries and learning online', in V. Carrington and M. Robinson (eds), *Digital Literacies: Social Learning and Classroom Practices.* Los Angeles, CA: UKLA and SAGE.

de Laat, P.B. (2012) 'Coercion or empowerment? Moderation of content in Wikipedia as "essentially contested" bureaucratic rules', *Ethics and Information Technology*, 14 (2): 123–35.

Dennison, G.M. (2012) 'Faculty workload: An analytical approach', *Innovative Higher Education*, 37 (4): 297–305.

Dewey, J. (2004 [1916]) *Democracy and Education.* Mineola, NY: Dover.

Downes, S. (2008) 'Places to go: Connectivism & connective knowledge', in *Innovate Journal of Online Education*, 5 (1).

Duh, K., Hirao, T., Kimura, A., Ishiguro, K., Iwata, T. and Yeung, C.M.A. (2012) *Creating Stories: Social Curation of Twitter Messages*, Sixth International AAAI Conference on Weblogs and Social Media, 4 June, Dublin, Ireland. Available at: http://www.aaai.org/ocs/index.php/ICWSM/ICWSM12/paper/view/4578. Accessed 10 September 2013.

Duhigg, C. (2012) *The Power of Habit.* London: William Heinemann.

EDUCAUSE (2012) *ECAR Study of Undergraduate Students and Information Technology, 2012.* Available at: http://www.educause.edu/library/resources/ecar-study-undergraduate-students-and-information-technology-2012. Accessed 9 September 2013.

Faktor, S. (2013) *The 10 Types of Twitterers and How to Tame their Tweets.* Available at: http://www.forbes.com/sites/stevefaktor/2013/01/04/the-10-types-of-twitterers-and-how-to-tame-their-tweets-twitter-users/. Accessed 10 September 2013.

Fitzgerald, R. and Steele, J. (2008) *Digital Learning Communities (DLC): Investigating the Application of Social Software to Support Networked Learning.* Available at: http://eprints.qut.edu.au/18476/. Accessed 9 September 2013.

France, K., Danesh, A. and Jirard, S. (2013) 'Informing aggression-prevention efforts by comparing perpetrators of brief vs. extended cyber aggression', *Computers in Human Behavior*, 29 (6): 2143–9.

Freire, P. (1996 [1970]) *Pedagogy of the Oppressed.* London: Penguin.

Gikas, J. and Grant, M.M. (2013) 'Mobile computing devices in higher education: Student perspectives on learning with cellphones, smartphones and social media', *The Internet and Higher Education*, 19: 10–17.

Giumetti, G.W., McKibben, E.S., Hatfield, A.L., Schroeder, A.N. and Kowalski, R.M. (2012) 'Cyber incivility @ work: The new age of interpersonal deviance', *Cyberpsychology, Behavior, and Social Networking*, 15(3): 148–54.

Goodfellow, R. and Lea, M.R. (eds) (2013) *Literacy in the Digital University. Critical Perspectives on Learning, Scholarship and Technology.* London: Routledge.

Green, H. and Hannon, C. (2007) *Their Space: Education for a Digital Generation*. Available at: http://www.demos.co.uk/publications/theirspace. Accessed 9 September 2013.

Greiffenhagen, C. (2013) 'Visual grammar in practice: Negotiating the arrangement of speech bubbles in storyboards', *Semiotica*, 195: 127–67.

Gruzd, A., Wellman, B. and Takhteyev, Y. (2011) 'Imagining Twitter as an imagined community', *American Behavioral Scientist*, 55 (10): 1294–318.

Hague, C. and Payton, S. (2010) *Digital Literacy Across the Curriculum: A Futurelab Handbook*. Available at: http://archive.futurelab.org.uk/resources/publications-reports-articles/handbooks/Handbook1706. Accessed 13 September 2013.

Hague, C. and Williamson, B. (2009) *Digital Participation, Digital Literacy, and School Subjects: A Review of the Policies, Literature and Evidence*, Futurelab. Available at: http://www.futurelab.org.uk/resources/digital-participation-digital-literacy-and-school-subjects-literature-review. Accessed 9 September 2013.

Hartley, J. (2009) *The Uses of Digital Literacy*. St Lucia, Qld: University of Queensland Press.

Hartz Søraker, J. (2012) 'How shall I compare thee? Comparing the prudential value of actual virtual friendship', *Ethics and Information Technology*, 14 (3): 209–19.

Hoffman, E.S. (2009) 'Social media and learning environments: Shifting perspectives on the locus of control', *In Education*, 15 (2). Available at: http://ineducation.ca/index.php/ineducation/article/view/54/532. Accessed 13 September 2013.

Hrastinski, S. and Aghaee, N.M. (2012) 'How are campus students using social media to support their studies? An explorative interview study', *Education and Information Technologies*, 17 (4): 451–64.

Hugenholtz, P.B. and Okediji, R. (2012) *Conceiving an International Instrument on Limitations and Exceptions to Copyright*, study supported by the Open Society Institute (OSI); Amsterdam Law School Research Paper No. 2012–43; Institute for Information Law Research Paper No. 2012-37. Available at SSRN: http://ssrn.com/abstract=2017629 or http://dx.doi.org/10.2139/ssrn.2017629. Accessed 10 September 2013.

Hughes, M. and Louw, J. (2013) 'Playing games: The salience of social cues and group norms in eliciting aggressive behaviour', *South African Journal of Psychology*, 43 (2): 252–62.

Jacobson, D., Rursch, J. and Idziorek, J. (2012) *Security across the Curriculum and Beyond*, FIE '12 Proceedings of the 2012 IEEE Frontiers in Education Conference (FIE): 1–6. Available at: http://ieeexplore.ieee.org/xpl/articleDetails.jsp?arnumber=6462297. Accessed 10 September 2013.

JISC (2007) *Student Expectations Study: Findings from Preliminary Research*, Joint Information Systems Committee. Available at: http://www.jisc.ac.uk/publications/publications/studentexpectationsbp.aspx. Accessed 9 September 2013.

JISC (2008) *Great Expectations of ICT: How Higher Education Institutions Are Measuring Up*, Joint Information Systems Committee. Available at: http://www.jisc.ac.uk/publications/publications/greatexpectations. Accessed 9 September 2013.

Jones, H., Johnson, P. and Gruszczynska, A. (2012) 'Digital literacy: Digital maturity or digital bravery?', *Enhancing Learning in the Social Sciences*, 4 (2).

Jones, T.D. and Swain, D.E. (2012) 'Managing your online professional identity', *Bulletin of the American Society for Information Science and Technology*, 38 (2): 29–31.

Karjala, D.S., Brown, J.E. and Day O'Connor, D. (2013) 'International convergence on the need for third parties to become internet copyright police (but why?)', *Richmond Journal of Global Law and Business*, 189, Spring.

Kayam, O. and Hirsch, T. (2012) 'Using social media networks to conduct questionnaire-based research in social studies case study: Family language policy', *Journal of Sociological Research*, 3 (2): 57–67.

Kirkup, G. (2010) 'Academic blogging, academic practice and academic identity', *London Review of Education*, 8 (1): 75–84.

Korsgaard, C.M. (2009) *Self-Constitution: Agency, Identity, and Integrity*. Oxford: Oxford University Press.

Kuhlthau, C.C. (1991) 'Inside the search process: Information seeking from the user's perspective', *Journal of the American Society for Information Science*, 42 (5): 361–71.

Kukulska-Hulme, A. (2012) 'How should the higher education workforce adapt to advancements in technology for teaching and learning?', *The Internet and Higher Education*, 19: 247–54.

Kummer, C. (2013) *Factors Influencing Wiki Collaboration in Higher Education*, Social Science Research Network. Available at SSRN: http://ssrn.com/abstract=2208522. Accessed 12 September 2013.

Lin, C., Kuo, F., Tseng, F. and Tang, W. (2012) *Motivating and Sustaining Women's Digital Literacy through ICT Learning*, AMCIS 2012 Proceedings, Paper 20. Available at: http://aisel.aisnet.org/amcis2012/proceedings/AdoptionDiffusionIT/20. Accessed 10 September 2013.

Loader, D. (2007) *Jousting for the New Generation: Challenges to Contemporary Schooling*. Camberwell: ACER Press.

Madden, M. (2012) *Privacy Management on Social Media Sites*, Pew Research Center's Internet and American Life Project. Available at: http://pewinternet.org/Reports/2012/Privacy-management-on-social-media.aspx. Accessed 9 September 2013.

Mannheim, K. (1943) *Diagnosis of Our Time*. London: Kegan Paul, Trench, Trubner & Co., Ltd.

Martin, K. (2012) 'Information technology and privacy: Conceptual muddles or privacy vacuums?', *Ethics and Information Technology*, 14 (4): 267–84.

Marwick, A.E. and boyd, d. (2011) 'I tweet honestly, I tweet passionately: Twitter users, context collapse, and the imagined audience', *New Media & Society*, 13 (1): 114–33.

Matusiak, K.K. (2013) 'Image and multimedia resources in an academic environment: A qualitative study of students' experiences and literacy practices', *Journal of the American Society for Information Science and Technology*, 64 (8): 1577–89.

MCEECDYA (2010) *National Assessment Program – ICT Literacy Years 6 & 10*, Report 2008. Available at: www.mceecdya.edu.au/verve/_resources/NAP-ICTL_2008_report.pdf. Accessed 10 September 2013.

McNeill, T. (2012) '"Don't affect the share price": Social media policy in higher education as reputation management', *Research in Learning Technology*, 20, Supplement: ALT-C 2012 Conference Proceedings: 152–62.

Meyer, K.A. (2012) 'The influence of online teaching on faculty productivity', *Innovative Higher Education*, 37 (1): 37–52.

Minor, M.A., Smith, G.S. and Brashen, H. (2013) 'Cyberbullying in higher education', *Journal of Educational Research and Practice*, 3 (1): 15–29.

Mounce, R. (2013) 'Open access and altmetrics: Distinct but complementary', *Bulletin of the American Society for Information Science and Technology*, 39 (4): 14–17.

New Media Consortium and EDUCAUSE Learning Initiative (2008) *The Horizon Report*. Available at: http://wp.nmc.org/horizon2008/. Accessed 9 September 2013.

Ng, W. (2012) 'Can we teach digital natives digital literacy?', *Computers & Education*, 59 (3): 1065–78.

Nichol, D., Hunter, J., Yaseen, J. and Prescott-Clements, L. (2012) 'A simple guide to enhancing learning through Web 2.0 technologies', *European Journal of Higher Education*, 2 (4): 436–46.

O'Reilly, T. (2005) *What is Web 2.0? Design Patterns and Business Models for the Next Generation of Software*. Available at: http://oreilly.com/web2/archive/what-is-web-20.html. Accessed 11 September 2013.

Park, Y.J. (2013) 'Digital literacy and privacy behavior online', *Communication Research*, 40 (2): 215–36.

Pearce, N., Weller, M., Scanlon, E. and Kinsley, S. (2010) 'Digital scholarship considered: How new technologies could transform academic work', *In Education*, 16 (1): 33–44.

Pearson, M. (2012) *Blogging and Tweeting Without Getting Sued*. Sydney: Allen & Unwin.

Pochoda, P. (2013) 'The big one: The epistemic system break in scholarly monograph publishing', *New Media & Society*, 15 (3): 359–78.

Poore, M. (2011) 'Digital literacy: Human flourishing and collective intelligence in a knowledge society', *Literacy Learning: the Middle Years*, 19 (2): 20–26.

Poore, M. (2012) *Using Social Media in the Classroom. A Best Practice Guide*. London: SAGE.

Postman, N. (1993) *Technopoly: The Surrender of Culture to Technology*. New York: Vintage Books.

Powell, D.A., Jacob, C.J. and Chapman, B.J. (2012) 'Using blogs and new media in academic practice: Potential roles in research, teaching, learning, and extension', *Innovative Higher Education*, 37 (4): 271–82.

Prensky, M. (2001a) 'Digital natives, digital immigrants. A new way to look at ourselves and our kids', *On the Horizon*, 9 (5): 1–6. Available at: http://www.marcprensky.com/writing/Prensky%20-%20Digital%20Natives,%20Digital%20Immigrants%20-%20Part1.pdf. Accessed 13 September 2013.

Prensky, M. (2001b) 'Digital natives, digital immigrants, Part II: Do they really think differently?', *On the Horizon*, 9 (6): 1–9. Available at: http://www.marcprensky.com/writing/Prensky%20-%20Digital%20Natives,%20Digital%20Immigrants%20-%20Part2.pdf. Accessed 13 September 2013.

Procter, R., Williams, R., Stewart, J., Poschen, M., Snee, H., Voss, A. and Asgari-Targhi, M. (2010) 'Adoption and use of Web 2.0 in scholarly communications', *Philosophical Transactions of the Royal Society A*, 368: 4039–56.

Quimbo, M.A.T. and Sulabo, E.C. (2013) 'Research productivity and its policy implications in higher education institutions', *Studies in Higher Education*, August: 1–17.

Rheingold, H. and Weeks, A. (2012) *Net Smart: How to Thrive Online*. Cambridge, MA: The MIT Press.

Rogers, D. and Coughlan, P. (2013) 'Digital video as a pedagogical resource in doctoral education', *International Journal of Research & Method in Education*, 36 (3): 295–308.

Rowlands, I., Nicholas, D., Russell, B., Canty, N. and Watkinson, A. (2011) 'Social media use in the research workflow', *Learned Publishing*, 24: 183–95.

Salaway, G., Caruso, J.B. and Nelson, M.R. (2008) *The ECAR Study of Undergraduate Students and Information Technology*, Research Study, Vol. 8. Boulder, CO: EDUCAUSE Center for Applied Research. Available at: http://net.educause.edu/ir/library/pdf/ERS0808/RS/ERS0808w.pdf, 52. Accessed 13 September 2013.

Sanchez-Franco, M.J., Martín-Velicia, F.A., Leal-Rodríguez, A.L. and Oliva-Vera, I.M. (2012) *Acceptance and Use of Social Network Sites: An Analysis Among Undergraduate Students*, proceedings of the 5th International Conference of Education, Research and Innovations, 19–21 November, Madrid, Spain. pp. 1433–44.

Settle, Q., Telg, R., Baker, L.M., Irani, T., Rhoades, E. and Rutherford, T. (2012) 'Social media in education: The relationship between past use and current perceptions', *Journal of Agricultural Education*, 53 (3): 137–53.

Shariff, S. (2008) *Cyber-bullying: Issues and Solutions for the School, the Classroom and the Home*. London: Routledge.

Shaw, D.B. (2008) *Technoculture: The Key Concepts*. Oxford: Berg.

Shema, H., Bar-Ilan, J. and Thelwall, M. (2012) 'Research blogs and the discussion of scholarly information', *PLoS ONE*, 7 (5). Available at: http://www.plosone.org/article/info%3Adoi%2F10.1371%2Fjournal.pone.0035869. Accessed 12 September 2013.

Shen, D., Cho, M., Tsai, C. and Marra, R. (2013) 'Unpacking online learning experiences: Online learning self-efficacy and learning satisfaction', *The Internet and Higher Education*, 19: 10–17.

SICTAS (2009) *Web 2.0 Site Blocking in Schools*, report published by Strategic ICT Advisory Service, Education.au. Available at: http://apo.org.au/research/web-20-site-blocking-schools. Accessed 11 September 2013.

Spence, E.H. (2011) 'Information, knowledge and wisdom: Groundwork for the normative evaluation of digital information and its relation to the good life', *Ethics and Information Technology*, 13 (3): 261–75.

Stutzman, F., Vitak, J., Ellison, N.B., Gray, R. and Lampe, C. (2012) *Privacy in Interaction: Exploring Disclosure and Social Capital in Facebook*, Sixth International AAAI Conference on Weblogs and Social Media. Available at: http://www.aaai.org/ocs/index.php/ICWSM/ICWSM12/paper/view/4666. Accessed 10 September 2013.

Top, E. (2012) 'Blogging as a social medium in undergraduate courses: Sense of community best predictor of perceived learning', *The Internet and Higher Education*, 15 (1): 24–8.

Ullrich, C., Borau, K., Luo, H., Tan, X., Shen, L. and Shen, R. (2008) *Why Web 2.0 is Good for Learning and for Research: Principles and Prototypes*, paper presented at International World Wide Web Conference, 21–25 April, Beijing, China. Available at: wwwconference.org/www2008/papers/pdf/p705-ullrichA.pdf. Accessed 11 September 2013.

University of Edinburgh (2007) *Guidelines for Using External Web 2.0 Services*. Available at: https://www.wiki.ed.ac.uk/display/Web2wiki/Web+2.0+Guidelines. Accessed 9 September 2013.

University of Melbourne (2006) *First Year Students' Experiences with Technology: Are They Really Digital Natives?* Available at: http://www.bmu.unimelb.edu.au/research/munatives/natives_report2006.pdf. Accessed 12 February 2008.

Vallor, S. (2012) 'Flourishing on Facebook: Virtue friendship and new social media', *Ethics and Information Technology*, 14 (3): 185–99.

Veletsianos, G. and Kimmons, R. (2013) 'Scholars and faculty members' lived experiences in online social networks', *The Internet and Higher Education*, 19: 43–50.

Weller, M. (2012) 'The virtues of blogging as scholarly activity', *Chronicle of Higher Education*. Available at: http://chronicle.com/article/The-Virtues-of-Blogging-as/131666/. Accessed 12 September 2012.

Xiao, B.S. and Wong, Y.M. (2013) 'Cyber-bullying among university students: An empirical investigation from the social cognitive perspective', *International Journal of Business and Information*, 8 (1): 34–69.

Xu, C., Ma, B., Chen, X. and Ma, F. (2013) 'Social tagging in the scholarly world', *Journal of the American Society for Information Science and Technology*, 64 (10): 2045–57.

Yelland, N. (2007) *Shift to the Future: Rethinking Learning with New Technologies in Education*. New York: Routledge.

Zhong, C., Shah, S., Sundaravadivelan, K. and Sastry, N. (2013) *Sharing the Loves: Understanding the How and Why of Online Content Curation*. Available at: http://pub.geekonabicycle.co.uk/icwsm13.pdf. Accessed 10 September 2013.

Zimmer, M. (2010) '"But the data is already public": On the ethics of research in Facebook', *Ethics and Information Technology*, 12 (4): 313–25.

Index

Added to a page number 'f' denotes a figure and 't' denotes a table.